# ABOUT FACE

# ABOUT FACE

Essays on Recovery, Therapies, and
Controversies of Addictions in Canada

EDITED BY DOUGLAS GOSSE

BREAKWATER

BREAKWATER
P.O. BOX 2188, ST. JOHN'S, NL, CANADA, A1C 6E6
WWW.BREAKWATERBOOKS.COM

COPYRIGHT © 2018 Breakwater Books Ltd.
ISBN 978-1-55081-688-4
A CIP catalogue record for this book is available from Library and Archives
Canada

We acknowledge the support of the Canada Council for the Arts.
We acknowledge the financial support of the Government of Canada and
he Government of Newfoundland and Labrador through the Department
of Tourism, Culture, Industry and Innovation for our publishing activities.
PRINTED AND BOUND IN CANADA.

      Newfoundland Labrador

Breakwater Books is committed to choosing papers and materials for our books that
help to protect our environment. To this end, this book is printed on a recycled paper
that is certified by the Forest Stewardship Council®.

MIX
Paper from
responsible sources
FSC® C004071

*This anthology is dedicated to Dr. Danielle Nahon*

# CONTENTS

## DIGITAL ADDICTIONS
### SEX, VIDEO GAMES, GAMBLING, AND SOCIAL MEDIA

## SERVICE PROVIDERS

# INTRODUCTION

*A*bout Face: Essays on Recovery, Therapies, and Controversies of
*Addictions in Canada* seeks to illuminate social justice and equity
in Canada germane to addictions. This collection is meant to be
accessible to a broad spectrum of the Canadian population, and
by highlighting the stories of diverse people affected by addiction,
we hope to increase public awareness, debate, and direction in the
understanding and treatment of addiction.

Some contend that addiction is a disease, or a spiritual problem
created by a lack of meaning and purpose in this twenty-first-
century era of increased social disconnect and loneliness. One
thing is for sure—people with addictions are our family members,
co-workers, healthcare professionals, teachers, counsellors, and
community leaders—people with addictions are present in every walk
of life. Addictions bypass social class, ethnicity, sexual orientation,
sex/gender, rural and urban locations, and the spectrum of
physical and mental health. Addiction is not a phenomenon of
the "other" but affects us all.

In our first section, entitled "Substance Abuse," several essays
relate the grip of alcohol and cigarette addictions, by far the most
common drugs used by Canadians. The estimated costs of cigarette

and alcohol harm to Canadians are in the billions. Among youth, while smoking and alcohol abuse has decreased in recent years, prescription-stimulant use is on the rise. In the twenty-first century, there is a marked increase in so-called "party drugs," including ecstasy, cocaine, ketamine, crystal meth, Percocet, and other various opioids. However, their use is not limited to youth, but involves mothers and fathers, blue- and pink-collar workers, and university educated professionals. Do you think of these drugs and automatically picture rave culture with tribal beats and strobe lights? Think again. In many circles, these drugs have replaced the evening or weekend cocktail or beer.

The second section of this anthology explores, "Digital Addictions: Sex, Video Games, Gambling, and Social Media." Growing numbers of Canadians not only excessively partake of alcohol, but also use the Internet to procure multiple sex partners while under the influence of drugs such as crystal meth. Legal ramifications of sexually compulsive behaviours are also discussed. Additionally, whether it be an addiction to dating or hook-up sites, Facebook, Instagram, video games, or online gambling, some Canadians spiral down a rabbit hole that is deleterious to their mental and physical health, social and familial relationships, and employment. Professionals who treat them, and who problematize the superficial characterizations of this new-millennium trend, complement this section.

The third section is "Food Addiction, Body Dysmorphia, and Eating Disorders." Awareness of eating disorders was brought to public attention in the 1980s in a proliferation of movies, television shows, talk shows, documentaries, and books. Obesity and compulsive eating are an ongoing problem, emphasising the intricate inter-play of mental and physical stressors in life. Moreover, in our millennium, men, women, and youth are exposed to unprecedented social-media messages to obtain the "perfect" body. Perfectionism is but one trait common to many of those affected with body dysmorphia. While increasing numbers of boys and men suffer from anorexia nervosa and bulimia, girls and women remain the majority. However, a significant number of Canadian boys and men display "megarexia" or "bigorexia"—the drive to become impossibly muscular and/or to have a lean musculature. Abuse of anabolic steroids, obsessive dieting, counting of calories, and embracing of so-called miracle foods, along with an overly regimented workout schedule, may lead to what some term the Adonis Complex. To conclude this section, therapists discuss the distinctions and overlap between body dysmorphia and those who suffer from substance abuse, delving into the question, "Are eating disorders addictions?"

"Contemporary Discussion of Addictions in Canada: Steps Forward," contains provocative essays by people working in the field of addictions, including social workers, therapists, criminologists, psychologists, lawyers, a journalist, and a psychiatrist. The lives of imprisoned men and women, many of whom are Indigenous, are accentuated, and links made to inmates' histories of childhood abuse and poverty. The need for increased government funding is a reoccurring theme. A final section, "Service Providers," provides an overview of several agencies across Canada known for their innovative and holistic treatment of various addictions.

In brief, *About Face: Essays on Recovery, Therapies, and Controversies of Addictions in Canada*, aims to question:

- Who suffers from addiction in Canada?
- How can we better understand addiction in the 21st century, and its myriad new forms?
- What are steps forward in the prevention and treatment of Canadians affected by addiction?

*About Face: Essays on Recovery, Therapies, and Controversies of Addictions in Canada* provides a timely platform for rigorous discussion and improved understanding of the contemporary evolution of addictions across our country.

Douglas Gosse
General Editor

# SUBSTANCE ABUSE

> "A friend's heart attack, two more
> friends dying of cancer, watching relatives
> carry around oxygen tanks,
> all of these would remind me that I shouldn't
> smoke, and then I would light up."

## MY LIFE IS GOING UP IN SMOKE

Jennifer Barnett

When my grandmother was a young mother of six children, she went to the doctor due to stress. Her family doctor told her to go out and buy a pack of cigarettes, keep them at home, and whenever she was feeling anxiety, to smoke. Thus, prescribed by her doctor, my grandmother picked up and set down cigarettes for years. Fortunately, she was one of those individuals who could behave in this manner and not become an addict.

My mother was not so fortunate. She started as a young woman as well, and smoked until she was in her fifties. She had her own experience with a doctor when pregnant with her first child, myself. She asked her family physician if smoking was bad for the fetus. He asked how much she smoked and, upon hearing it was just under a pack a day, told her she had nothing to worry about. She thus continued to smoke through her pregnancies, with us in the car as children and in the house, and didn't quit until we were adults living away from home. Though it was over twenty years ago, today at seventy-nine she still chews nicotine gum and, on occasion, when feeling stress, will go out and purchase nicotine patches.

I am my mother's daughter.

I had my first cigarette around grade seven. Over visiting friends whose parents were out of town, I had one after being offered. Everyone else was and so, being the typical eleven-year-old girl, I didn't want to feel different, and so I lit up. I coughed terribly, but felt such pride at doing something so adult that I went home that night and kissed my mother. Thus was my introduction to the fact that cigarettes smell.

In grade eight, after witnessing that many of my friends' parents had given permission to their children to smoke, I asked my mom for permission. She was so upset with me that she lit up a cigarette to calm down. I gave her the expected teenage glare and the conversation was over.

What proceeded through my high-school years were instances of smoking at school, out at parties, and mom finding my cigarettes and taking them. By this point I had a part-time job and could easily replace them. Smoking was easy back then. Just as when I was a child and my mom used to send me to the store for cigarettes, no one asked for ID when I was in high school. You simply went in and asked and they were given to you. At school, there were no lessons on the evil of tobacco; instead, there were smoking areas on school property, and the teachers smoked in the staffroom. I remember smoking on the bus, smoking being allowed on airplanes and in restaurants, and smoking during a movie in a movie theatre.

In the later years of high school, I do remember thinking that I wouldn't smoke when I turned twenty, but this auspicious birthday came and left with me still smoking. It was not until I was in university that smoking started to become 'not in vogue.' I quit for the first time in my third year of university. I remember the initial days feeling angry and upset, but didn't recognise the wild mood swings I was having as withdrawal. I had experienced similar times in high school when I had to go away for a few weeks with my parents on family trips, but never associated these terrible angry moments with the cigarettes. I quit for over a year, until one night at a university party there was this guy whom I really liked. He was having a cigarette. I walked up to him and bummed one in order to strike up a conversation. At that point, I was working in a student pub, and given smoking was still allowed indoors and the customers and staff smoked, it was nothing to pick up the habit again. Back then, smoking was still considered a habit. I have to say, there was something so deliciously social about having a cigarette with another person. I still feel this way.

By the time I had my first job whether or not you could smoke at your desk at work was dependent on your employer. While many provided breaks and smoking rooms, more still provided ashtrays beside your typewriter. I was successful in the career I chose, but due to a series of events, ended up going to teacher's college. I smoked all the way through teacher's college though there were times I would abstain due to the fact that less and less of my friends seemed to be smoking. I also found it was interfering with my sports as digging for the ball in volleyball, or swimming fast in water polo became challenging. I seemed to have the muscle tone to be competitive, but would occasionally get winded. I also started to feel tingling in my hands and feet on occasion. This always occurred when I smoked and seemed to disappear when I did not. The social rewards of smoking, though, always outweighed these symptoms, and so I continued to light up. It was not really an issue as smoking was allowed at the university, just not inside anymore, and smoking still occurred inside bars and cars and restaurants and, while on teacher placement, on public-school property. We would step outside and smoke on the steps of the school.

It was within my first years of teaching that school boards began to demand that teachers and students leave school property to smoke. I remember the first warning from the board office that announced that if teachers did not leave school property they would be fined, and their principals would be fined three times the amount. Having your principal fined because of something you "chose" to do was enough to cause a mass exodus of vehicles every lunch hour from the school parking lot. Snowstorms, rainstorms, scheduled meeting with parents, nothing would deter us from our lunch-hour drives. I can remember bundling up and going out to my car, sweeping it off in blowing wind that cut my face and hurt my hands, driving off school property and up the road in zero visibility, just to get that one cigarette in me. Boy, could I suck that one cigarette back. It was such a pleasure! I always kept perfume in the car and would try to avoid everyone upon reentering the school, making a beeline to the sink to brush my teeth. I didn't want anyone to smell it on me. With a sense of shame that I owned this addiction, I would cower over the sink and brush like crazy, making sure my clothes didn't smell, and my hair was re-hairsprayed. This sense of shame was not enough to make me quit, though, as smoking was still considered acceptable in many social places, whether in a bar or at a ball diamond, at people's homes, or in the car. The only place I felt shame was at work or when in a situation with nonsmokers. However, this shame was as intense as the desire to smoke. The desire to smoke, the addiction, overrode the shame on most occasions, but not always.

I remember one weekend being at a volleyball tournament with my students. By lunch, my normal cigarette time, I was dying for a smoke. I knew I could have one, but then the parents and students would smell it on me, so out of a sense of shame, I resisted. I was wound up tighter then a drum by the time the tournament ended. Even forming sentences when talking with parents seemed difficult.

My nerves were drawn like violin strings and I was trying very hard not to shake. My eyes began to lose their ability to focus, and I clenched my hands to prevent the shakes from spreading to my arms. One cigarette would have solved the problem, but I could not allow myself to be seen as a smoker by these others. In similar situations, there were times I even cried upon finally having that first cigarette, such was the relief.

During the next twenty years, I quit numerous times. Sometimes it lasted only a few days, but during other times it lasted months, and on one occasion it lasted a year. It was always finding myself in a social situation with another smoker that caused me to fall off the wagon. By this time I knew I was an addict, and accepted the label. At this time, society had changed enough that the dangers of smoking were better known. Gone were the days of advertisements on the television, on billboards, and in magazines for different brands of cigarettes. In their place, we had health warnings, documentaries on cancer, and then later some pretty awful pictures on cigarette packages. Yet, despite all this new information, I continued to find myself smoking. A friend's heart attack, two more friends dying of cancer, watching relatives carry around oxygen tanks, all of these would remind me that I shouldn't smoke, and then I would light up.

Beside social situations, the other big catalyst for me was stress. A bad day at work, favouritism by a boss that hurt others, a dispute with a friend or partner—any of these could stimulate the need for a smoke. In fact, just being in a room with someone who smoked could prompt me to light up as well, despite how long I had quit. Of course, when others felt the same way as I did about a stressor and they smoked, then the urge was doubly strong. It was common to find myself sitting on a patio with a peer or a group of peers from work, discussing the situation with a beer and cigarette in hand. We were venting. We were seeking solace. We were releasing stress. Of course, once the meeting was over, I would have a cigarette or two in the car on the way home and then continue to smoke through the evening. The following morning, after brushing my teeth, the first thing I would do is have a cigarette.

After numerous years of smoking in my car and in my house, I decided to only smoke outside. The catalyst for this change was a new car and then a new house. I couldn't stand the smell of old cigarette smoke on my clothes and didn't want to spend hours cleaning yellow off the inside of the car windshield, off framed photos in the house, nor tackle cleaning the yellow stains that ran down the walls. It occurred to me more than once, since this residue was left on glass and walls, to question what must be left in my lungs. I would have a smoke as I thought about it. These visual facts were not enough to stop me from smoking. It could be a snowstorm or pouring rain, and yet outside I would go, cigarette in hand, to suck back the nicotine into my lungs.

My battle with cigarettes continues. I am an addict. I quit frequently and for months at a time. I have found if I want to stay off cigarettes I need to not drink alcohol or coffee, avoid heavy foods and large meals, avoid social situations with any friends who smoke or who like to talk about stressful things, and walk a lot. Basically, if I want to be a non-smoker, I must be a hermit. I have done so on many occasions, forgoing social invites and ostracizing myself from a social life. I can quit for five months in this manner until I find the smell of cigarette smoke on others so repulsive that it physically turns my stomach. And yet, with a beer or two in me while sitting with a friend who smokes, it is likely I fall of the wagon. The craving to have one is immense, even though the smell and taste disgust me. The smoke enters my lungs and after the initial revulsion, it is like I relax. My muscles relax, my nerves relax, my entire being slows down, and my mind finds peace.

When I am not smoking, after the initial five days of withdrawal that is present even with the nicotine patch, and despite the vivid dreams of cigarettes I frequently have at night, I find myself happier. I feel together and in control. I feel complete. I feel energized. When I find myself experiencing this intense happiness and completeness, I remind myself to remember these feelings and to never light up again. I always think I won't; and then I do. All it takes is for me to find myself in a social situation, have a few beers, and be around a smoker. My friends who still smoke are only too happy to give me one when I ask. All it takes is one, and I am hooked again.

I am an addict. I am always hooked, always craving, always one decision away from having a smoke. I never wanted to be an addict. I never set out to be one. I feel shame frequently and try to hide it all the time. I sneak out the back door at work and look around to make sure there is no one I know before lighting up. While sucking the smoke into my lungs, I keep my eyes peeled for other people so I can hide. I continue to fight the addiction every day.

I have thought about going to Alcoholics Anonymous or Narcotics Anonymous to see if it will help. The problem is that what frequently happens at these meetings is that people share and then, at break, have a coffee and go out for a smoke. For addiction meetings, smoking is considered the lesser of two evils. Cigarette smoking, as much as it is considered disgusting by many today and recognized as an addiction, has a different history than other drugs. While it was never considered okay to watch porn on an airplane, in vogue to have a joint in the workplace, or socially acceptable to drink while watching a movie in a theatre, for a long time, smoking was socially acceptable and even encouraged. For this reason, there are no meetings for me, and I must continue to struggle on my own. Though a narcotic, when cigarettes are your evil vice and addiction, you are alone in coping. I had a friend who was an alcoholic who explained to me that he could never do drugs, as it would stimulate the need to drink. I had another friend who was in Narcotics Anonymous who explained he could never drink, as it would create the desire in him to do drugs. Smoking, though a narcotic, due to its social history of acceptance, is still allowed by these twelve-step programs. I have friends who have quit for twenty years who have started smoking again. It is still out there and accepted by segments of society. Cigarettes are still sold in corner stores with milk, bread, and deodorant.

I do not want to smoke. And yet, upon the smoke entering my lungs, I feel whole again. I am in recovery frequently, but I am always a smoker. Despite the negative attitude, given the permissiveness and acceptance that still exists in society, I suspect that I will always be a smoker. I know I am an addict. I know smoking has killed some of my friends and relatives. I try to abstain, but then I light up and feel shame. I occasionally cry. And then I will have a second one.

I know the essays in this book are to be those of people in recovery. I have not had a cigarette since July 2017, and yet I find myself wondering if we are ever really in recovery. Are we ever recovered? I also find myself wondering how many of those with alcohol, drug, porn, or sex addictions are also still smokers. Smoking has a unique place among addictions. It is still accepted in certain situations. How I wish the world were different when I was young, and how I wish the world were different now. Writing this was stressful; I think I'll have a smoke.

"I had seen what happened
when you turned on people,
and I saw your Jekyll-and-Hyde
personality. I had seen you use people until
there was nothing left."

## DEAR ALCOHOL

Michael Parsons

2

Dear alcohol,

We can no longer be friends, ever. For many years, I thought you were my friend. I looked to you to comfort me in times of pain and sorrow, and I even hung around with you during the happy times. For many years, we seemed to have a good relationship, but as time passed, I sensed our relationship was going bad. People even warned me that I should hang out with you less. I became too dependent on you and needed you more and more. This was not a healthy relationship. You were always there, every day, to "take the edge off." At first, you seemed to make every day a little better, and even spending a few minutes with you in the evenings was enough for me to forget about whatever was bothering me. You whispered to me even when I wanted to be alone with my thoughts. You assured me that no matter what I had going on, I could count on you to see me through the day. You made subtle suggestions that one more would make things just that much better. You kept my demons at bay.

The signs were there from the start, and I should have paid attention. I had seen what happened when you turned on people, and I saw your Jekyll-and-Hyde personality. I had seen you use people until there was nothing left. I had seen you ruin families, relationships, and lives, but you assured me that you were not the cause. You said, "It was really the people themselves who were screwed up. They were the weak ones." You told me time and time again that I was not one of those people and we could be friends forever. You told me I was stronger than everybody else and what we had together was special and unique. I believed you. For years, I believed you. I convinced myself that our relationship was different and that I would never become "one of those people." You boosted my confidence and made me feel special. You convinced me that any problem could be overcome just by having a drink. It seemed to work for a long time.

Then I started noticing the change. You became more demanding. You wanted to spend more and more time together. You became jealous of the time I spent with others. You wanted me exclusively to yourself. You whispered dark things to me. For years, you held the key that kept my demons locked away. Whenever they threatened to break free, you could push them back into that locked box in my mind. For years, you were the only gatekeeper that worked, and with you, I could keep them at bay. When I attempted to distance our friendship, you blackmailed me. You would let the darkness peek out, and then you would threaten to release it if I stayed away from you. You used your powers of persuasion to always reel me back in. We were living a lie together, right under the noses of the other people I loved. I became your prisoner instead of your friend. Despite my best attempts, I could not break free. I felt guilty about you, but felt helpless to do anything about it. I was afraid that my demons would finally come out and I would be left dirty, discarded, and alone.

In the days leading up to our breakup, you convinced me that nothing else mattered, only our friendship. You convinced me that I didn't need anybody else but you. You made me push everybody away. You made me believe that if we couldn't be together then life was not worth living. On this dark day, I saw no light.

Thankfully, something pulled me back from the brink and I asked for what I had been too afraid to ask for all my life—help. I discovered that there were people who loved me more than you. I found that in my darkest hour of despair, I was worthy and, if I were strong enough, I could face my demons. I reached out for a hand to hold and realized there were many hands that wanted to hold mine. I realized that maybe I could not do without you on my own, but I could with the help and love of others.

Since our breakup, I have learned a lot about you. I see that you were never a true friend and were only using me to get what you wanted—control. You wanted to control me like you control many others. My body, my mind, and my soul were only pawns that you toyed with. You made many promises, but kept very few. I now know that even though you made me feel special and strong, I was not unique, and you cheated on me with countless others. I was a fool for believing you could fix anything. All those evenings and weekends we spent together and the problems you said you were fixing were all there the next day. We never fixed anything together; we only made things worse. All those times you told me our friendship would "take the edge off," we only ever masked the symptoms and never addressed any of the issues. All those mornings you stayed and offered me comfort from the night before was a lie. You just wanted to keep me on your leash so that I couldn't stray from your firm grasp. All those bad decisions we made together seemed like fun at the time, but only served to hurt myself and others. Looking back, you always seemed to come out unscathed, and I was the one with the hurt, shame, sorrow, and guilt. You were never my true friend.

I think this breakup will be harder on me than you. I know you have many other friends and have a long list of young people that want to be your friend. I know you are still there and will make many attempts to rekindle our relationship. I know your appeal. I know how intoxicating you can be and how the sight and scent of you makes me susceptible to your charms. I know that I must be on my guard for fear of losing myself in you all over again. I still see you with my friends and family, and I see you playing the same tricks with some of them as you played on me.

I have faced my demons, and I have grown stronger without you. I have learned that love and life are far better friends than you ever were. I have learned that each precious moment in the day is worthwhile, and if I need you to be happy, then something else in my life is broken and needs fixing. My body and my mind are healthier since I left you, and my true inner spirit has taken your place.

So this is goodbye, forever.

"My new, sober world was a scary one. My confidence left me. In a strange way, my motivation was gone, and I could no longer put in the marathons at the office without the promise of the beer-soaked reset button at the end."

3

## THE WEEKEND ALCOHOLIC

Gareth Mitton

M ine was a weekend alcoholism. The kind you can brush aside, as I did, for years by saying things like, *"It's just a few drinks. It's not like I do it every day. I work hard; I deserve it."*

I grew up in England and later moved to Newfoundland. From a drinking culture perspective, you could say that's the frying pan to the fire. Add my field of work—creative marketing—to the mix and you've just thrown on gasoline.

There are many drinks I can't recall, but I remember my first one well enough. It should have served as a warning, but at fifteen I lacked the perspective I've earned today. I loved the way that cold, crisp, bubbly beer made me feel. I remember standing in the bathroom, the taste on my lips, the warm feeling in my stomach, thinking, "Oh yes. I'm going to be doing much more of this." I sure did. Only much later did I learn that the disease worsens the younger you start.

We were at my Mum's friend's place when I had that first one. She was a journalist and, I would later discover, an alcoholic herself. "Go on," she said, that way we alkies do, "Let him have a pint. He's old enough now." Mum was reluctant but such was the culture. Safer, I'm sure she thought, to be here when he tries it than not. (That friend of my Mum's would later lose her driver's license and career to the bottle.)

That wasn't my first time being close to beer, or smelling its hoppy odour. My earliest memory of beer was sitting on Dad's lap as a toddler, being entertained as he wrote my name in the thick white foam of his Guinness and showed me how it was miraculously still there at the bottom of the glass after he'd quaffed the thick black liquid below.

Nor was it the first time I was drunk. That came a little later, at a cousin's house party. They'd let me off the leash that night. Introduced me to the joys of whiskey and coke, and made the mistake of telling me to help myself. I did, and, as it turns out, I most certainly didn't. Mum stood over me tutting as I threw up from alcohol abuse for the first time, but far from the last.

As the years went by, my love of booze continued to develop. University made it easier than ever to overindulge. Fifty-pence-a-pint days at the Student Union. Vodka-Red Bull 'Pitchers of Happiness' (oh, the irony) at the local student bar. Endless cheap tins of the bubbly stuff to bring back and drink at home, sometimes with friends, but increasingly alone.

Five years sober and I still sometimes do that thing that addicts do. I question if I was really an addict at all. What if I overreacted to a few bad nights and a few bad choices and cut the booze I loved so much out of my life for no good reason? What if I'm missing out?

Then I pull out the little scrap of paper I keep in my satchel at all times, in the little Velcro pocket with a plastic comb I never use.

The scrap of paper where I jotted down the words, *Why you are an alcoholic*:

*Drinking alone.* I started this as a teenager. I loved nothing more than being in my bedroom, knocking back beers and singing along to my blasting music. Sometimes with a friend, often not. It hardly seemed to matter. Check one.

*Unable to stop at one or two.* I remember coming home for Christmas after my first semester at uni and going to visit my next-door neighbour. He gave me a tall can of beer. I drank it. He didn't offer me another, so I asked. My friend asked me, "Do you ever have just one?" I thought it was a silly question. At eighteen years old, I already regarded having one drink as a waste of time, a waste of an opportunity to get lit. If I knew I'd only be able to get my hands on one beer, I'd opt not to drink at all. Later, stopping at one *case* of beer would become a challenge. Check two.

*Becoming very convincing.* "I don't have a problem; I just had a rough day / I'm celebrating / I just played soccer / it's Friday, etc." Check three.

*Struggling through workday hangovers.* Today, when my addict brain says, "Hey, why don't we have a beer?" those are the days I think of. Head throbbing, body aching, stomach nauseous. Your soul itself begging you to just lie down, close your eyes and sleep. But you can't. *This is a get-through day*, I'd have to keep telling myself. *Just get through today.* What a horrible way to live. Check four.

*Can't stop for a period of time.* I remember telling my now-wife (then-girlfriend) that of course I could go a whole weekend without drinking. I think I even believed it myself. I lasted till about 7 p.m. on Friday night. Check five.

*The clock hits five and you're drinking immediately.* Only on Fridays for the most part, but then I didn't even always wait till five o'clock. Towards the worst stages of my disease, I'd go to the liquor store at lunch and crack the first beer around four, usually bringing one to a colleague or two. I wasn't an alcoholic—I was a cool boss. If my wife was working late and picking me up, I'd happily stay at the office, drinking alone till she arrived. I was often already drunk by the time she did. Check six.

*Leaving a place without alcohol to go to a place with alcohol.* The pattern of my Friday nights for the last few years of my drinking days was, I'd start drinking after work (if not just before). I'd continue drinking through the evening while listening to music, fiddling on my guitar, watching sports, or playing videogames. Then, once my wife had gone to bed, I'd sneak out to the nearest bar to drink alone among people. Sometimes I'd sing karaoke (I can only imagine very badly). Check seven.

I made terrible decisions. I put myself in danger. I chipped away at my self-esteem. My weekends became a Friday-night explosion of self-abuse, followed by two days of either dragging myself around in a state of abject misery, wanting to be home in bed rather than out enjoying my free days with my wife. Or, in the worst instances, in bed because I couldn't rouse myself to play along.

It was exhausting, not least because during the week I was successful in my career. I was getting promotion after promotion. I was pretty much at the top of the tree by age thirty-two. But my life was an unsustainable cycle of overworking followed by overindulging. My weekends flew by in a drunken-hungover blur. Then it was Monday again.

One Friday night I left the club, came home, and fell on my face—physically and figuratively. I remember breaking a coffee table on my way down. I remember my nose pressed to musty carpet. I remember my glasses digging into my skin as my arms tried to remember how to prop my paralytic body upright again. The next morning I tried to explain the broken table and the scars on my face to my wife in a way that didn't make me seem like a hopeless drunk.

I'd hit bottom, and I knew it.

They say that if you relapse, it's back to where you stopped drinking, not where you started. That's not somewhere I have any interest in returning.

I was lucky. My wife stuck by me, on condition that I got help and cleaned up my act. AA followed and (knock on wood) sobriety stuck around too. But here's the thing: my struggle wasn't over. That's the kicker with addiction. You don't just stop and suddenly it's rainbows and butterflies. There's relief that one kind of battle just ended, but immense apprehension and trepidation in the face of a whole new challenge. One that has no visible or comprehensible end. One that might just be life and death.

I do believe that. I think if I started drinking again, I might die. There were enough nights spent alone on cold bathroom floors, clinging to consciousness long enough to get all the vomiting done. If I hadn't managed to time that out right, even just once, I may not be here to type this now.

But beer had also been my crutch. For all the pain and damage it caused, it had gotten me through hard times. The death of my father. School and work stress. It had been my companion in solace and joy. It had been the light at the end of my workweek. What I only came to realize once I stopped drinking was that I'd been living for drinking.

My new, sober world was a scary one. My confidence left me. In a strange way, my motivation was gone, and I could no longer put in the marathons at the office without the promise of the beer-soaked reset button at the end. I tried switching jobs; it didn't work. I tried switching provinces; nada. Five years on, and I'm still trying to figure out how to cope with everyday life.

I also got to witness the darker side of mental health "care" in Canada. I went on stress leave from work and was eventually asked by the insurance company to call a psychologist in Ontario. Based on a one-hour consultation with someone I never met in person,

I was diagnosed bipolar and prescribed medication. When I asked if this meant I needed to be on medication for the rest of my life, she replied, "If you ever want to live a normal life, yes."

I didn't fill that prescription, nor pop one pill. I don't say that to suggest that taking medication for addiction recovery or mental illness is wrong, just that it's not for me. Generally, I'm wary of pharmaceuticals, and my addiction issues have only added to my resolve to stay clean in every way.

I do have days when I wonder if we, as people, are ready for the modern world, with its constant bombardment of media and technology. Whether we are evolved enough, or if it's all too much, too soon for our brains and for our health. Maybe we need medication to help. But for me, clean means clean, and I want to be stimulant and sedative free, whether it's the kind I get over a liquor store or pharmacy counter. (I certainly don't trust myself not to become addicted to an addictive prescription medication.)

Instead, I've chosen to invest in stress- and anxiety-management techniques. I've trained in meditation and practice it regularly. I do yoga. I play sports and keep active running, swimming, and jogging. My wife is a nutritionist, so I eat well, for the most part, though I do allow myself some comfort food when I feel like it.

There are times when I recall my red-eyed days through rose-tinted glasses, but I know I'm better off without booze in my life. It isn't easy, though. Our social culture is based around the bottle. Being the non-drinker in the crowd can make others feel awkward. They often want to talk about how they "don't drink that much" or are "celebrating" or drinking because "it's Friday." I know most of them aren't like me. They are in control. They can stop at one. Many could go a weekend or several without a drop.

But there must be some stuck in that cycle of denial that almost took everything from me. For them, I wish nothing but sobriety.

"You are a big boy now,
  two already,
too big to be up sitting on someone's lap,
  too old to be cuddled and kissed."

## A MOMENT IN TIME

Ann Dwyer Galway

Tuesday, April 8, 1961, 3:07 p.m..

"Happy Birthday to you, happy birthday to you…"

Five voices, at least three off key, resounded, and excitement buzzed in the air. My little brother, Jack, had all the attention today. He looked like a little man in his red plaid shirt and blue overalls. His face had been scrubbed until it shone. Dad had trimmed his hair and it was slicked back on his forehead.

It was Jack's second birthday. There would not be a birthday party, but our mom might bake a cake if she had time. My heart was full of love as I watched him bask in all the attention. His eyes sparkled as he ran around the kitchen giggling and laughing when one of his siblings caught him and tickled him. As the oldest, I was always on guard. On that day I was keeping a careful watch from the pantry off the kitchen, making sure no one got hurt.

The small kitchen was hot from the fire burning in the woodstove. The children's faces glowed red, and beads of sweat were beginning to gather on foreheads and necks.

My mom might not get around to baking a birthday cake, but my dad never failed to celebrate our birthdays in the old traditional way. He faithfully brewed a keg of beer days before and invited uncles, cousins, and neighbors in for a drink. It was the perfect excuse for a party.

Then the old wooden door opened and blew shut. A wave of cold air swept into the kitchen. But it didn't cool the excitement. The door opened and closed like this until the room was full to capacity. The birthday boy was lifted into the arms of uncles, bounced on knees by cousins, and patted on the head by friends. No one resented the little guy getting all the attention; after all, it was his birthday.

I waited impatiently for the next part of the tradition, and I knew my siblings were as well. Finally, an old uncle began to dig around in his pocket and came up with a coin. With much ado he offered it to Jack, whose eyes bulged as he took it in his chubby little hand. On cue, they all reached into their pockets. Jack went from one to another collecting pennies, nickels, and maybe a couple of dimes. Oh, the danger of him swallowing one! Not to worry! Dad knew to take them from Jack and slipped them into his pocket. Later, Dad would buy treats for all, at the shop down the road. The little fellow's face fell slightly. He quickly recovered though, buoyed along by the increasing jovial laughter of the men in the room. Everything was good. He was still a happy little boy.

Just as he had been doing all his young life, Jack held up his arms to be lifted onto a lap, cooed to, cuddled, and kissed. Even if I had been prepared for what happened next, there was nothing I could have done to stop it.

"You are a big boy now, two already, too big to be up sitting on someone's lap, too old to be cuddled and kissed."

This came from my dad and was echoed in unison by the others.

My father meant no malice, said it with pride even. It was the way of the times. A rite of passage. The little guy turned to one man after another and received the same sentence for turning two. He stood still, a look of astonishment on his tiny face. He waited as if expecting laughter at some joke. He returned to our dad, arms uplifted. But the answer was the same. That was the moment I knew nothing was ever going to be the same for my little brother.

His big happy smile disappeared. His mouth trembled. Tears trickled down over his still baby cheeks but no sound accompanied them.

To add to his grief, one of the men told him, "Big boys don't cry!"

He stood alone in the middle of the room, a look of shock on his face. A wall of sadness seemed to close in around him. In my twelve-year-old mind I knew something big had just happened, but I didn't know exactly what. I only knew I didn't like what I had witnessed. I didn't like what it had done to my two-year-old brother. The party had ended. I gathered him into my arms and it was a while before he settled down. Soon he was running around again. No obvious wound. I was relieved that he was young enough to forget the incident.

That was the exact moment his path in life was determined. The moment that he stopped hoping, believing, and trusting, even if neither of us could identify or understand this at the time. One moment in time that need not have happened at all, but did. There were no child-rearing books or advice from child psychologists. Just traditions passed on from one generation to the next, no one having any idea of the consequences.

I didn't know that at the time, of course. It was years later that I grasped the significance of this single event. It was a scene that played out in my mind for decades as I watched Jack grow up. He was a serious child, withdrawn and shy. I worried about him as he became a teenager and a man.

As I watched his life unfold and I learned more about child psychology, I began to understand what I had witnessed that afternoon on his second birthday. I had watched as the innocence of a child was wiped from his very being. He would never be the same again. I could not fix this with a cuddle alone. Jack's trust in human kindness had been severed.

Jack had no way of knowing why he started to drink at age twelve, why he fought his way through the teenage years with no memories of good times without alcohol. When he drank, anger reared its ugly head. When he was sober, he was kind, giving, and willing to help anyone who needed help. Jack was smart, a talented carpenter and a hard worker. His drinking didn't take away these wonderful traits. However, most people around him began to see him as nothing more than a drunk who couldn't be trusted to be at the job in the morning, someone to avoid because of his anger.

I loved him but I didn't know how to help him.

His relationships were always turbulent and didn't last. It wasn't that he didn't want love. He did. But for Jack, love was painful and was not to be trusted. For reasons he couldn't understand, he wasn't staying around long enough to be pushed aside, to experience the hurt that was sure to come. Over the years, I got glimpses of the hidden Jack. He didn't believe me when I told him that he was kind, caring, smart, and talented. He drowned his thoughts and feelings with alcohol. He floated along life in a daze. Alone. It was hard to watch.

Jack never doubted that I loved him. I tried in many ways to get him to follow the plans that I thought would change his life and make him happy. The whole journey with him was taking its toll on me, so I joined ALON, a group to help relatives and friends of alcoholics. Over time, I let go of the idea that I could change his life, but to let him know I loved and accepted him without judgement. At one point, I persuaded him to go to an AA meeting. He stayed long enough in the program to accept that he was an alcoholic. But he was not equipped to stop drinking. He didn't get counselling to deal with his pain. He had only one social group and couldn't be there without being drawn back into the old habits.

Jack had a daughter from whom he walked away. He told me he did this because he didn't want her to grow up with a father who was an alcoholic. He wanted better than that for her, he said. This decision was not made lightly. I saw firsthand the pain it caused. Jack began to drink more.

His drinking took him on a path of self-destruction. He couldn't hold down a job, he served time in prison for disorderly conduct and for driving while under the influence of alcohol.

Then one day he moved away from home to a community where he didn't know anyone. He cut himself off from the family. He didn't come for visits. But he called me every three months or so to let me know he was doing okay. And I went to see him from time to time.

"I am happy here," he told me. "I have good friends. No one judges me here."

I am happy for Jack. His drinking buddies are more than just friends. They are also his family. They are the same kind, caring people that Jack has been all his life. He has other friends who see him as the talented person he is, who hire him to do carpentry work for them, and praise his skills. He hasn't stopped drinking, but he is drinking less and more responsibly. He has blossomed under the love and caring of friends who accept him as he is and make time to get to know him.

I have never told Jack about the events of his second birthday. I'm not sure he'd understand anyway. That's okay. His life has not been the life I would have chosen for him. I can't undo the damage that happened at that moment in time many years go. It's been a long, turbulent road for Jack. I take solace in knowing he is happier and stronger now.

"I came to realize with every beer I drank,
     what I was really doing was sipping on fear
and pissing out confidence. Every haul on a
     joint meant inhaling more fear and
exhaling a critical part of my power."

## A QUESTION OF SPIRIT

Christopher K. Wallace

We don't often talk of spirit when discussing substance use. Go big or go home seems to be the order of the day: all-in belief or nothing. I suppose this might be due to our physiology. After all, our eyes see out. We should be forgiven for seeking answers to big questions out there somewhere. As if looking to the heavens will reflect some perfect truth we can use to guide our actions. There's merit to this: it often does.

But first, let me ask you something: Have you ever been afraid? Where you momentarily had the wits scared out of you? What happens?

Your breathing shallows, your heart rate increases, blood pressure rises, and thinking narrows as you focus on escape or resolution. We all know these symptoms as classic fight or flight. Now, think of what happens after you drink a couple of beers or smoke a joint or take any other mood-altering chemical. Sure enough, it's the same thing: breathing shallows, heart rate goes up, blood pressure rises, and most importantly, thinking narrows. Using these substances puts your physiology into a fight or flight state

The body doesn't distinguish between medicines; moreover, it has no idea it's "just a joint," or "just a couple of beers," or "doctor prescribed." It's all the same, considered as a threat to your system from foreign poisons, where your body is put off-balance, and out of something called homeostasis. And once in this state, the body counters by doing everything it can to restore itself back to normal, including engaging the sympathetic nervous system to help (Spencer and Hutchison, 1999).

Perspiration, breath, heart rate, liver and kidneys are all put on overtime use. Adrenaline and cortisol course through your veins in preparation for fight or flight—or freeze or feint, the other two Fs of the 4Fs, and often overlooked when your being is under attack. Meantime, the feel-good neurotransmitter dopamine provides cover for the habituated user, making them think the buzz signals everything's okay. It's not.

Let me give you some examples.

If you think of your first experiences with any of these substances, you may recall how your body and mind reacted with fear. It could be dizziness or vomiting from alcohol use, or an intense fear from using cannabis. Some people say they don't get off on pot the first time they try it; that's how good your body is at countering its effects. People stick with it and adapt; eventually, they feel it. Cocaine is another one which typically induces intense fear. And for some people, first LSD use is the scariest thing ever, resulting in a "bad trip."

Remember in high school being over at that one friend's house with the cool parents, where a garage or basement became a drug zone after school or on weekends? Maybe you passed the bong around until you were all pretty much unable to speak. Oh sure, maybe someone says, "Hey dude, do you think your cat's stoned? Do you think it knows we're high, man?" We all thought we were buzzed; when in truth, we were immobilized by fear.

Nietzsche said, "All credibility, all good conscience, all evidence of truth comes only from the senses" (Kaufmann, 2000, p. 134). The brain relies on what comes in from touch, taste, smell, hearing, and sight to log onto our world. Experience is derived from the senses; therefore, undermined sensory inputs means compromised experience. Alcohol and drugs create a fear response in the body while using dopamine to trigger your reward centers, keeping awareness of fear symptoms at bay. Beneath the surface, a tug of war is going on while you sit and get high.

The brain and body are not separate entities. In fact, your whole physical being is the universal address of your existence. As such, feelings live as equally in the body as they do in the brain through the tenth cranial nerve. Known as the Vagus Complex, it connects your brain stem to most of your internal organs, including the heart and gut (Porges, 2011).

Feelings come from experience. Think of what kinds of feelings a baby has compared to an adult. As the baby matures, it's capable of a variety of emotions in increasing complexity as its experience grows. And feelings are predictive, not reactive as we often think (Barrett Feldman, 2017). Much of the brain works this way. Let me explain.

Your brain predicts your sleep and wake cycle and builds up levels of melatonin to prepare you for slumber. It predicts the eventual need for food by signaling with the hormone ghrelin well in advance of mealtimes. Even your visual cortex receives inputs from the eye, but also has neurons running the other way, from the cortex, which carry predictions affecting what you see. At any moment, beneath awareness, the brain predicts what state is required and scans your bank of previous experiences for matching emotions in preparation for what's ahead.

In this way, science tells us we live emotionally and use our thinking brain to explain things after the fact. Emotions rule because they occur milliseconds faster than we can think, acting as our early warning system. The line between reality and imagination blurs during substance use, while the body tallies the score. The brain's memory doesn't discern between stoned or drunk and straight. It's all just input.

After decades of smoking hashish, the last ten or more years as a nightcap to my day, the way others use a glass of wine to unwind, I noticed (and for the first time really took stock of) my physical symptoms. Then I asked myself this question: "Can you be afraid and confident at the same time?" Most people's gut answer to this is to say, No, it's one or the other as the feelings are mutually exclusive. If you are in fear, you may still be in action, but it is unlikely to be with much confidence. It's more likely you are going through the motions, rather than giving things your best.

Moreover, if emotions rule my actions, without me even realizing it through my databank of recalled events, I had to ask myself what compounding effect substance use was having on my confidence? I'm talking about real confidence here, the kind gained from trial and error. Sometimes, it comes from taking a great leap of faith. Other times, it arises from a series of small victories adding up to a quiet competence. Either way, it's always hard earned.

Math is like that, so is spelling or writing. Even riding a bicycle results in a lasting physical confidence, whereas doing something like public speaking for the first time can vault a person into a new sense of self. Think of the first time you climbed high into a tree or jumped off the high diving board at the local pool. So much of our progress in life is because of these quests to add to our personal repertoire of skills and emotional durability. Life usually gets better when we get better at life.

The times on weekends where I'd drink a half-dozen beers on a Friday or Saturday night, or both, I'd find not much got done during the day. I would also fail to connect with my wife and children in a meaningful way. The things I'd planned to do on my days off were often put off or started but never finished. Once, I built half of a fair-sized shed, became unsure of my plans, so just dismantled it. I stacked the wood behind my house, and never returned to the task. Confidence.

And small things, the ordinary demands a man rises to meet during life, were not being handled with any urgency. It didn't take much to put me off my game. I came to realize with every beer I drank, what I was really doing was sipping on fear and pissing out confidence. Every haul on a joint meant inhaling more fear and exhaling a critical part of my power.

Who needs this confidence thing anyway? Turns out, we all do. I've heard it said that confidence is the stuff we use to turn thoughts into actions. This has wider implications. Let me ask you, "How then, do you live confidently when you regularly subject your body to a fear state which cannot be resolved with action?" In my case, when I was honest with myself, I had to admit I could not.

I'd work hard at gaining confidence, and yet, doubt would creep back into my life. It meant I didn't invest in all the technological wonders that have arisen in my lifetime and which I could have easily participated in. It meant I took jobs that kept me safe. It also resulted in me not standing up for myself when I should have. Overall, it kept me playing small. It was two steps forward, and one step back. Sometimes, admittedly, it was just one step back. Though I had all the trappings of the middle class, I was living a charade.

I'm not talking about occasional substance use. I'm referring to habitual use, from more than once per week to daily consumption. Under the fear-load this engenders in the body, assuredly, confidence wanes. In time, this steady assault on confidence can become something called "learned helplessness." That's when you tell yourself a story about confidence. You may realize it's for other people, something off in the distance, far from your existence. Or, more likely, it's something we don't talk about at all because it means we have given up aspiring to becoming something more. In a measure, we abandon our dreams.

Can you live this way and survive? Sure. You can get by. But even now you'll realize it's not what Mother Nature or God had in mind when you defied the odds by beating all those other sperm to the egg, when you won the race of life. Damn it. This was not supposed to be our destiny. The Universe wants more from you, from me, and confidence is key to allowing our spirit to fly, to soar with the eagles in full view of the sun.

But here's what happens. Twenty years may go by. If you're lucky, one day you'll have an epiphany like I did. You may realize you have not lived those twenty years at all. Instead, what you have really done is lived one year...twenty times.

Let that sink in a bit. I had to soak in it for a while.

Why did I need this jolt of fear every day? When I searched a little deeper, it dawned on me. I'd been creating fear like this since I was a kid. I figured out my family of origin likely set me on this path through its uneven attachments and unpredictable violence. Paradoxically, I was a fear seeker. Early on, fight or flight had carried the day for me and I survived, thereby searing its red-hot brand upon my soul. I lived by it. It meant life or death to me. If there was no fear in my life, I'd seek it out, create it out of thin air if needed. As I recalled the decades gone by, I could see a significant part of my time was spent re-enacting a deep need for fear. Imprisoned this way as a little boy, I carried these emotional shackles into adulthood.

Fact is, I meet fear at an entirely different level than most people. I have been strangely attracted to it, mostly beneath my awareness. It's as if my body survived it before and needed to prove it could survive it again. I was stuck in a loop. Perhaps it's why I stand up to bullies. My first question when encountering people is to unflinchingly think or say, "How can I help you." It's why I act best when I'm protecting my tribe, a brother's keeper. My self-concept silently commands: "Stand aside, this is for men." It's because I can, capably, fearlessly.

Yet, this was the gift I'd allowed to wane over time. The difference between how I saw myself and how I really acted, caused me untold dissonance. Once I understood why I continued to use drugs and alcohol, and how this diminished my confidence, the allure soon faded. I must live true and free. I have a destiny to fulfill, a pact with the universe: to let loose my spirit as a guardian to others. When honourable men use their power for good, in service of themselves and those around them, life becomes meaningful.

This, then, is the key to our freedom.

More questions I asked myself: How much of your confidence are you willing to sacrifice to keep a fear habit for another year? How much more of your spirit can you compromise? We think we have time: we don't.

And so, it was for me. I had been using drugs and alcohol to narrow my thinking. Instead of finding my personal tract, where my spirit could expand and answer the universe's calling, I was running from it. Narrowing my focus was a good objective, but not this way. I have experienced the zone before: it's a place where a mighty congruence of my ability and drive and concentration allows me to feel as if I am forcing time to stand still. It's a place of command, where my spirit lets loose and flies high. And there, fully aware now, filled with meaning from serving myself and others, and connected by purpose, I am set free, powerful once more.

It was Oliver Wendell Holmes Sr. (1868) who once said, "Every now and then a man's mind is stretched by a new idea or sensation, and never shrinks back to its former dimensions." I say to you then: let this be one of those times.

Stretch, my brothers and sisters, and we will find each other up there.

REFERENCES

Barrett Feldman, L. (2017). *How Emotions Are Made: The Secret Life of the Brain.* Boston: Houghton Mifflin Harcourt.

Holmes, O. W. (1868). *The Autocrat of the Breakfast-table* (Author's unabridged ed.). London: G. Routledge.

Kaufmann, W. (Ed.). (2000). *Basic Writings of Nietzsche.* New York: Modern Library.

Porges, S. W. (2011). *The Polyvagal Theory: Neurophysiological Foundations of Emotions, Attachment, Communication, and Self-regulation.* New York: W. W. Norton.

Spencer, R. L., and Hutchison K. E. (1999). "Alcohol, Aging, and the Stress Response." *Alcohol Research and Health,* 23(4), 272–83.

"When I get preoccupied with
the business of life, I forget that
I am not like other people who can
casually consume alcohol or other
mind-altering drugs. Most can take it
or leave it. I cannot.
My life depends on always
remembering this fact."

6

## PIXIE DUST AND EVERLASTING PLAY

Kathryn Eve

For reasons I may never fully understand, I became an alcoholic and addict. Of course, I never planned on growing up to become this way. No one does. But here I am in all my wounded glory. Even though I have been in recovery for some time now, it is still easy for me to forget that this disease lies dormant inside me. Close calls with relapse over the years have taught me that my addiction is always in the wings, patiently waiting for an opportune moment to sneak up on me when I least expect it. I guess you can say I have what one person in the twelve-step program calls "a built-in forgetter." When I get preoccupied with the business of life, I forget that I am not like other people who can casually consume alcohol or other mind-altering drugs. Most can take it or leave it. I cannot. My life depends on always remembering this fact.

*Remembering when* serves as a critical reminder for me to take care of my recovery on a daily basis. In Narcotics Anonymous, I learn to do this by paying vigilant attention to triggers or what they call the three Ps: People, Places, Playgrounds. A big part of growing up for me has been learning how to cultivate new playgrounds that don't always involve escapism. Some days I do well in this department. Other days I feel lost like Peter Pan, unafraid of death but adverse to growing up and living the ordinariness of adulthood. Hence the constant need to fly away from the rules and pressures of reality. Because I suffer from this Peter Pan Syndrome, I have a habit of turning away from the chance to love and be loved. Like Peter, I have spent years turning away from the Darling family's bedroom window (a symbol of home), to fly back to an even emptier Neverland. This plays itself out in urges to binge drink and drug. My version of pixie dust and everlasting play.

If the truth be known, I have always struggled with trying to manage the mundanity of everyday life without self-medicating. My addiction, like the cravings that feed it, point to my not wanting to be in my life, in my body, or on the planet. This makes sense. I have always craved interplanetary experiences. Why? Because throughout my life, I have felt unsettled to the core. Carl Jung, in a 1961 letter to AA co-founder Bill Wilson, understood it perfectly. He believed that to heal from addiction, a person requires a spiritual recovery. I guess you can say I suffer from a poverty of spirit or what spiritual researchers describe as addicts being "sick for God."

Thankfully, I came to a place in my addiction where the artificial magic stopped working for me. Today I recognize that I am both Peter and Wendy. Mother and child. I still cling to the magic and wonder of childhood. But now I am at least open to loving and being loved by others instead of pills and pot. And without love, what do any of us have to live for? So often I see in my clients who struggle with addiction and other mental-health issues, a deep-seated disconnection not only from themselves, but others. I recently read that the opposite of addiction is bonding. What it means to be fully human.

I find hidden and profound spiritual life lessons not only from the recovery rooms, but from the gospel according to Peter Pan. I think Peter was onto something. I could use a little more pixie dust in my life, just not the chemical kind. Today I dream of a good life. A life of healing because I am broken and sick for God. I am like Humpty Dumpty who has had a great fall and needs to be put back together again. This requires bravery. In recovery, I am learning to be brave and live out of my true north. Live real and purposeful with eyes wide open and mind clear. I do this by moving through the madness in meditation and turning to prayer because *prayer does not want.*

Yet, I am a child of consumerism. So, I do want. My wanting is in fact relentless. But in sobriety, I've learned that consumerism isn't just a powerful marketing strategy. It is an indominable spiritual force. The good news is today I see these "urgent wants or longings" for what they truly are. The starting point of a spiritual life. Looking back, I recognize that my spiritual thirst emerged at six years old when I began to explore a deep connection with God. But then I hit adolescence, and something shifted in my brain. Then my values. The same brain I inherited from my alcoholic father and valium-addicted mother. My biography was becoming my biology.

I still wanted heaven but found praying was too slow. So, I turned to something other than the spiritual life to give me supersonic relief. It would be some time before I learned how to untangle what was behind my compulsive chemical cravings and learned to beat them at their own game before the insatiable desires destroyed me. Of course, the global market ideology wants me to believe that I need more. It insists that I buy into the lie that who I am and what I have is not enough. Ever.

The way I counteract these lies is by telling them to fly away, along with Peter. I can do this because I am willing to live in the here and now and face life on life's terms. Recovery is a liberating paradox. Anne Frank, in one of her famous Holocaust diaries, wrote about personal liberation, "Our lives are fashioned by our choices. First, we make our choices. Then our choices make us." Now that I am living in the solution instead of the problem of addiction to alcohol and drugs, I feel empowered to make healthy, life-giving choices for myself. The process is untidy, unpredictable, and certainly uncomfortable at times. But life is a beautiful mess after all. I wouldn't have it any other way.

"We cannot fix this.
We did not cause it.
    Meghan can be a drug addict
and also a cherished
            family member."

## BLINDERS

Kelly S. Thompson

When I present my sister's crack pipe to our mother, I pretend I found it while looking for a sweater to borrow, because that's the kind of thing normal sisters do. Even though Meghan is slowly killing herself, Mom and Dad believe we should respect her scattered belongings, lugged to and fro in black garbage bags to each new locale: an addicted nomad. Mom is mad that I went through her things without permission.

But I explore her room routinely, digging under the mattress and patting down her sock drawer, not out of spite, but fear. Every pipe, bong, residue, and rock makes me vibrate with anger before the feeling dissipates into anxiety. I know the sharp tang of crack, the smell synonymous with my sister who used to smell of Herbal Essences shampoo.

We are a polite family: typical Canadians who *please* and *sorry* our way through life. Middle class—only just—proven by our suburban neighbourhood with the wide garage doors and more bedrooms than we'll ever use. Dad and I are both military officers, and soldiers and their families don't do drugs, right? We're law-abiding folk. We follow the rules as much as we enforce them.

Our privileged existence comes with a hefty set of blinders, donned since birth. They provide just enough guidance to keep us believing in the lies we tell ourselves—that we are buffeted from the pressures and pleasures that can come with addiction.

When I miss my big sister, who defended me from bullies and read me bedtime stories, I look at our first shared Christmas photo. It's horrible, really. Me, a wailing newborn and Meghan, mid-cancer battle, her kidney sporting a tumour the size of an orange. In this picture, Meghan's bald head is stark and white against the red background and plaid skirt, chubby three-year-old hands folded neatly in her lap, a smile barely present. My eyes are swollen and red as I squirm in Santa's arms, clutching his synthetic beard in my tiny fist.

In the photo, Santa is smiling at Meghan in the placating, nervous way that adults always gazed upon her illness. Heck, we still look at Meghan like this, no matter that she turned fifteen, then twenty, then twenty-five, each year marking another step towards a decade of addiction. We still treat her as though she might snap in two, because her vulnerability is a palpable thing, and without diligence, she could die. The weight of that fear gnaws at our family like a hunger, but it's the lack of control that makes us all crazy. We cannot fix this. We did not cause it. Meghan can be a drug addict and also, a cherished family member.

Looking at the photo, I find it ironic that me, young and healthy, promise of a hearty life ahead, cannot keep her emotions in check, while my sister, riddled with disease and something worth crying about, is an adorable bundle, relatively composed, telling Santa about her dreams of a Cabbage Patch Doll.

Since I'm the only one in the family able to face the stark reality of my sister's crack addiction, which will later morph into opioids, my sister and I walk a line of awkwardness teetering precariously towards acceptance, then back to animosity. I stop socializing with her or calling to check in. I'm an important military officer these days; no time for her shenanigans, which is what I tell myself they are. She can stop anytime, right? She can just call this whole thing off, put down the lighter and step away from the boyfriends and low self-esteem that curl a finger in her mouth like a fishhook. Her weakness makes me angry enough to cut her out of my life, or at least, the decision feels easier when I tell myself it is a choice of bitterness and not a recommendation from the Nar-Anon support group I went to. *Enabling.* It is a word I vow never to espouse.

I decide that what the Thompson family needs is some good old-fashioned holiday delusion. We need a new Santa photo, I tell my sister, and although she sounds high enough to hardly remember the conversation, Meghan shows up for our meeting wearing a baggy pair of jeans and a zip-up sweater that looks like one of those sporty polyester numbers from the seventies, although she's never played a sport in all of her life. She fidgets with her upper lip, picking and tugging at the tender skin there until blood stains the tips of her fingers.

Georgian Mall is full to the brim with last-minute Christmas shoppers and people mill around us, laughing and chatting. I stand to meet my sister, find myself awkward as she hugs me with arms like overcooked spaghetti. I pat her back uncomfortably, her eyes level with my chest, no longer the big sister, figuratively or literally. To look at us, you would never know we were related. I'm tall, she's short. I'm blonde, she's brunette. My skin tans to dark brown, she burns at the first exposure to light. We could be strangers, my sister and I.

"Hi," I say, stepping back.

"Hey."

"Thanks for meeting me."

"No problem."

There is no mention of the fact that it's been three months since we saw each other, when she moved to the other side of town from our parents. A whopping five-minute drive. She gathers her sheet of brown hair into a ponytail, wisps of grey sneaking through the box dye. It's only then that I take stock of her tiny five-foot-one frame, her cheeks sunken into skin the colour of an elephant. Her gentle curves have given way to jutting hip bones attached to a skeletal frame.

"You're crazy thin," I say, reaching out to tug at the loose waistband of her jeans. She swats at me with her hand.

"I'm fine. Gawd." Spittle gathers at the corner of her mouth. Her brows furrow into creases, and her blue eyes, the exact shade of my own and our sole shared feature, turn stormy and dark. And then, as though the hurricane has passed, she lifts the veil of anger and adjusts her sweater, a veritable Jekyll and Hyde.

"We better line up," she says, moving towards the throng of children.

I want to walk through the mall first, but for the last two years, every time I shop with her, we get home to her having stolen so much booty that I have no idea how she managed the stealth. Perhaps the store employees wear their own pair of blinders. *I can relate*, I would tell them. *Addiction is easier to ignore than trying to enforce the rules.*

We wander towards the line that curls around Santa's workshop. Kids rally around us from every angle, pointing and dragging their parents to coloured toys that have been enticingly placed in shop windows. Their excited energy makes me nervous while Meghan seems to be revelling in it, her crusty demeanour softened, a woman who despite all actions indicating otherwise, was born to be a mother. She coos at a pair of twin boys in a stroller in front of us, their matching blonde curls twirling around their ears.

Santa's workshop is pieced together out of painted wood and cardboard additions that look somehow polished since they're covered with fake cotton snow. A small gingerbread house is perched next to wooden elves that mechanically nod their heads while Rudolph's nose shines tomato-coloured light on the painted sky ahead. We slowly move forward in the lineup, photo after photo snapped as kids whisper their dreams of dollhouses and Nerf guns. The eighty-year-old Santa smiles happily into the camera for each shot. His motorized scooter, the reminder of real life, is tucked inconspicuously behind the giant present display.

Meghan alternates between picking her lip and scratching at invisible, nonexistent bumps on her arm. I repeatedly check my BlackBerry for messages that need tending to.

"Busy with work?"

"Super busy." I say as I click a few more words before dropping the phone into my purse. "What about you?"

"It's okay. Busy, I guess."

Last week, I went to the tanning salon where Meghan said she was working as a receptionist.

"Fired her," the clerk said, snapping her gum in a series of machine-gun pops while spraying the counter with disinfectant. "Sick of her coming in here high as all hell."

Meghan looks at me nervously, picking and picking until I feel like I might slap her. We've spent the last few years like this. Meghan lies. I know it. We're essentially the FBI of sisterhood.

"Ho, Ho, Ho!" Santa waves us over with his gloved hand.

"Hi Santa," Meghan says meekly, staring down at her feet as though this man really will determine if she's been good or bad.

"Tell me, what brings two ladies to see me?"

Meghan and I hover over his knees, aware of Santa's frailty, our thigh muscles wavering under our weight. I adjust myself uncomfortably, try to lean against the arm rest.

"We're redoing our Christmas photo for our parents," I say through clenched teeth.

"And what was wrong with the last one?"

Meghan's bottom lip quivers as a warning and then she blubbers into her hands, tucking her chin to her chest and leaning into the non-judgemental shoulder of Santa.

"Whoa, hey now, it's okay," Santa says. He keeps looking at his elven wranglers, then back to Meghan, then at me, as though somehow I will assuage the situation. I shrug my shoulders assuring Santa that I, too, am powerless. Also, Thompson women are hideous criers. Our eyes swell, our lips puff out, and our skin goes all red and blotchy. This photo doesn't stand a chance in hell.

"We weren't really happy in our last photo," I say, trying to keep my own unexpected tears at the back of my throat. "It's not a very happy picture for our parents."

"Well then, let's create a new memory," Santa says, a line straight out of a Hallmark commercial. His eyes dart to the fifty-odd waiting children.

"Ready girls?" Santa asks.

"Ready," we say in unison.

Just as quick as the tears arrived, Meghan reveals a plastic smile that is frightening in its suggestion of happiness. I could almost believe it myself. Our eyes connect, her glassy, dilated pupils wide and black like the big marble we used to fight over as kids. My face goes prickly and hot. I hate her. Or I want to hate her. Or maybe I want to save her. Tuck her tiny body into my arms and keep her safe.

"Say Christmas!" says the camera operator. Her finger hovers over the shutter button while she waves a stuffed reindeer. I hear the jingling of bells somewhere distant as the flash snaps, and for a moment, I am blind to everything, a shiny orb following my line of sight.

Later, when Meghan asks me why I'm crying, I explain that it's just allergies. My eyes are watering from the flash, of course. I'll lie. Meghan will know it. Another secret kept.

Meghan calls, and I answer. I always answer when she calls, ever since she finished treatment and got clean.

"Going to get some Santa photos done with Rowan." I can hear her smiling and then the sound of my nephew suckling. I can't control the smirk that appears on my own face. "Going this Thursday. Want to come?"

I tell her no, but thanks, I'm busy. I could make it, if I'm honest, but I want her to have this moment with her son, with the family she deserves, so that when she looks upon it twenty years from now, gazing at her child with the same blinders we all sported for years, she will recognize what happiness looks like, and how easy it can be to stray from.

"During my treatment for my addiction,
I learned that it's not wrong to be upset.

It's not wrong to cry, or to want attention.
It's not wrong to scream and throw a fit.

What is wrong is to keep it all inside."

## MY HEART NEVER GAVE UP

Rebecca Dawe

How can I put into words something that can only be experienced? I cannot believe the person I was a few years ago. It's been a long rough road, and if it wasn't for my family who constantly supported me, I would never have become the person I am today. As Babe Ruth said, "It's hard to beat a person who never gives up." Although it felt like I gave up multiple times, and fell into my dark place again, my heart never gave up.

My name is Rebecca Dawe. I am nineteen years old, and I am currently dealing with alcohol addiction. It all started when I was five. I was one of seven girls who was sexually assaulted by an adult man. Unfortunately, it was not a one-time thing. This went on for about three years. I never told anyone until I was twelve years old. Eventually, my case went to court, but ended up being dropped. It always felt like I never got justice.

That was my trigger. Then came my behaviour changes. I was

always lashing out, and never listening to my parents. I refused all help that my parents tried to give me, all the counselling, and the therapy. I used to say that I didn't need help, that I didn't have a problem. Then I started running away, hiding away from everything. Hiding away from reality. I ended up moving away from my family. I moved out on my own when I was sixteen, so nobody could tell me what to do, or what I was supposed to do. I was my own person. That's when I found a way to really get away from reality. Forget everything for a little while, and black out. I started drinking. Excessively. I could barely remember my name, let alone what my past was, and I loved it. I was not worried about school, or my family. I did not have time for relationships like a normal teenager. I only had time for those few hours that I could forget everything and everyone. I only had time for the bottle.

Each time I drank, though, I was realizing that it was taking more and more alcohol to get the feeling I wanted. The numbness that I needed. Those few hours were not enough anymore. My tolerance for alcohol was getting higher. I could drink more and last longer. Then it got to the point where I wouldn't sleep. I would stay up all night drinking. I was skipping school. Sometimes, I wouldn't eat for days at a time. Everything I had went to alcohol, but once again it got to a point where even that wasn't enough for me either. I needed more.

Then I started drinking as soon as my eyes would open. At this point, I dropped out of school. The only thing I had time for was the booze. There were many hospital visits, and many stupid decisions. Nothing stopped me, or so I thought.

I started losing everything, including my mind. I was getting violent when I was drunk, fighting with people who were only trying to help me. I was also getting destructive. I got kicked out of my apartment for destroying it one night that I ran out of booze. This is when reality hit me like a ton of bricks when I sobered up, of course. I had a problem. I needed help.

I finally moved back home with my family, to mend the relationship. They helped get me the counselling that I needed. I was told about the treatment centre in Grand Falls- Windsor, NL. So I gave it a shot. I was finally ready for it. I wanted my life back. I wanted to graduate from grade twelve. I wanted to get my license. I wanted to go to college. I had all these dreams that I could only do if I got control of my addiction.

My time in the treatment centre was not easy. It took a lot of opening up, which I was not used to. I had to come to terms with why I was drinking so heavily, and how what happened to me was not my fault. I blamed myself for everything that happened to me as a child. There were many group discussions, as well as a lot of one-on-one time with counsellors to get to the root of my problems, and how to fix them, and get back on the right path. I learned a lot of techniques to help me cope with my problems, and some healthy ways to deal with them also, instead of turning to the bottle.

I wasn't looking to give up alcohol altogether; at this point, I was not even nineteen. I just didn't want to use alcohol as a coping mechanism anymore. I wanted to be able to have one drink, and it just be one drink. I didn't want to black out anymore. I wanted to be able to have a social drink, and know how to control myself. I succeeded. Yes, I do have a drink every now and then, but I've learned how to control myself, and not use it as a cover-up.

During my treatment for my addiction, I learned that it's not wrong to be upset. It's not wrong to cry, or to want attention. It's not wrong to scream and throw a fit. What is wrong is to keep it all inside. To blame and punish yourself for being human. What is wrong is to never to be heard and to be alone in pain. So today and every day, share it, let it out. Everyone needs someone there to talk to. You are not alone.

Now, I've finally finished my grade twelve. I got my license. I just graduated from College as a Heavy Equipment Operator. I'm still living with my family, and I could not be happier with how far I have come, and the person that I am today. I don't know what I would have done or where I would be today without my family, who never gave up on me. Even though sometimes I felt like my mind gave up on myself, my heart never did. My heart knew what was right.

Always believe in yourself. You can do anything you put your mind to. Christopher Robin (*Winnie the Pooh*) said, "You are braver than you believe, stronger than you seem, and smarter than you think."

"Why can't the world be like this always—
        a wondrous place of joy and happiness?
Like an ancient tribal religious ritual,
    where you all dance yourselves into a frenzy
before a big hunt, to bond into a single entity—
    a team, a group, a tribe.
        It's like we're all one being here now...
Group Mind...Transcendence...Nirvana."

## PSEUDO WORLD

William Stromich

### I THE BEGINNING—OVERTURE

Where do you start? Sometimes people start stories about themselves by telling you all about their parents and childhood and crap like that. I don't know about you, but I usually find that incredibly boring. I think it's enough to say that, growing up, there was a lot of drinking and yelling and throwing things, but my parents stuck together because of the ancient rites of Catholicism. But this isn't a story about them. It's about me. Obviously, if that's your life, you get away from that shit as fast as possible—move to the big city, start over. Get a job. Make new friends. Come out. Live a kind of dull, routine life.

And so I lived a dull, routine life. A government job with a desk in a small office. Sober. Realistic. Reliable. Serious. Interested in movies, classical music, lousy TV, novels. Hard work and career stress navigating bureaucratic intrigue. Community groups. See what I mean? D-u-l-l. Time passes. You have friends you do stuff with but still feel kind of alone, in a way, isolated. Until...

I met Jeremy and Brian at an LGBT barbeque in Vancouver. Brian came across as a successful corporate guy, tall with blonde hair and blue eyes, WASP to the core—pleasant, from a rich family, maybe a bit dull, or so I thought at the time. On the other hand, Jeremy seemed more interesting. I was immediately drawn to him, and he to me. We became best friends. Tall, freckled, with straight, floppy, ginger hair, Jeremy looks like he was a student at Oxford in the 1920s. He works out a lot, and is smart and gregarious. He's unusual— an intellectual combined with an athlete is a strange mix you don't see too often. He got me into reading pop-culture sage Marshall McLuhan. We'd go out to movies and dissect them to pieces afterwards over coffee at Starbucks.

We also used to go out dancing periodically. One of the things I liked about Jeremy was we could have a lively debate on some obscure topic, and then we could go out and drink ourselves silly and dance. But lately, he's been preoccupied with a new job he landed, and I've been really busy being depressed about my lonely, loveless life. He's cancelled on me at the last minute five times over the last few weeks saying he was really busy. Then one day, he suggests going out dancing, to the next big party, as we haven't done it in a while. He says for sure he won't cancel. Then, after me getting the tickets, he tells me at the last minute he can't go as he's got some kind of work emergency. Shocker! So, rather than not going out, I decide to call Brian. He's going with a group of friends, and he's cool with me tagging along with them. I go to his place to meet for a drink before going out. I meet some of his eclectic friends.

They're actually quite nice—an actor, a waiter, a security guard, a student, a guy in finance. I'm a bit surprised to see they're also all getting their party drugs organised. Brian says he has some extra Ecstasy if I want to try it.

It seems that behind the corporate guy mask, Brian is seriously into partying. So 9 a.m. to 5 p.m., Monday to Friday, he's at the office working hard, making a good impression and all, with promotions and bonuses. But weekends, he becomes a totally out-there, try-anything, party-boy drug machine. Not just Ecstasy, but Ketamine, GHB, coke, crystal meth, the whole catastrophe. So I feel a little trepidation about the whole thing, but also more than a little curiosity. I've spent my entire life being a good boy, and I must admit the dark side has a kind of strange attraction. Was this the low door in the wall leading to the enchanted garden that Charles found in *Brideshead Revisited*? So anyhow, I go, and take him up on his offer and take some E. And, I have to admit, I had an absolutely incredible time!

## II THE MIDDLE—ALLEGRO CO FUOCO

How do you describe Methylenedioxymethamphetamine-MDMA? Ecstasy. How can mere words, the crude symbol system we use to communicate pleasantries and actions and esoteric concepts, capture or even hope to express the total overwhelming intensity of the emotional experience? How can a symbol system where, as Iris Murdoch said, any statement beyond "pass the gravy" is at best, an ambiguous approximation of our thoughts, subject to endless debate and interpretation of subtle facets of meaning, how can such a system express the unbridled euphoria, the blissful calm? How can it possibly convey a state of mind where you become the Dalai Llama, and a joyful lottery winner? Where you feel the love and compassion and empathy of Mother Theresa, and the giggly happiness of a child? A transformation that's so complete, it seems like some modern-day alchemist has succeeded in unlocking the mystery of magical transmutation. It creates a state of mind unlike anything you experience in the "real" world. A real world that, afterwards, seems so sullen and grey and sad. Sometimes, words don't create beautiful mellifluous poetry. Instead, they ring hollow and empty, a shrill, tuneless clanging. Martin Luther King said, "Occasionally in life there are those moments of unutterable fulfillment which cannot be completely explained by those symbols called words." Although I'm sure he was talking about something else, it certainly applies to E. It was a throwing off of the chains of my bondage to the quiet, shy persona I had lived inside my entire life.

So I become one of Brian's clubbing posse, and we go clubbing on a regular basis. The first couple of times we go out, I just go out for the night, and go home in the morning when they go to the afterhours club. At this point, Jeremy and I stopped talking. If I called him, he wouldn't answer or call me back. He got wind of what was going on and mightily disapproved.

A typical week now sort of rolls out like this:

*Friday 10:00 p.m.*

Go to the bar, the meet-up. See friends not seen for a week— have a jovial beer together. I forget, is it operant or classical conditioning when the conditioned response precedes the stimulus? Classical, I think. So when the jaw is already starting to clench up a bit and I get jittery and giddy in the bar—it's the classical conditioning kicking in—I'm Pavlov's dog! Hey, who knew Psych 101 was actually true?

Head down to the club. The lineup. The anticipation. The bouncers. The pat down. Inside, finally. A few quick calculations about when the headliner starts, and when to peak—it's time now. The drop!

The waiting—anxiously checking the time. Not yet. Check again. Not yet. God, I hope it's not bad shit! Calming smoke outside. Clock check. Wait. Then—the scalp begins to tingle, the feet get lighter, it suddenly starts to feel a bit warmer, you smile for no reason— the world seems more beautiful, and better and happier. You realize it's happening now, and then, The Rush comes—euphoria! You're dancing now—you can't not be. The music, the lights, the people, the bodies, the motion is all One with you, floating over it all, within it all, in a cloud of blissful love and joy. You're Rolling now! This is good stuff. The music, God, the music. Following all the melodic layers as they weave together, the way they communicate with each other, like a Bach fugue. I hear them all, see them all dancing together. Flying! Here comes some tempo doubling—guess that means the arms go up in the air soon. Feel the beat. Build. Build. Release! Love the tonic pedal now! New rhythm starting to emerge—a new tune coming in now. Great mixing! Wow, this DJ is Totally Sick! Really loving The Beat—I am...the beat. I mean, I'm not just dancing to it, it's *inside* me. I'm Floating. Time dilates. You don't just exist anymore. You're alive! Why can't you be like this always? Why can't the world be like this always— a wondrous place of joy and happiness? Like an ancient tribal religious ritual, where you all dance yourselves into a frenzy before a big hunt, to bond into a single entity—a team, a group, a tribe. It's like we're all one being here now...Group Mind... Transcendence...Nirvana.

Been dancing a long time now, nonstop. We sit and chill and talk for a while. I have the best friends in the world! I mean, we really understand each other—we connect in a really profound way. No boundaries, no differences, no separations, just all of us togeth- er, part of the same whole. A friend gently strokes my forearm as we talk, not in a sexual way, just a friendly way. The nerves tingle with a gentle electricity and send little waves of pleasure through my body.

Funny how the senses are heightened but you don't feel tense, just calm and content. Everyone is so nice here. Starting to gently coast down, I think. Time to dose again. Waiting. Takeoff. Time to dance some more. Flying. Coast, dose, wait, flight. Again.

## Saturday

Closing time at the club but we're too high to go home. So, we head to the afterhours club. It's really a total shithole, and the crowd is kind of weird and skanky and totally fucked up, but the music is really hard, and any manner of drugs is readily available. Most patrons seem messed up on a wide variety of letters of the alphabet: E,K,G, not to mention coke and crystal and weed. A more diverse mix of people here. The gays in one area, the ginos and ginas over there. The homies in the back corner. People mix on the dance floor and everything's cool—we're all doing our own thing, and people are pretty nice, and there are huge bouncers walking around to quickly deal with anyone who gets out of line. We're all into the music and the beat is really hard and pumpin', not ethereal and uplifting and trancey like it was before; it's dark and dirty. We dance. Chill. Dose. Keep on going. What a crazy otherworldly vibe in this place, like one of those bars on another planet in *Star Wars*, full of really weird looking aliens with appendages sticking out everywhere. You know, the places people go to buy things they're not supposed to have and learn things they're not supposed to know. Who knows what time it is in this dark and dingy and crowded place? Afternoon? Already? Maybe it's time to come down and go home? They turn the lights on and stop the music—that means it's time to leave.

We start the long journey home. The sun is Really Bright! How strange the world looks out here in the daylight, people going about their normal lives—it all seems so—odd? How sad and awful for them—or is that what they think of us, coming out of that place, at this time of day? So, am I one of them, again, now, instead of whatever sort of being I just was, back in there?

Imagine, a teeny little pill, and all it does is swoosh the serotonin in the neurons in your brain out into the synapses, and then inhibit its re-uptake for a while, so the receptors just soak it all up. Kind of like Prozac or Zoloft or Effexor, only more intense. And that little process caused this night of rapture. What are "real" emotions and thoughts then? Why was this chemical-induced feeling of ecstasy less real than "normal" feelings? "Real" emotions are intermediated by the same neurotransmitters, over the same synapses, aren't they? So doesn't that make them the same? Which state is really more real? And by knowing the "unreal" state of bliss is *possible*, does that mean that it can be achieved *without* the chemical assistance? Whoa—deep thoughts!

Tired, sleep deprived, coming down and getting totally sketchy. So tired, can hardly walk. Enormous dilated pupils—hard to focus— people say I look really fucked up—don't feel that bad though—just tired. Cabbies zoom right past us, despite outstretched arms—I guess we look pretty bad? Get home and try to sleep, but it's pointless— must pee every fifteen minutes—overdid the water maybe? Can't read more than two sentences in a row—no attention span—is this what ADD is like? Try and choke down a bit of food—should eat, since it's been nearly twenty-four hours since I last ate anything, but not really very hungry. Pills were a bit speedy, I think. Only menial tasks are possible. The day, or what's left of it, is a write-off— another sketch-out day...the vast empty desert expanse that must be crossed, returning from the land of bliss, to the land of...what... reality, I guess. Early to bed—sleep at last!

*Sunday*

Afterglow. A not unpleasant day–some chores and tasks and reading yesterday's papers. Still a bit sketchy—a bit hard to concentrate on anything for a long time—back to maybe seventy-five percent of normal capacity. Phone rings. It's Brian. He tells me about the post-afterhours club sketch-out party. Talk about how much fun the weekend was—too short though. I think maybe I'll go to the sketch party next time. The day since the afterhours club has been a waste anyways.

### Monday

Office. The world is a nice place, placid and satisfied. Still a bit tired though. It takes a long time to catch up on a whole night's missed sleep! What a great weekend though. Can't wait to do it again! Bit uncoordinated and clumsy though. I keep dropping my water bottle. Odd that. Hungry again, ravenous, in fact.

### Tuesday

Work. The weekend seems remote, distant, long gone—another world, another planet even—a long, long time ago in a galaxy far, far away. Was it fun? Did I have a good time? Or was it all just an illusion, some sort of hallucination? I don't think so, but…I wonder. I wonder. Some weird shit on the weekend.

### Wednesday

Sad. Morose. Depressed, even. The world sucks, life sucks, everything sucks. So lost and miserable. Must be The Crash, a big one. I guess it's Newton's third law in action, with a small update, i.e., for every Rush, there is an equal and opposite Crash. God, my life sucks. Cranky and irritable. Does it show? I don't think so. I try to act "normal" but people at work keep asking what's wrong, say I seem a bit bummed, on edge. Dunno why, because I'm really trying hard to act "normal." I just wanna go home and get the fuck away from them all.

*Thursday*

A nice day. The air is fresh and crisp. I forgot how great Armin is! What did people do before portable music? How did people stand the subway? Now, riding the subway is like your own personal music video. I don't even mind when the train does one of those annoying mid-tunnel stops. It just means more time with the headphones and the music, and less time in the office. Work. The day goes by, getting lots of work done. Brian phones. Do I maybe wanna go out this weekend? Not sure. Maybe a week off would be good? Recharge, like. Nah? Who's spinning? Shit, can't miss him. All the "accoutrements" are organized? Ok, I'm in. See ya tomorrow.

*Friday*

Hey, it's Friday. Thank God. Rough week at work. Day goes by. Time to head out. The bar, the meet-up. Friends not seen for a week— a jovial beer together. Hide the drugs. Time to head down to the club—must admit, getting a bit giddy now!

In no time at all, my life changes pretty dramatically. I could lie and say I was all reluctant-like, but what's the point? It all happened incredibly fast, really. It didn't take very long at all from the first time I did it, until I started doing it every week. It was so much fun, and felt so incredibly good! Pretty soon, it starts to take up most of my free time. Pretty soon, I start to spend less and less time with my other friends. I'm busy every weekend and too tired during the week. And when I do see them, they say I look like shit, ask what's going on. If I give them a little outline, just some highlights, they get all worried and concerned. Tell me to be careful. Lecture and criticize like some fucking afterschool special. Idiots. Who needs that shit? They have no idea what they're missing.

The ecstasy-based weeklong mood swings create a different kind of texture to my emotional life. I begin to question all of my feelings on the basis that it's all being affected by the ebb and flow of serotonin and dopamine and who knows what other neurotransmitters in my brain. I almost feel sort of removed from myself in a mildly Buddhist kind of way. I start to feel aloof from all the problems, worries, and concerns in my life, and the new problems all the drug use is creating. Being really high much of the time, and recovering the rest, is a great way to accomplish that. Generally, it works pretty well. For a while.

Pretty quickly the ecstasy starts to lose its magic. You can't really do it every week the way we did. Your brain needs time to replenish the serotonin it's used up on the weekend, and a week isn't long enough. I buy some 5-HTP at the vitamin store to try to help the process along, but it's a waste of time. I get the energy, but the ecstatic euphoria fades into a feeling of being just happy, which then fades into being just sort of mildly pleased. I learn what to expect and how to control it, and it becomes routine, almost mundane. It's so fucking maddening that something that was so amazing for a while has become a big fucking boring routine! That's when you start to branch out into the other stuff: G, K, crystal. They give you a new kind of kick, a new kind of high, each intense in their own ways, and there's no limit on how much of those you can do.

After the club, and after the afterhours club, you don't really want it to end, you don't want to stop, so I started going to the sketch parties. So-called because everyone is pretty sketchy from a night of dancing, drugs, and sleep deprivation. You go to someone's house and lounge around. Brian's place became the weekend hangout.

So at Brian's, we listen to chill out music. Have something to drink, Gatorade, coffee. No one really eats anything. The drugs kill your appetite. Maybe smoke some weed. Do some more drugs. This is where the G really comes to the fore. It relaxes you and makes you horny, so a little casual groping and sex usually result. If you do too much G though, you G-out, i.e., pass out and sleep for a few hours, like in a coma. If you get too mellow, then a line of crystal will make you clear and sharp and alert. You never really know what's in the pills sold as E. Sometimes its pure MDMA. Those are good for the first couple of doses on the weekend. Some have amphetamine—speed—in them. Those are better for the rest of the weekend. Sometimes the dealer has an idea which are which, sometimes not. It's not like they're made by a big pharma company with all those labels and warnings. They're made by some guy in a "lab," probably more like a shed, in China or somewhere. Over the course of the weekend, I guess we'd end up taking a lot of speed, not just MDMA. So if you want to perk up and feel a buzz, a little trail mix is in order—ground up speedy-E mixed with some K and snorted. Just K will perk you up, or give you a nice sort of slightly disoriented euphoria, depending on how much you take. If you take too much, then you end up in a K-hole, where you are no longer in control of your body but your mind is still active. It's a dissociative anesthetic after all, so that's the anesthetic dosage. But the right dose gives a great euphoric, trippy high, that's a lot of fun to dance to. Things kind of go in slow motion, then speed up. Objects have speed trails. The music slows down and speeds up. You feel like you're underwater and then in the air flying. You feel like you're falling over and then you find your balance. The party can go on for hours. Days. People come and go. It goes on basically until you run out of drugs. That's when someone calls a friend who deals a bit, or until it's time to go to the next club, 'cause hey, it's night again! This is how a Friday night out turns into a whole weekend. A couple of nights out, a couple of sketch parties, and the weekend's gone and it's Sunday night and it's time to go home and get some sleep to go to work on Monday.

It's odd. It's a prepackaged world of friendly people, of instant social bonds. The E makes you all open and loving. People are nice, welcoming. The G makes you horny as hell and enhances performance—blood flows where it's needed with great alacrity—I mean like someone touches you and Boing! There is easy sex. It's a world of delirious, delightful happiness in pill or powder or liquid form. You're so fucked up, that you don't really feel responsible for your actions and just do whatever feels good at the moment. No consequences. Isn't that how you're supposed to live anyways, on some level? You don't say to yourself, what the fuck was I thinking, until about two or three days later. How can't that be enticing and alluring when you're miserable and depressed and lonely? You feel this "us against them" bond and feel sorry for the sad losers in the real world who can't share this kind of bliss. Is this the real world or a fake world? A pseudo world...or not. What is "reality" anyways? When you're in the pseudo world, the other, "real," world seems distant and unreal and irrelevant. But when you're in the "real" world, like say, sitting at your desk at work, the drug world seems really far away...but you can hardly wait to get back to it next weekend.

## II THE END-CODA

It went on this way for maybe a year or so.

Then, one night we went out to hear Digweed spin. An old-time DJ, but he's still got it. He was amazing, building to an ecstatic crescendo over five hours. It was incredible. Only did a couple of Es and few bumps of K, so pretty light on the drugs. After, we went to the afterhours club. I did a cap of G and there was something really fucked up about it. Must have been some K in there? I felt kind of odd and disoriented—distracted by light and movement. I guess my eyes and head were sort of darting around, and I had a funny reptilian expression on my face. Brian made fun of me, laughing at me, ridiculing me. I tried to limit my movement and expressions to try to cut down on the ridicule, and he just made fun of that, calling me a vegetable and not even human. He took me around to people we didn't even know and asked me questions, and when I couldn't answer, he laughed maniacally at me. People told him to stop being so mean, but he just kept going on and on. I felt like a prisoner inside my body being tormented by a psychotic jailer. I wanted to go home, for it to end, but it wouldn't end. After what seemed like a long time, Brian sat me down in the back chill-out area, and left to search for more G.

This was the beginning of Brian getting more and more weird. There was this dark undercurrent of malice that began to creep out from him. He was doing a lot of meth. Sunday nights, I would go home and try to get some sleep for work on Monday. Brian would go back to the afterhours club until it closed on Monday at 6 a.m., and then go home and get ready for work with a big line of meth. The afterhours club had a "green room" where they put people who had G-ed out to sleep it off—just a dingy little back room with some old puke-stained mattresses on the floor. Brian got put in there a few times. He was argumentative with the bouncers when he woke up, and they told him to go home. He didn't want to go. So they banned him from the club for weeks at a time. He started to hear voices and had these wild mood swings. One minute, he'd be his old, happy, laughing self. Then he'd become that angry version. Then he'd be all catatonic and unresponsive, like a zombie. We were all getting worried. If we said anything to him, told him to maybe ease up a bit, he would get all mad, paranoid-like, and tell us to stop interfering. Some medical-type person told me later that all this was pretty standard stuff for a speed/meth user: anger, violent outbursts, and paranoia are part of something called amphetamine psychosis.

One Wednesday, when I hadn't heard from him for a few days, I got a call from his sister. Sobbing, barely able to get the words out, she told me that Brian had died of a heart attack. I was stunned. I got together with the other members of the posse and told them. They were all shocked. One of them thought we should call a dealer and get something to give him a proper send off. I was appalled at the idea and left.

I took all of this as a cue to take a break. Brian's death made it clear to me where this was heading, so I stopped seeing almost all of the other members of the posse. All of the magic and fun had gone anyways. The whole scene had started to feel more and more like a boring routine. A compulsion. Then this shock about Brian sent it from being a comedy that was getting sort of boring into the realm of tragedy. Even though things got kind of weird at the end, we had been through a lot together. I really cared about him. Loved him, in a way, even. So his death had a big impact.

I had lost about thirty pounds over the last year and looked like shit. Not eating anything at all every weekend is a great way to lose weight. My real world friends, the few whom I still saw, were very concerned. Some had given up on me completely. After I decided to stop partying, some of the party people tried to get me to come back to the fun. But I stayed clean. The rest kept on going. I stayed friends with only one of them who toned things down a lot, although he didn't stop completely. But the two of us started doing "normal" friend things. The effects of the drugs on your body and brain slowly build up, so you hardly notice the cumulative deterioration. But it adds up. After a month off, as you start to recover and feel better, you realize just how bad things had gotten. How shitty you felt all the time. How terrible you looked. But you didn't care because feeling good was just a pill or a snort or a smoke away. It takes a long time to really recover and start to feel like your old self again.

Really, the end for me came just as fast as the beginning. I got out of that world as quickly as I had fallen in. Was I an addict? Certainly, over the year or so that I lived in this pseudo world, many of my friends in the "real" world thought I was, and said as much, over and over again. Who can say for sure? I certainly danced on the razor's edge of the abyss for a while. I think I fell one way and Brian fell the other. Was I just lucky? Who knows. The time between when you don't think you need to stop, and when you know you can't, passes by in the blink of an eye. I've known a few people for whom the only way out was to leave town and go back to their families somewhere else. It works for some people. It wasn't unusual for people you saw around all the time to suddenly disappear. You weren't sure if they went to rehab, left town, went to jail or what. Sometimes they would turn up again, the day after they got out of rehab, ready to party. Sometimes they just disappeared and no one knew where they'd gone. They just stopped responding to calls or texts.

I've gone back to my normal, somewhat staid life. I even became friends with Jeremy again. Every now and then I think about that strange world. I can't say I don't miss the fun part at the beginning, a little. The thing people don't get when they say they don't understand how someone *chooses* to become an addict, is that they look at the mess you are at the end. They don't realize that, at the beginning, it's fun and exciting. It gives you a kind of unbridled happiness you can't find in your normal life. An instant world of acceptance, love, and friends. A profound feeling of connection. An escape from all of your problems and worries. It takes time for this illusion to crumble. By then it might be too late. It takes time to see it's all fake, a delusion that doesn't, can't, last, and that the dull, boring real world is better than the pseudo world after all.

"It's been almost three years since I injected
        myself with morphine. It's been almost
three years since I hit rock bottom.
                I lost a lot, but I've gained so
much more than I could ever have imagined!"

## NOT TODAY, BUT SOMEDAY, I WILL BREAK FREE

Amanda Murphy

Some days, like today, are bad days. Days like today, I lack passion for life and motivation to move forward. I feel numb and disconnected, and it scares me. It's like being paralyzed, tied to the middle of a merry-go-round, being stuck while the rest of the world passes you by. I'll be okay. I've been here before and I hated it then, too. It's days like today that have taught me to appreciate the good days. Not today, but someday, I will break free. When I do, I'm running, and I'm never looking back. Until then, I guess I'll just do what I have to do. I'll choose to find enjoyment in the misery. This too shall pass. I just need to hold on to hope with all my might and never let go.

I've grieved the loss of myself more times than I can count. I'm not referring to suicidal behaviour, but to the feeling of living as an empty shell; the feeling of your soul having left your body, but still I have a pulse. I'm living a constant identity crisis. I've spent most of my life running, fighting to survive, working to get as far from the danger as I could. Now, I don't have anything to run from anymore. All my skeletons are out of the closet. All my wounds are open and exposed for everyone to see. I've made mistakes, and my past still haunts me, but I've chosen to face it rather than let it own me.

It's hard to explain, not being able to imagine a future. For so many years, I lived within the confines of depression, anxiety, addiction, and PTSD. I was what I was going to be; I felt insufficient at my job, socially disconnected, toxic. I was miserable. I was living day by day because I didn't see a future for myself. Drugs, pot then pain killers, numbed my pain, but they kept me trapped in a black hole of self-hatred and isolation. I didn't know life could be different. I didn't know how to exist without emotional torture. I thought wellness was something health professionals said existed, a mythical concept to keep you busy instead of destroying yourself.

It's been almost three years since I injected myself with morphine. It's been almost three years since I hit rock bottom. I lost a lot, but I've gained so much more than I could ever have imagined! It's rough. Not only do I still have to deal with the anxiety, depression, and PTSD, but I also have to face the consequences of my actions and redeem myself, all while stone cold sober. I've spent so many hours in counselling, in courtrooms, telling strangers intimate details about my life, being judged, both by people designated to do so, and by small-minded individuals who think they're better than I am. I've been working an average of fifty to sixty hours a week at low paying jobs that I'm overqualified for. Most days I feel stuck, and it really friggin' sucks!

But I'm worth it. I am so lucky to be where I am today. I am alive. I am well. I am surrounded by family, friends, and strangers who care about me, and believe in me. I have the opportunity to redeem myself and get back to the career I worked so hard to have in the first place. I guess it's not luck. I've worked damn-well hard to pull myself up, own my shit, and work my way back up. Looking back, I really don't know how I didn't kill myself when I hit rock bottom. I don't know how my body didn't shut down with all the chemicals I was pumping into it. I don't have to figure these things out; I just have to make sure I don't go back to that place.

I don't know what my future will bring, but I have a future, and that's pretty cool. One thing is for certain: I want to be an example. People don't usually talk about things that make them look weak, ill, or socially unacceptable. When I was fourteen years old, crying on my bedroom floor, thinking I was abnormal, I could have used a "fuck up" to look up to. Well, I'm a fuck up, a mental case, a worthless addict, and a criminal, and I'll wear it on my sleeve. I have been all of those things, and I still am, but now I'm a functioning mental case, who is clean, well, has no criminal convictions, has a bright future, and self-respect. If I can make it to the other side, so can you.

"The next day, I attended my first
twelve-step meeting where I got a
feeling I had never experienced before.
I felt like I fit in.
These people knew exactly how I
was feeling and what I was talking about."

## YOU ARE NEVER ALONE

Sheri Kilmury-Ginther

A wise man repeatedly told me in early recovery, "You are never alone." What did that mean? After battling a thirty-year addiction to drugs and alcohol, an addiction that made me try and take my own life. I could never figure out what that man meant when he said those words to me.

I grew up in a very dysfunctional alcoholic home. I was a child whose life consisted of repeated sexual, mental, and physical abuse on a regular basis. My family would always laugh and tell the story of the first time I got drunk at three years old, sitting under the kitchen table drinking all the little bits of beer left over in the empty beer bottles. So I guess you could say I had an early start.

My mother was just a child when she had me at thirteen years old, so my grandmother raised me after my parents divorced when I was four years old. My life from that point forward was just a downhill spiral until the day I walked into Addictions Foundation

Manitoba (AFM) in Winnipeg.

I remember always being alone as a child. My mother had abandoned my two younger brothers and myself as soon as we were in the care of my grandmother. Occasionally, my father would come around. My grandmother was definitely not the loving person a child needed in her life.

I can remember walking around my neighborhood as a child looking in everyone's windows and longing for a family, someone to tell me they loved me and put their arms around me. I remember being resentful of the kids that got dropped off at school, their parents kissing them good-bye and telling them to have a good day, and telling them they loved them. I would stand in the background trying to figure out why my life was so different, why no one loved me, and feeling so alone.

At ten years old, I had my first real drink. My mother came back into my life when I was twelve years old and we became best drinking buddies. At fifteen years of age, I was drinking and using drugs every day. She introduced me to prostitution by pre-rranging "dates" for me, and that is how she paid for our addiction. Life was a big party, or so I thought. I was so happy I had her back in my life and did everything I could to keep her in my life.

The next few years of my life was nothing but drinking, drugging, abusive relationships with men, an absolutely chaotic life that an alcoholic lives. Not only was I destroying my life but also the lives of the people around me. I always felt different, like I never fit in. I was like a chameleon, always playing someone. I was trying to fit in and fill this lonely feeling up in my chest. I just wanted to feel accepted. I didn't want to feel the way I was feeling anymore.

At twenty-seven, I found myself pregnant. I couldn't take care of myself, and now I was going to have a baby. I somehow managed to stay sober throughout my pregnancy but could not wait for the day that my child was born so I could use some kind of substance.

I thought I would be happy, that my child would fill the lonely void deep inside me, and once she was born I could drink and drug again. My alcoholism took me to the beer store on my way home from the hospital with my brand new daughter, so I could buy beer and have a drink as soon as I got home. My second child was born fifteen months later. Again, I somehow stayed sober throughout my second pregnancy. After my son was born, I really wanted to try and stay sober and be a good mother to my children. Unfortunately, it didn't last too long. When my children were two and three years old, I left the family home, and left my children behind. My addiction won. The power it had over me was stronger than the bond between a mother and her children.

My daughter moved in with me three years later when she was six. I was devastated that she wanted to live with me because all my addiction told me over and over in my head was, how would I continue to live this lifestyle with her in the way. The only thing that mattered in my life was where was I going to get my next fix. My daughter soon became the victim of an alcoholic parent, living with the mental and emotional abuse that alcoholics burden the ones we love with.

I was a blackout drinker. I aimed for that goal every time I brought my first drink of the day to my lips. One night, while out with friends in a total blackout, I had no idea where my ten-year-old daughter was. Nor did I really care at that point in the night. When I woke in the morning, the first thing I would do is go to my daughter's room to make sure she was okay. However, this morning was different! She wasn't there, and I had no idea where she was. Instead of going to look for her, I sat on my couch and opened another drink. She did come home and had been with a friend of mine who found her wandering around the streets at 3:00 a.m. Once I sobered up a bit, this was the day I started to think that maybe I had a problem with alcohol and drugs.

Two more years of drinking, drugging, and blackouts were my future until I finally hit my rock bottom. By the time I hit my rock bottom, neither one of my children would have any contact with me. All of my friends and family had given up on me. I was homeless and living in a tent next to the river. I was totally alone. I couldn't not stand the constant spinning in my head from all the negative thoughts, the shame, guilt, and fear. I was emotionless on the outside, nothing but an empty shell of a body that was so scared to die but did not want to live anymore either. I was the loneliest I have ever been in my life. I couldn't see any hope. I could never see things getting any better than what they were sitting next to the river one night, looking across. That night was April 8, 2012. I tried to take my life that night.

Being the lowest I have ever been, I decided that maybe I really needed some help. I truly didn't believe that alcohol and drugs were the problem in my life, but all the things that happened to me were the problem. I called the Addictions Foundation Manitoba and decided to go to an orientation they held once a week. Maybe I could find someone there to talk to and I would be okay after a few sessions? After my orientation, I was put in contact with a woman who would change my life in ways I never could have imagined. I had my first appointment with her and told her everything about my life. All she said to me was, "If you let me, I can help you." No one had ever said those words to me before, and I was instantly drawn to her. I trusted her, and I had never trusted anyone before. I did not want to feel the way I was feeling anymore, and she told me I didn't have to. She recommended that I enter the twenty-eight-day, in-house rehab program at a place called River House, and that she would be my counsellor.

My journey began on August 14, 2012. I entered River House as a forty-year-old woman who, when I look back now, is unrecognizable to me. I remember sitting on my bed being so scared of the unknown, but also so scared of myself. I did not want to hurt myself anymore. The next day, I attended my first twelve-step meeting where I got a feeling I had never experienced before. I felt like I fit in. These people knew exactly how I was feeling and what I was talking about. At the end of the meeting, an elderly lady came to me, wrapped her arms around me and said, "If you keep coming back, you will be in for the ride of your life." I was puzzled because I had no idea what she meant, but I will never forget that moment.

That was the beginning the wonderful life I live today. I wanted what all these other sober people had, that I saw every day at the meetings, the laughter and smiles on everyone's face, the look in their eyes. I craved to have that in my life.

I completed treatment, and before I left, I asked a wonderful lady to be my sponsor, and she agreed. I worked with her one-on-one, once a week, and went through the steps with her. I wanted this, and I knew I had to become willing and open-minded. Once I committed, it didn't take long for little things to start changing. I was also told that I had to believe in a power greater than myself, my own conception of a higher power. I struggled with this at first until it was explained to me that this higher power didn't have to have a face or name. I just had to believe.

I did everything my sponsor suggested of me, and also what everyone else suggested of me. One day at a time, I stayed sober. I continued to do the work, and my life started to fall in place. I have my children back in my life, and have an amazing relationship with my daughter. I have a great place to live, and great friends and support, a life I never thought was possible. The only thing I aim for today is to be a better person than I was yesterday.

A wise man told me, "You are never alone." I understand that today. The wise man that had such an impact on me in early sobriety was my sponsor's husband. He was understanding, caring, patient, and there for a hug whenever I needed. My sponsor and her husband gave me the family I have never had. They loved me unconditionally until I could love myself.

Today I have a deep faith in my higher power, because I was able to surrender and open my eyes and heart to the idea that something greater than me existed. I have been able to see how my higher power works in my life, fully understanding that my higher power has a plan for me. I also believe that something had to be watching over me during my active addiction, and guided me to the point of bringing me to my knees, to seek the help I so desperately needed. I have a deep spiritual connection with that higher power, a feeling deep down inside of me, that no matter what life challenges me with, I will be okay. When I sit down and think of what my spiritual connection feels like with my higher power, the only way I can explain is the feeling you get when someone puts their arms around you and tells you everything will be okay. I am never alone even when I am. Today, when I am alone, I feel serenity and peace. I truly believe that higher power brought me to the doors of the AFM almost five years ago.

"The pastor came and
shook my hand telling me,
"You belong here."
His simple act of kindness
toward me gave me hope."

## YEAR ONE

**12**

Morgan Longjohn

Addiction has plagued my world for over a decade, and my life did not go according to plan. No one plans on being addicted, but it happens too often in today's society. At thirty years old, I tackled my first year of sobriety. I know addiction, and it has been my way of life. I was not a bad person, but in the addiction world, I did bad things until I grasped hope and discovered freedom in my first year of sobriety.

Addiction took root in my childhood and it grew like weeds in a beautiful garden. Over time, the overgrowth of addiction became out of control choking out what was meant to be beautiful and prosperous. It was too late, and the seeds of substance abuse were sown in my garden of life. These unfortunate seeds grew amongst the precious fruit in my life, devouring the goods and eventually tearing my life apart.

My childhood was modest and decent. My father raised me in

a working-class home after the divorce. I excelled in school, a bright child participating in extra-curricular activities and loving sports. I was outgoing, and I had numerous friends throughout my youth. Humor has always been a good friend of mine, and I hid my sorrows with a smile.

Immoral and unethical abuses were inflicted upon me in my childhood. These abuses became the major roots of addiction in my life. I carried these dark, heavy burdens upon my little shoulders for years. I was secretly tormented by the abuses that occurred in my childhood, which sprouted into the growth of several negative traits such as fear, shame, low self-esteem, and problems with drugs and alcohol.

By age twelve, I started meddling with substances, and I easily became addicted. I tampered with cigarettes, alcohol, marijuana, and sniffing/inhalants. By age fifteen, I left home to live with my addicted mother. Addictive substances had a grip on my life, and the bad habits escalated. Not only was I getting high and drinking, but also I was lying, stealing, running away, skipping school, and fighting. I was fifteen years old breaking and entering into homes with other broken youth, and it seemed normal. I was a rebellious youth without help and hope, so I acted out and no one seemed to care.

My mother was a powerful woman in her lifetime. She was an educated First Nations woman in a society that was discriminatory toward women and Indigenous people. She was Band Manager in our reserve and also worked with northern communities across Saskatchewan. Prescription drugs became her addiction. She became an addict by the medication she was prescribed by her doctor. She suffered from fibromyalgia, and she was usually in great pain, but family and friends only saw the addiction. She slithered from prescription drugs to IV drugs and lost all the power and prestige she held in society. My mother was deeply bound in addiction, but I loved her still.

I became a parent early in life and I was living with my mother at the time. We lived in an old rundown, war-era house in the ghetto area of town. My mother found stability on the methadone program, and I returned to high school as a teen mother and graduated. Together, we made a good team, living by faith in a dark, weary world. Our ghetto house became a loving home occupied by imperfect, hopeful souls, and it was good.

By age eighteen, I was a full-blown alcoholic. I glamorized the party life, and drinking alcohol became a regular, everyday thing. I over did it, and it started to interfere with my family, my relationships, my education, and everything else. Then I was introduced to a "new" high: crack cocaine. Over the years, my life spiralled out of control, the alcohol and crack controlled me over and over again. My children were apprehended, I dropped out of university, and my life was a vicious cycle of being drunk, high, and hungover.

One seed was planted into my life that never really budded, but I carried it genuinely: the seed of faith. At age eighteen, I optimistically enrolled and enlisted in every type of addiction program available to man, but for the next decade, I failed at maintaining sobriety. I had faith in the Living God, Creator of heaven and earth, believing there was more to life than what I was living, and that gave me hope.

I ended up at rock bottom, over and over again. Twice in a mental-health facility, the psych-ward, once in a single-vehicle rollover, numerous times in drunk tanks and jail cells. I became a terrorist toward those around me, and I was destructive—I did not care who I hurt along the way. My substance abuse was all over the map: crack, shrooms, rails, alcohol, pills, meth, IV drugs, marijuana, and ecstasy. I smoked, sniffed, snorted, injected, popped, and drank during these dark days of my life, but crack cocaine and alcohol were my main highs. I got taken advantage of by men and even raped, which I blocked out in my darkest times. I was stealing money from my father to support my bad habits, and I lived a very twisted lifestyle. I literally went from dope to hope.

My mother and two sisters passed away during this dark decade of my life, and mixing grief with addiction was a tragic mess. Many times I did not care if I lived or died, but I did not have the strength to take my own life. Suicidal tendencies crept up numerous times, but I knew I could never do it. Thank God! Losing my family members leaves me quite alone. My mother died from an accidental methadone overdose, and I discovered her lifeless body. That traumatized me for a long time. My oldest sister died from a blood infection using a dirty intravenous needle. My stepmother died after she had a brain aneurism in our home, and ten days later, my only living sister died from brain cancer. Grief and loss were added to my plate, and it was difficult for me to function as a normal human being in society. Today, I am a warrior strengthened by my journey, and my strength comes from above.

I lived in the dark world of addiction for a long period of time. I am fortunate to "get out" of that darkness today. This is my *Year One* of sobriety. I am able to choose freely—legitimate, clean, zero tolerance for the drugs and alcohol lifestyle. Coming out has not been easy, but it has been worth it. I overcame many hard times and continue to overcome the barriers and burdens of life, as I clean the mess addiction has left behind. The lack of genuine support from friends and family hurts the most, and I carry the stigma of addiction over my life, which has ultimately strengthened my inner-self to quit the bad habits once and for all.

After ten years of intense battle with addiction, grief, and loss and all the other gloomy issues I faced, the seed of faith started to bloom. Many times I tried to get sober and clean and fell back into addiction, but sobriety finally became real and I discovered it. I am where I need to be today, and that is 365-plus days sober and clean. The dark clouds of addiction have started to clear up, and it's a beautiful life. Forgiveness is key in my recovery and obedience to the good in life. I forgive myself and others, as well as seeking the forgiveness from those I hurt along the way. Life has meaning and purpose as I continue day by day in my sober life.

A year ago I walked into church hungover, wearing an ACDC T-shirt, seeking hope for my lost soul. I was utterly alone, none of my so-called friends or family supported me anymore because I was known as a failure. The pastor came and shook my hand telling me, "You belong here." His simple act of kindness toward me gave me hope. Over the months I fought the addictions by resisting temptations with the support of the entire church. This church offers a faith-based addiction program known as Reformers Unanimous, and I love it. This addiction program is the only program I attend today, and I dedicate my Friday nights to RU. I drive fifty-five kilometres one-way from my reserve, Sturgeon Lake First Nation, to attend RU every Friday night in Prince Albert, Saskatchewan. I believe that, if I am meant to be there, God will provide the transportation, and He has every single Friday for the past year. I live my life as a Christian today, and it is an abundant life. The fruits of my spirit are finally blossoming into the beautiful life it was created to be. I have joy no man can take from me. The weeds of addictions have been cleared out of the way for me to experience life as it is meant to be.

The doors of opportunity have opened for me to grow and prosper. I returned to the University of Saskatchewan and successfully completed four classes this academic year. I was recently employed full-time as a janitor: a quiet, peaceable job, and I was obedient in my operations no matter how futile the job seemed to the world. Today, I have new employment on reserve driving a medical taxi and sharing my story with clients, which is closer to my undecided career choice in the health field of nursing and/or criminology and addictions. My average in university is very decent, and I am thankful to still have a functioning brain after years of substance abuse.

I have also gained credibility in the past year as well as several other healthy, productive traits to add to my new character. It is a wonderful journey to live life with clarity, hope and love.

I have passion for the addicted, leading me to pursue goals and dreams that reach out to the addicted in society. I invite and encourage all people to give RU a try; it is an international addiction program that was founded in Rockford, Illinois. I had the opportunity to meet the cofounder of RU recently at a nationwide conference in Prince Albert, Saskatchewan, which encouraged me on my sober journey. Reformers Unanimous can be "Googled" for more information and it really is a great program. I also write testimonies each month that are distributed to every Baptist church across the nation to encourage others in hope and with love. I was published in Kapuskasing, Ontario, in January 2018, which distributed my letter to 9000 homes; I also receive feedback from places such as Nunavut and British Columbia, where I encouraged others, and it is totally amazing!

I am finally able to function in society in ways I could not before actively in addiction. My family is being restored, and my life is renewed. Trials and temptations come and go, but that is when I reach out to my pastor and the church to help me overcome the obstacles, and they are faithful to do so. I am blessed today like never before because I got plugged into the right source and the wrong ones soon fell away. That source is my hope and faith in God, who rescued me from the foul addictions that kept me bound for years.

I share my story with people as I meet them in the streets of everyday life or on the methadone van that I now drive from the reserve to the city and in the church with doctors and pastors from all across North America. I love to encourage my brothers and sisters in humanity that there is hope after addiction is tackled and under your feet. I truly believe life is a garden and you gotta dig it. Life after addiction is a celebration of life.

"I'm not going to lie to you,
      being high feels great.
Like your brain is filled with pale fire
            snatched from the sun.
Therein lies the problem."

## THE FUTURE IS AN
## UNLOCKED DOOR

13

Jim Conley

*D*ad, *when was the last time you relapsed?*

Tough question with several answers.

*What does that mean? You either did or you didn't.*

I have a wide range of addictions, boyo. Some things I've kept clear of, some things I haven't. What matters is where I am now. I take it day by day, and today's a good day. There are a lot of things I could be on today—crack, meth, magic mushrooms, ecstasy, painkillers, pot, alcohol—but right now, I'm not on any of them.

*You're still not answering my question.*

And I don't plan to. I tell you most everything, but some stuff is mine alone to know. Let's just go with it's been long enough that you don't have to worry.

*I'm not angry. I just want to know. You're way better than you used to be.*

It's hard to talk to you about these things, boyo. It makes for hard conversation. It started long before you were born. I've been doing drugs since I was your age. The only reason I even tell you about this stuff is because I hope you make better choices than I did.

*Did you do drugs with Mom?*

Yes. We did a lot of things for a long time. It was a big part of our life. Your sister knows a lot more about it than you do. Ask her about it sometime.

*I'm not all brain-damaged because Mom did drugs, am I?*

No. She didn't do anything once she knew she was pregnant with you. Give her credit for that. Taking care of you is something we both tried to do as well as we could.

*Are you going to relapse again?*

I hope not, but the statistics are against me. Long-term drug use combined with mental illness doesn't usually work out so well. You know that Dad's been diagnosed with bipolar depression, and that's resulted in being hospitalized half a dozen times over the last thirty years. Between hospitals and treatment programs, I've spent far too much time in the care of others.

*You mean like when you went to that halfway house place last year?*

Yes. I've done that twice now. Neither of them did a bit of good, but it's what the courts wanted. I'll let you in on a secret, boyo. No doctor or treatment program or priest or psychologist or medication will cure you of addiction or depression. They can all help you manage it, but only you can control it. Do you know why I tell you all this?

*Not really.*

Because I don't like lying to you. It's easy, but it stays with me. You're growing up fast, and there's a lot of this I'm ready to tell you. I've learned to lie very well over the years. I don't want to lie to anyone anymore. Can we talk about something else now?

*I'm not mad at you. I just want to understand. Does your new girlfriend know about all this?*

Yes. She knows, and she understands. She worries, but she understands.

*So how long ago was it? It's important.*

Time is relative. It's been long enough that you shouldn't worry, but it's been recent enough that it still scares me. What's important is how I am right now. I've spent enough time in my life behind locked doors for one life.

*Can I do anything to help?*

Just be here, boyo. That's all I ask.

*What's it like being high?*

I'm not going to lie to you, being high feels great. Like your brain is filled with pale fire snatched from the sun. Therein lies the problem. Addiction is so easy. What starts as fun grows into something you can't stop. It's all you think about, and the world starts falling apart. You lie. You steal. You become something awful before you even realize things have come undone. I went from a casual user to spending hundreds of dollars a day in a matter of months.

*Where did you get the money?*

I put it on credit cards, nearly a hundred thousand dollars. I didn't care. I decided I would just kill myself when it ran out.

*I'm glad you didn't. When you were messed up you told me you wanted to do that.*

I'm sorry, boyo. I really am. I never wanted you to see all this, and I'm so glad we made it through it all. I'm still closer to the sun than I want to be, but it's like I said—every day is a new one, and we've got to leave the past where it belongs. I've wanted to die many times, but I've wanted to live more.

*Why did she leave?*

Your sister? She knew something was happening even if she never saw me doing anything. I just got worse and worse, and she couldn't take it anymore. She knew even if she couldn't say what it was. She knew my wings were melting.

*That was when we lived in the apartment with the view, right?*

It was. I had a good job back then, eight thousand a month, but I was living a double life. Work all day, party all night. Then it all started to spin out of control. I've had problems with drugs most of my adult life, boyo, but it never got like this. I got fired in late May, two years ago now, and everything exploded in less than a month. I had no structure, nowhere I had to be, and I just did more and more and more drugs.

*You were never home. I remember calling Grandpa when you didn't come home for the second day. He was really mad.*

He was, and I felt guilty as hell. It didn't stop me though. It hit a threshold when my ex-girlfriend called to say she didn't want to be involved anymore. I gave up on a lot of things when that happened, myself mostly. I did about a thousand bucks worth of crack in two days, and the voices just got worse and worse. I thought policemen were following me and broadcasting messages in my car. That's why I started the fire. I thought there were tiny policemen hiding under the seats monitoring my movement, and they were going to hurt you unless I became a police informant.

*Wow.*

You have no idea. I was a long way from the real world and thought I was being followed everywhere. I think I was trying to commit suicide by cop. I really don't know.

*That's when you're trying to get the cops to kill you, right?*

That's right. I remember standing on the hood of the car pouring gasoline over it. Nice car—late model Mercedes coupe—and I almost poured the gas on myself instead, but it just didn't seem the right thing to do. The car went up in flames and the roof started melting, and I just sat there smoking crack while I waited for something to happen. The police arrived, and I was on the ground in cuffs before I knew what was happening.

*I remember when the policeman came after you set fire to the car. He stayed with me until Auntie came. He was nice to me. I didn't know what was going on but I was worried about you. You never answered your phone.*

I'm sorry. I always will be. In some ways we had a better life back then. There are so many things I can't give you anymore.

*You're better. That's good enough.*

I suppose it is. More than anything else, you keep me healthy. I slip up sometimes, but I come back from the way I used to be because I love you. It's like seeing shore when you're being pulled out to sea. There's a poem by Stevie Smith called "Not Waving but Drowning." The title says it all and explains what addiction feels like. It looks like you're happy, but you're waving your hand looking for help and nobody realizes what's happening, especially yourself.

*Please tell me when the last time you used was?*

It doesn't matter, boyo. Whether it was this morning or a year ago. I did, and it left me feeling guilty and broken. I'm already a disappointment. No reason to compound the pain. Just understand that I try as hard as I can not to do it again, and you're the reason why.

*Who else did you do drugs with, besides Mom?*

I mostly did drugs by myself. I've never been much on being social, and I preferred to be alone when I did them. In some ways, that was the biggest mistake I made. I became paranoid and had no reference to the real world. Another addict wouldn't have been the best person for a reality check, but it would have been something. I spent months thinking the police were following me. Do you remember that time I had Auntie come get you from the apartment for the night?

*Yeah. That really bothered me.*

I thought police were going to break in the door and take me away. I didn't want you to see that.

*I knew something was wrong. You were all sweating and your eyes were funny.*

I'd left you alone for the night, again, and I thought they were following me from work. Your Auntie knew something was wrong, so she just got you out of there.

*She sort of knew everything, didn't she?*

We never talked about it, but she knew something was way out of control. Grandpa did, too, but I never talked to anybody about it. I was too far gone to reach out for help. Your sister left around then, went to live with friends and called Social Services. It always surprised me they didn't come around to check on you.

*Didn't you know something was wrong when she left?*

I did, but I couldn't do anything about it anymore. It had gone too far. I was spending my nights with homeless people in the park who could get me drugs. I was sleeping in my car because I couldn't drive. I was seeing things.

*What were you seeing?*

Shadows were coming at me out of the walls. Windows were melting. Everything was wrong. Everything.

*I'm sorry.*

Thank you, boyo, but it was a self-inflicted hell. I did it to myself, and I wish I'd never started. I'm so glad I stopped.

*But you haven't.*

I slipped up, but I came back. I didn't get dragged into hell again.

*You got lucky.*

Maybe I did, but I'm here now, and I'm healthy, and I'm raising you the way I should, and I have a job and a girlfriend and I'm becoming.

*What does that mean?*

I'm becoming. It means that I'm changing into something, and it's better than I was. I can't explain what's going to happen, but I feel it running through me.

*You're never going to tell me when you relapsed, are you?*

No. It doesn't matter. Just watch me and judge me by the actions you can see. I'm so far from perfect that I'm barely here, but when you look at me, try to see the good, the brightness in the black.

*I never said you were bad. I'm just trying to understand.*

Me too, boyo. I've done a lot of bad things in my life, but I'm making up for them every day. I've made my amends to people, apologized for the way I hurt them.

*I know. Thank you. That was important to me.*

I want you to remember that everybody is drowning in their own way, and they have to remember to call for help when they need it. It took me a long time to do that, and that's what keeps me clean.

*Are you really clean?*

Today I am. Tomorrow I want to be. That's all I've got for you, boyo. Any addict who says more is lying to themselves and everyone around them.

*You're never really going to be better, are you?*

If you mean "cured," then no. It won't happen.

*But are you going to be "okay"?*

As best I can, I promise I will be. I am becoming.

*Who did you do the drugs with? Were you by yourself?*

No. It was with somebody. You know them. Don't bother asking.

*Why would they do that to you, when they know what's happened?*

Because they thought I could handle it. It's not quite what you think, but it did happen. It wasn't one of the drugs I used to do when I got in trouble.

*Why won't you tell me what it was, or when it happened?*

Because it doesn't matter. What matters is that I didn't lose myself in the void.

*Can you promise me something?*

I'll try.

*If you ever want to do that again, will you talk to me first?*

You're not old enough to bear my problems just yet.

*You kind of made me old, Dad.*

I deserved that.

*When was it?*

Three months ago.

*I know.*

"Although I had a good education,
professional employment, and a small
family, I still struggled with drug and
alcohol addiction, as well as other
self-defeating behaviour, like engaging in toxic
relationships, places, and behaviours."

# DEALING WITH PTSD, ANXIETY, CHRONIC PAIN, AND HARM REDUCTION

Melissa Cook

In 2007, I was diagnosed with Post Traumatic Stress Disorder (PTSD) and anxiety by the head of the addiction unit from the Health Sciences Center in Winnipeg, Manitoba. Although I had a good education, professional employment, and a small family, I still struggled with drug and alcohol addiction, as well as other self-defeating behaviour, like engaging in toxic relationships, places, and behaviours. Basically, once the abusers in my life were no longer around, I took it upon myself to continue the abuse by abusing myself. I was always getting hurt when I was younger: I had numerous broken bones, sprains, fractures, and bruises. I now know that my clumsiness and recklessness is a direct result of the PTSD, and when

I started noticing bruises as an adult, it was a sign to switch gears, slow down, and determine why. The first time I got high I was eleven; it was within months of my mom leaving my stepfather. Getting high became my "out," and by the age of thirteen, I had already had my first run-in with the local police. I was reported for selling drugs. This lifestyle and behaviour would last for another two decades (and a bit longer). I embraced the numbness, and it engulfed me in turn.

As I got older, my life was so high risk it was hard for me to understand, and I was on the verge of an early death at my own hand (in one way or another). This was my behaviour, and the truth was that I actually wanted to live. I would not accept this life I was dealt: my life born to struggle. Despite all the failure and falling to my knees, I kept on getting up. I spilled my guts to my nurse practitioner and a family doctor at the time. I told them all of my dark ugly secrets: the long nights of insomnia or drug and alcohol abuse, the loss of self and my dignity. I was totally lost and empty inside. I was starting to believe that it was, in fact, all my fault and that I was bad and hopeless. These are the messages that I had always heard growing up in a dysfunctional environment. Don't get me wrong, my mom worked hard, loved us, and there are good memories, but there were times when other people rocked our world to the core.

I was a patient at a local clinic, and I asked my doctor for a referral to try to figure out where my self-defeating behaviour was coming from. Despite all of my best attempts, I just could not escape my vicious cycle. I had tried every way possible on my own. Nothing worked, so I finally gave in and asked them for help. I then became part of the shared-care program at the clinic, and with more of a team approach to my healing, they all stepped in. I was so relieved when they sent me to a therapist. We met, and spoke, shared, and he made his conclusions.

With his final recommendations came a plan for exercise and meditation. There was a suggestion for medications, but I refused. At that time, he told me that I was "fighting a spiritual battle." From a Western doctor, this was confusing for me. He confirmed the post-traumatic stress, concluded my "cravings" were actually anxiety, and that when I dealt properly with these feelings, the urges would wane (never go away, but decrease or become less powerful). I told him of my night terrors, a common theme of which was a loss of some sort, or a personal invasion on my body like parasites, maggots in me, falling on me, falling from me. The loss was often of my teeth, breaking apart, falling out, becoming loose, for example.

My long history of compulsive coping, flashbacks, night terrors, self-destructive behaviour, weeks of insomnia, and other symptoms, finally had a name. When I was a child, everything felt "in fast forward." I used to have dreams of floating or flying. I acted out a lot. I used to zone out and daydream. I had experienced child sexual abuse and witnessed violence. I was a victim of physical violence and emotional trauma. All of this later resulted in PTSD and an anxiety disorder, as stated.

Fast forward to me finally moving from the large city to a small city in rural Manitoba. I now live in and own a one-hundred-year-old schoolhouse. I run my own consulting business, and I love to write. The schoolhouse sits on four acres, and my house is enclosed entirely by majestic 100-foot tall spruce, pine, cedar, and poplar trees. It's my heaven on earth, my forever home, my safe place. By day, my yard is full of birds singing, and in the summer birds flying over. At night, I listen to the lonely cries of the coyotes whose dens surround me. Is it loneliness? It's just amazing and humbling to live here. I have the rescue animals I always dreamt of saving. I have my children, who are my whole entire world. I have just enough support to be happy and well loved. After all of my struggles, my high-risk life, and feeling lost, I am finally home. I'm home safe.

Now, to put a wrench in my healing journey, for the last five years I have been battling a chronic-pain condition. This includes being a patient at cancer care for two years. I once was sick. I vomited, and the entire right side of my face and neck swelled so fast I was terrified. I ended up at the emergency department, and it stayed swollen for three weeks. I kept getting infections in my jaw and ear. The pain unbearable. They were very worried that I had cancer in my salivary gland, and I was sent for every test imaginable. My life flashed before my eyes so many times. There were times I was convinced the news would be bad, and that all of the self-abuse had caught up with me. It was the worst pain I have ever felt in my life, and with my life of hardship, but my tolerance for pain was and is higher than many people.

I was on morphine, 5 ml only, but it was for roughly six months. I felt worried and guilty about the morphine, so I asked to switch to Tylenol 3 and then gabapentin consecutively. I was worried because of my history of compulsive coping, my addictive behaviour that wreaked havoc on my life since the age of eleven. The gabapentin was horrible. It didn't work, and my pain stayed. My depression skyrocketed. I felt low and hopeless.

Because of my history, I was not comfortable being on all of the pills, and I was trying to manage without. I ended up just suffering in pain a lot, and as of today, I will take a Tylenol 2 and a baclofen to try to relax the muscles in my neck and jaw. I sleep when I can, although I am up four or five times a night. On a good night, I will go to bed with my four year old at seven or eight in the evening and wake up at 4:30-5:00 a.m.

The temporomandibular disorder (TMJ) I was finally diagnosed with on October 21, 2017 (not cancer thank you God) resulted from my PTSD/Anxiety. Never in a million years would I have made that connection—the body, mind, and soul. It's amazing the connections we are not aware of. When I am in times of elevated stress, anxiety, or my past comes back to haunt me, I get more nightmares. I clench my teeth harder. I am up for weeks with hardly any sleep.

Part of my condition has been compared to an eating disorder at times, with how it affects my eating habits (periods of not eating/periods of eating too much). The combination of all of this, including the switch from pain medication to gabapentin, which led to depression, caused the worst flare-up of my pain, and my condition, in my whole life thus far. Let's factor in the theme of my recurring nightmares, broken teeth, teeth falling out, and then my reality: having a tooth pulled to try to relieve the pain in my jaw, and a cracked molar resulting from grinding and clenching. You can only imagine my horror.

In October of 2017, I was diagnosed with TMJ and reconfirming my PTSD/Anxiety. A day before the diagnosis, I testified publically at the National Inquiry for Missing and Murdered Women, as a living witness and survivor. Also around this time, I was attempting to move forward with a civil suit against one of my abusers. I was receiving follow-up calls and emails regarding this. My forever home and my life were completely disrupted with my past and unfinished business knocking on my old schoolhouse door.

I chose to write this story, to share my story to help someone else. I was so blown away by the reality of the situation, and how it was all connected. I've successfully accomplished most of what was needed to be done (the diagnosis, the inquiry, reducing self-harm by switching meds). It was painstaking. It was horrific at times. It was hard, and it was worth it. My hope and prayer now for me and my family is that I once again move forward, that I can once again manage; I can look for and create "my imperfect balance." All I want to do is live: free from harm, free from pain, full of peace, and most importantly, free from shame. It's spring soon here and out in the country. It will be amazing. I cannot wait to walk the old country roads, feeling fine. Be strong if you are also struggling. I never thought I would make it through, but I finally see the light.

All of the love,
Melissa.

"I've completed my high school,
            and I'm currently a year into my
post-secondary program. I have not
    touched or wanted to touch any drug
                since April 7, 2015. I have
spoken on panels about the opioid
        crisis going on in Canada."

## ENOUGH OF
## THE PARTY DRUGS!

Casey Dalton

I started using drugs when I was just eleven years old. My whole childhood, I watched relatives struggle with drug and alcohol problems, and yet there I was, eleven years old, trying cocaine for the first time. By the time I was thirteen, I was smoking crack and doing meth. I entered rehab for the first time at age fourteen, and I celebrated my fifteenth birthday in rehab. The rehab I attended was in another province, so I did not have the support I needed from my family. I left rehab not long after my fifteenth birthday because I was scared and afraid, and I was in a treatment facility with people who were five plus years older than me, and who had much more serious addictions. At the time, seeing those people deterred me from wanting to do drugs again. I stayed clean for one year after I left rehab.

When I was sixteen, I moved out of my mother's house and into my own apartment with a few friends. I thought I was living the best life possible. We would stay up and party for days. We always had people around, and there was always an endless amount of drugs. We were doing hallucinogens such as mushrooms and LSD, something I did not have an addiction to. It was more just for fun and because everyone else was doing it. Occasionally, there would be cocaine around, but I kept telling myself it was okay to do it because I wasn't addicted. I was terribly wrong. My addiction quickly came back. We were partying every single day and staying up for three to six days at a time. This went on until I was seventeen.

When I was seventeen and had enough of the 'party drugs', I tried OxyContin for the first time. A relative had an addiction to OxyContin for eight years and was also on methadone, so I saw how these drugs ruined his life. I didn't care. The first time I tried it, I fell in love with it, and it took over my whole life. I would wake up in the morning and the first thought through my mind was, "How am I going to get high today?" For three years, I was doing OxyContin or morphine every single day. I was hiding it from everyone, and most people did not know any different because I was still working, and still maintaining a fairly normal life.

When I was twenty years old, it became harder to hide. I had to move back into my mom's house, and I was getting money off her every day so I could get my drug of choice. She became increasingly suspicious. In September of 2011, I found out I was pregnant. I knew I could not have this baby because I was still doing a very heavy amount of drugs. I broke down and finally told my mother that I was addicted to OxyContin and that I needed help. The end of September 2011, I went to my first doctor's appointment to get on methadone.

When I started methadone, I was scared, ashamed, and nervous. I had known a little bit about the methadone program, and I knew the stigma attached to methadone: "It's just another way to get high" and "People on methadone are junkies and steal" were just some of what was said about people on methadone. I did not do any drugs for the first two years I was on the methadone program. I had my first child on methadone, which is something I did not want to do. Luckily, she was great and did not withdraw. After I had my first child, I started using cocaine again. This habit became an everyday thing very quickly. I was doing cocaine every day, or every second day, for fourteen months.

I was twenty-two years old, and almost off the methadone program. My pop was in hospital dying. I thought I could do one OxyContin and be fine. I was terribly wrong, once again. That one pill turned in to a full-blown relapse, and I stopped going to my methadone doctor. I was doing more OxyContin this time then I was the first time I got on methadone. No one knew. I was very good at hiding it.

On my twenty-third birthday, my whole life changed. My then boyfriend, and father of my child, had gotten arrested, and police were in my home to search it. Knowing I had a child living there, social workers got involved, and they placed my child with her grandparents, so they could supervise me and my then-boyfriend because they were concerned about drug use. Three days after he got arrested, I found out I was pregnant with my second child. At this point, I had come clean to the social workers about my very heavy drug use, and I was in the process of getting back on the methadone program. Almost having my child taken from me was the worst feeling I've ever felt in my life. All of this was a blessing in disguise because it made me realize that I was taking everything for granted and I was being very selfish. On April 7, 2015, I did drugs for the last time.

I'm currently twenty-six years old, and I have been sober for over three years and successfully completed the methadone program. I've completed my high school, and I'm currently a year into my post-secondary program. I have not touched or wanted to touch any drug since April 7, 2015. I have spoken on panels about the opioid crisis going on in Canada. I have spoken at workshops about my addiction, and I speak to the university every year about the stigma attached to methadone and how to help get rid of it.

"Then I moved to Banff where it went to a
whole new level, as in massive daily
usage of two specific drugs: cocaine and ecstasy.
I bought and did drugs with several different
groups, so nobody really noticed
how bad it had got."

## TAKING IT DAY BY DAY 16

Jenine Glynn

Last week, I arrived here in Winnipeg to do six weeks of Management Training, meaning six weeks away from my family. How do I go six weeks without my kids? I need to see those faces! The biggest adjustment to being away is that I've never put myself first, and this has forced me to do so. I've done lots of reflecting, and spent countless hours inside my head. I've challenged myself to improve my self-care while I have this time away, and I have decided to start with journal entries. This has been quite the journey, both professionally and personally. My parents taught me that "The more difficult a conversation is to have, all the more important it is to have it!"

In a couple of weeks, I'll be finished my training and ready for my new job to start at the beginning of March. The first week of March is significant to me, as it marks twelve years clean from daily, heavy drug usage. I started dabbling in drugs while in college, and I found that they helped numb me from personal issues and pain. I "thought" this was awesome; I didn't have to bother anyone with my issues, and I got to continue to be the life of the party, and party I did.

Then I moved to Banff where it went to a whole new level, as in massive daily usage of two specific drugs: cocaine and ecstasy. I bought and did drugs with several different groups, so nobody really noticed how bad it had got. The work and lifestyle in Banff meant that there was always a group partying, and I was always there, even with people I didn't really know. Those closest to me at the time "think" they knew, but nobody truly knew the severity.

I loved being numb. I hated sleeping. I felt that I had to keep going flat-out. Then one night, I went out like any other night, but this night I ended up with drugs that were laced with something else. I overdosed, flat-lined several times that night, the doctors said. I have never, and maybe never will, get into the disgusting details of that night, but it forever changed me. It was brutal and terrifying. Things happened to me that I will never speak of. I have been diagnosed with post-traumatic stress disorder (PTSD) due to said night's events.

This is where my then friend, now husband, Jay, came into my world. We had been friends since we arrived in Banff, but this event brought us closer. Most people around me in Banff heard the rumours of what happened that awful night, but only Jay truly listened to the real story from beginning to end. He never judged me, and he showed me unconditional love that got me through the rough days. He didn't quit on me. He supported me and kicked my ass to a clean and sober self. He knew I could do it, and he was right.

Twelve years ago, I walked away from those two drugs and

never looked back. Cold turkey. The struggle didn't end there. My body no longer naturally produces serotonin. As well, I have physical damage, brain damage, short-term memory issues, depression, and anxiety. I now take medication to help with these issues, which I am slowly decreasing as time goes on. My biggest current issues are with my self-confidence. Although I quit my drug addiction cold turkey, I found a new addiction of eating whatever I wanted. This added new prescriptions and their side effects of water retention, loss of energy, and weight gain—massive weight gain. I am terrified of going out in public, afraid of running into someone I haven't seen in a while because I know I'll see that "look" on their face like, "Holy shit, what happened to you?"

Emotionally, I wasn't ready, so I've hid in my house like an anti-social hermit for the past few years. Then with encouragement from my husband and kids, I made the leap and joined a weight-lifting gym. I was terrified, but I did it, and I love it! It gave me new confidence, a new outlook. I've started on a path to a healthier me from the inside out. I must start with one step forward. The pace isn't important, just keep heading in the right direction. Surround yourself with people who love and support you, no matter what! I have a long journey ahead of me, but I'm taking it day by day. I still have rough days, but with the amazing support of family and friends, I can do this. I'll continue to work on me, and I've accepted that I'm not going to be back to a fully healthy self overnight. Years of damage takes years to reverse.

So be patient, be kind, and be awesome!

"How many of each drug could I take
every day to maintain the "high" without
running out before it was time for a refill?
How far into withdrawal could I push myself
before I would give into
temptation and just take more pills?
My addiction robbed
me of ten years of my life."

## MY ADDICTION JOURNEY

Rachel Marzetti

I was born and raised in Sault Ste. Marie, Ontario, and currently still call this home. I am thirty-nine years old, and my ten-year-long addiction was just revealed two years ago. It's been a long and often tough road for me, but my tenacity and resilience push me forward each and every day.

My addiction to prescription medications started innocently, as most probably do. Once in the throes of addiction, though, I became a master of disguise. I was able to hide my addiction from anyone and everyone in my life: my family, friends, partners, and others with whom I had limited encounters.

For ten years, I was addicted to prescription medications, as well as some over-the-counter drugs. In particular, I tended to abuse my prescribed opiates and pain-management medications (Tylenol 3s, Percocet, Dilaudid, fentanyl, amitriptyline) and benzodiazepines (Ativan, Clonazepam, Temazepam). However, this pattern of abuse quickly began to include such things as acetaminophen (Tylenol) and Gravol—the things that were easy to obtain and were not controlled substances.

My addiction was borne of multiple medical issues and diagnoses, both confirmed and unconfirmed, as well as an end result of abuse: verbal, emotional, and physical. Test after test became my life for many years, combined with the constant exposure to abuses from partners. One script was added to another to try to control the "pain," an emotional roller coaster that had become my life. It took years for a formal diagnosis to happen, both physical and psychological. And, therefore, it took years of my life. Everyday, I spent hours calculating medications, numbers, and combinations. How many of each drug could I take every day to maintain the "high" without running out before it was time for a refill? How far into withdrawal could I push myself before I would give into temptation and just take more pills? My addiction robbed me of ten years of my life.

Like most people, I never thought that addiction would ever happen to me. I put my trust in my medical professionals. At the beginning of my journey, everything seemed to be well controlled. I had no urges to overuse my medications, often even forgetting to take them altogether. However, combined with the medications came the frustrations of not knowing what was wrong with me, and the daily abuses that ensued. I became very depressed and anxious, and that perpetuated the prescriptions. More and more pills. It became difficult to even keep track of them all. It became easier and easier to take more than the prescribed dosages. In turn, it made everything feel so very different. The intense physical pain wasn't there anymore.

The emotional and mental anguish would dissipate, and I would often just sleep through my "problems." These pills were fixing all of my problems. They helped me to just escape. They made life tolerable again.

It wasn't until May 28, 2016, when I intentionally overdosed, that everything became real again. I thought I could escape everything and not have to admit to my faults, addictions, and feelings if I weren't around anymore. After what felt like hours of fighting with my partner (at the time) and my father, the ambulance was called, and I was able to be convinced to be taken to the hospital. I was treated for my first overdose that day and, surprisingly, by 10 p.m. was discharged home. This was just the beginning of the downward spiral for me. Now I had to admit my addictions to my family and friends. I had to explain to them that, for the past ten years, I was nothing more than a performer to all of them. Not one of them had any clue as to the extent that I would go to appear "normal."

For seven of the ten years, I was even able to maintain a job. A job that became increasingly more stressful as I moved my way up the corporate ladder and into management positions. I really did have myself convinced that I had everything under control. It wasn't happening to me. How could all of this be happening to me?

After I admitted that I was a powerless contender in my battle with addictions, I sought out professional help. At the time, I had the support of my family and friends, who just wanted me to be better. On July 19, 2016, I attended a walk-in counselling session with a trained addictions counsellor. I spent one hour trying desperately to find the right words to convey the state that I was in and how desperately I wanted things to be different. I lucked out. She was able to refer me to one of the very few local doctors in our small city who dealt with addictions and withdrawal management. As well, she added me to her personal caseload at the agency at which she was employed. I literally walked out of the counselling appointment and went directly to see the suggested doctor. Within two hours, I was seen by the doctor and provided a script for Suboxone. This was going to be my lifesaver! Or, so I thought.

As it turned out, despite the Suboxone, the withdrawal was painstaking. There were many times that I recall thinking that a slow death would be easier to endure than the withdrawal. Despite feeling absolutely horrible, the Suboxone seemed to work well for the first while. That was, until I figured out how to stockpile that medication as well, with the sole purpose of facilitating taking the remaining opiates that I still had in my possession. I had found that fine line again. I also realized that acetaminophen and Gravol were also still options to me. So, I began my course of abusing those instead. You see, Suboxone doesn't work on those two medications, and I learned quickly that I could even take them all together. My mask was back on.

I had regularly scheduled counselling appointments with my addictions counsellor and my mental-health counsellor. I attended every appointment faithfully. I had an already established relationship with my mental-health counsellor of nearly two years, and to say the least, she was quite taken aback when I admitted my addiction to her, as well as how long I had been an "addict." Between both of these counsellors, and the multiple doctors that I was under the care of, a referral was made to an in-patient treatment centre, outside of my small, sheltered city of Sault Ste. Marie, Ontario, which continues to have nothing more than a level-one detox facility. I definitely needed more than that.

Time! It was time that was the most unbearable. Everything was a wait. I was on the waiting list for treatment. I was still suffering from withdrawal, despite the Suboxone, which I was being weaned off of in preparation for acceptance into residential treatment. It felt like my life wasn't my own anymore, and that I was in a perpetual loop of doing what everyone else demanded of me.

My mental health declined rapidly, and in September of 2016, I had not only my second, but also my third intentional overdose. These ones were different though. They were not prescription medications that I overdosed on. They were the over-the-counter, easily accessible medications, specifically acetaminophen. These garnered me my second and third ambulance rides. The second time though, I was treated with an antidote to acetaminophen, known commonly as Mucomyst, and required hospitalization for five days. I was referred to yet another doctor, a psychiatrist this time, who felt I required time in hospital, and to be weaned off the benzodiazepines. This was the longest five days of my life, or so I thought at the time. As it turned out, I was readmitted again within one week of discharge, for the very same reason, overdose.

The light at the end of the bleakest tunnel of my life was that I was finally offered a date to begin my residential treatment. October 16, 2016, was to be the day that my life would change forever. And, believe me, once there, it felt like forever. The thirty-five-day treatment program felt like it took years. On November 20, 2016, I returned home, having graduated the treatment program with honours, "clean and sober," with no urges overtaking me. It was as if someone had finally handed me the life that I felt I deserved on a golden platter. I felt like an entirely different person. This was it! This was my second chance! I did really well for a very long time. I remained abstinent of any unnecessary medications, and actually followed the directions for the few medications that I absolutely had to have.

I recall clearly when this all changed again though. It was May 2017, coming up on the one-year anniversary of my sobriety from opiates. I became fixated on the date. Despite continuing all of my counselling appointments and follow-up appointments with my doctors, I saw the train wreck that was about to happen. I felt all the urges return. I reached out to whomever and wherever I could for more help. I practically pleaded with anyone in the field of addictions who would listen, to help me. I didn't want my story to be this way. I was supposed to be stronger than a relapse.

Sadly, from May through to August 2017, I returned to abusing over-the-counter medications. I felt like no matter what I did, whom I reached out to, or what skills I tried to utilize, nothing was working. That damn train wreck was so much closer now, it was hitting head on. In August 2017, I overdosed on acetaminophen again, coupled with all of my newly prescribed medications (none of which were any of my drugs of choice). This happened multiple times in a very short period of time. Eventually, I was hospitalized again. Again, I received the acetaminophen antidote. However, unlike other times, I was also forced to drink what seemed like a never-ending glass of charcoal.

From the end of August 2017 until March of 2018, I remained abstinent of all previous drugs of choice, including over-the-counter medications. Sadly, in March of 2018, I again had a slip. I cannot even say for certain what the trigger was, but I ended up purchasing another bottle of acetaminophen. Luckily, this was a slip and not another full-blown relapse. I am back on the path of sobriety again. Yes, again. Every day is not easy. Every day is a struggle. And, everyday, I fight with all that I am to live my life, to really *live* it. I still have my medical conditions and issues to contend with, but my tenacity to overcome the many obstacles that life has thrown at me is paramount.

Throughout my journey, I have lost family members whom I thought would never abandon me, but I have also been fortunate enough to have constant championing from friends and family who have stood by me throughout everything. And, of course, I have been fortunate to now include new people in my life, who each enrich it in their own individual ways.

This is simply the tip of the iceberg of my life with addiction and all that has contributed to it over the years. To include all of the minute details would be unfair and disadvantageous, as these could simply be interpreted as excuses for my poor behaviour. I own what I have done. I take personal responsibility for my actions that led me down the path that they did. But the most wonderful part of all of this is that the struggle and strife have made me into the person I am today.

And, my story isn't over yet! This quote often helps me get through each day:

> BREATHE. You're going to be okay. Breathe and remember that you've been in this place before. You've been this uncomfortable and anxious and scared. And you've survived. Breathe and know that you can survive this too. These feelings can't break you. They're painful and debilitating, but you can sit with them and eventually, they will pass. Maybe not immediately, but sometime soon, they are going to fade and when they do, you'll look back at this moment and laugh for having doubted your resilience. I know it feels unbearable right now, but keep breathing, again and again. This will pass. I promise it will pass."
>
> – Daniell Koepke

"I repaired relationships I never thought
possible, bridged seemingly insurmountable
gaps with my family, and have found
the love of a wonderful woman who has
cultivated incredible personal growth.
Against all odds, not only am I alive,
I am happy."

# 18

## A CHOICE

Stephen Miller

Whenever people learn about my past, about how bad things used to be, they never seem as interested in how I became an opiate addict as they are in how I stopped being one. It makes sense. These days opiate addicts are a dime a dozen. Everyone knows someone who set out to dip their toes in the water and ended up drowning. Ex-addicts are far more rare, unfortunately, and known to revert to their former status more often than not.

Even at two-and-a-half years sober, I'm not out of the woods. I haven't had a slip, never even came close. Doesn't matter. Hubris is a luxury afforded only to the naïve, and naivety and I parted ways several tragedies ago.

Truthfully, despite the common question, no one ever stops

being an addict. That potential, unbeknownst to me, had always existed inside me. I was an addict long before I ever snorted that first line of Percocet or pierced my skin and flooded my veins with liquefied OxyContin. I just didn't realize it until after I had let the tiger out of the cage.

What they really want to know is how I learned to stop feeding the tiger, who by all accounts was ravenous. How exactly did you lull it back to sleep? How did you learn to ignore all the teeth and claws and appetite?

I tell them it all started with a choice. And that much is true. I tell them how I moved from Marystown to St. John's to start the methadone maintenance program after I finally accepted that my will power was no match for my withdrawals. In reality, this was no great epiphany. I had accepted my weakness in the face of my addiction long before.

Truthfully, my journey to sobriety started the moment they told me she was dead.

My relationship with Joy was what you might call typical, considering the circumstances. Two addicts deeply enamoured with one another but engaged in the toxic rat race that is drug addiction. All day every day spent trying to scratch that incessant itch by any means necessary, up to and including at the other's expense.

Did we love each other? Undoubtedly. In fact, the only thing we loved more than each other was the drugs.

We lied, cheated, short-changed, and betrayed whomever necessary, up to and including each other. Forgiveness was always inevitable. We knew the score. Nothing is sacred when there's a monkey on your back, not even love.

Most of the time, though, it was us against the world. The vast majority of our deceit coordinated together for our mutual benefit. Backing up each other's lies, cooperating in criminal activity. At the time, it seemed terribly exciting…romantic almost.

We made a hell of a team. Conniving, creative, relentless—
we were truly a force to be contended with when it came to getting
our own way. I often wonder what sort of laudable goals we might
have achieved if our motivations had been less perverse. In the life
of an addict, success is measured by your ability to stay high. Me
and Joy were very successful addicts. We were constantly under the
influence, numb to everything, just the way we liked it.

Our success would be her downfall.

Both of us had developed quite a tolerance to opiates, but we knew
our limits, and Joy was adamant that we stay within them. I was the
risk taker, secretly doing much more potent hits than she realized.
That was why I was so certain that I, if anyone, would be the one who
overdosed.

The hit that killed her was paltry. Three quarters of an eighty
milligram Oxy. We were doing between three and six a day regularly
at the time of her death. At that point, sixty milligrams should have
been like a coffee and a cigarette.

Unbeknownst to us, Joy's organs had been deteriorating rapidly
from the consistent drug use. That seemingly innocuous hit was the
straw that broke the camel's back.

It happened fast, faster than I could've ever imagined. Her throat
started to swell shut and her face began to turn purple. It was like
witnessing a terrible allergic reaction. The fear I saw in her eyes
defies description. The only thing that I can compare them to are
the eyes of an animal caught in a snare. Joy instinctively recognized
the direness of the situation and told me to call the ambulance,
struggling to speak.

The ambulance took less than fifteen minutes to arrive. Joy lost
consciousness before it did. She never regained it.

Her vitals were critically low when the paramedics first assessed
her. They allowed me to travel in the ambulance with them as we
rushed to the nearby hospital. Although the hospital was little more

than ten minutes away, she crashed before we even arrived.

The staff at the Grand Bank Healthcare Centre worked tirelessly for about an hour to resuscitate her. It felt more like a year. I refused to give up hope right up until the moment the doctor informed me there was nothing left to hope for.

Looking back on it, it's as though the first few days after her death happened to someone else. Almost like an out-of-body experience. I can recall what I did, who I saw, but it might as well have been someone else. I was on auto-pilot. I guess it was shock.

I wasn't allowed to attend Joy's funeral. Her father and some of his side of the family held me responsible. Her death seemed as salacious as her life. The funeral home had informed the staff I was to be allowed entry under no circumstances. An RCMP police unit patrolled the parking lot to dissuade me, should the thought of disobedience arise. They need not have worried. I had no intention of turning her funeral into a fiasco.

Perhaps I didn't blame myself directly, but I felt the crushing guilt of the survivor. It should have been me. I should have intervened long ago and set us down a better path. She had so much potential. So many years ahead of her.

Most people thought that the countdown on my life had begun the moment Joy passed. Many knew that it was Joy who had kept me alive by demanding I ration my pills and enforcing limits as to how much I consumed in each hit. It would have been the easy thing to do. Double down on my escapist tendencies, numb myself to all the pain until there was no one left to feel it.

And that was when I really had to make a choice. I had to choose between what was right and what was easy, between what was expected of me and what I was capable of.

Seemed to me that there would be no greater insult to Joy's memory than for me to purposefully snuff out my own life. Intentionally or not, she had paid the ultimate price to provide me with the ultimate wake-up call.

I decided that I would live. That I would devote my life to getting better and living up to the potential I know we both had within us. I could no longer plead ignorance to what was at stake, and I wanted to become someone that we could both be proud of.

At the time of writing, I have been free from illicit drugs for well over two years. I completed the methadone program on December 21, 2017, and have been running on my own steam ever since. After a decade out of school, I have completed two semesters of my journalism program. Recently, I was fortunate enough to be chosen for an internship at a broadcasting corporation. I recently spoke about my experiences at a convention in Gander and intend to speak publicly about my recovery whenever possible. I want people to know that if I can do it, anyone can.

I repaired relationships I never thought possible, bridged seemingly insurmountable gaps with my family, and have found the love of a wonderful woman who has cultivated incredible personal growth. Against all odds, not only am I alive, I am happy.

And it all started with a choice.

"Her last turn in rehab had gone well.
She saw me the day she returned, clear-eyed and
cheerful as usual when she was clean;
she was full of enthusiasm, in touch
with her AA sponsor, and was going to
contact her family and her better friends."

## JESSICA

Kirsten Emmott

J essica is dead. The coroner called me early on Saturday morning, waking me from sleep. I heard a dog barking and a child chattering in the background. It took me a minute to realize who was calling and even longer to understand what she was telling me: Jessica was dead of a heroin overdose.

She'd overdosed two days before, been brought in to the emergency ward, walked out after being revived, and I couldn't reach her after that. On the night she died, her boyfriend told the police she'd gone into the bathroom to shoot up and she hadn't come out. He found her unconscious. By the time the ambulance got there, she was gone.

I had been Jessica's GP for a number of years. I liked her and liked working with her; in contrast with some of my addicted patients, she seemed to have a basically optimistic outlook on life. She was slim, pretty, looked younger than her years.

Her last turn in rehab had gone well. She saw me the day she returned, clear-eyed and cheerful as usual when she was clean; she was full of enthusiasm, in touch with her AA sponsor, and was going to contact her family and her better friends.

Jessica had many supports in the community. Her parents, both alcoholics, were dead, but four of her siblings were still alive; she had a grown child, who had given her grandchildren; and she had her ex-husband, Bill. Bill had stopped drinking years ago. He was endlessly patient with Jessica when she was trying to stay straight.

"She is the sweetest person when she's not drinking," he used to say to me, "but when she's drunk, or stoned, she goes completely crazy."

Bill didn't take any shenanigans from Jessica. When she wouldn't straighten out, he threw her out. He had other responsibilities, and he couldn't manage Jessica's problems. Drunk, she had committed a number of assaults; in the past three years, when she became addicted to heroin and cocaine, she was arrested for break-and-enter and then for parole violations.

I never saw Jessica at her worst. When she was straight, she was utterly charming and determined to beat her substance abuse. When she was using, she would come to the office depressed and defeated looking, trembling from withdrawal, pleading to be detoxified. Never did I see her drunk or stoned. Never did she pretend to have lost her prescriptions or give lying stories to get drugs. Every time she wanted to withdraw, I was supportive, calling the residential centers and several times admitting her for alcohol withdrawal. She bore the shakes poorly, and twice she eloped from the hospital after a day or so of Valium loading. But we both persisted.

In April, she wavered. A suicidal gesture, pills and alcohol, led to a short stay on the psychiatric ward. Sitting on the edge of her bed, I levelled with her.

"You can't go on treating your body like this, Jessica," I said. "Something's got to give. Already I see the changes in your health. You're not the beauty you once were; you're getting tired."

"I know," said Jessica. "I want to change."

We got the social workers organized, the court workers, the psychiatrist. Jessica increased her Prozac. She went back into rehab. And when she returned, she came in on Monday, clean and sober, things seeming to be going her way. She had plans. She was going to look for work. Maybe, I thought, she would get back together with Bill, as she so often did after a few months of sobriety.

But Bill, unfortunately, had continued to smoke. Not long ago, I heard that Bill had lung cancer. And later that same Monday, Bill died.

It must have been that loss that pushed Jessica over the edge. She found some heroin that same day. And by Friday night, she was dead.

"I've talked to the family," said the coroner. She named the band they belonged to. "They wanted to come in and wash the body, so that was arranged. Sad."

I answered something and hung up. Sad it was. At her funeral, at least sixty members of her extended family packed the first six rows of the chapel; scores more filled the room, which rang with sobs and sniffles during the ceremony. The loving eulogy in the little booklet the family handed out told me all sorts of things about Jessica that I never knew. There was no judgment here; the eulogy spoke frankly of her drug and alcohol problems as something Jessica struggled against, but could never defeat. As for Bill, all I read was that Jessica loved him and craved a stable life with him. Yet I knew nothing of that.

Jessica's family had weathered storms that people like me just read about in novels, at least until we start practicing family medicine. Was her parents' alcoholism to blame? The misery of residential schools? Racism? I have no idea. Two of her relatives were suicides. Others have had problems with drugs, alcohol, crime, and psychiatric hospitalization. One of her siblings has also come to me with drug and alcohol problems. Perhaps this will snap him to attention, I thought. Or maybe it will just add one more straw to the camel's back. All I can do is hope, and soldier on.

But what if that's not good enough? What if my best efforts don't work any better than they did with Jessica? After all, I never really got to know Jessica really well. I dealt mainly with her substance abuse problems, as she careened from one crisis to the next. I could have spent more time with her, delving into her childhood, or propping up her sense of self-worth. She was a fine person, despite her self-destructive ways.

I'm sorry, Jessica.

"Then we were introduced to Oxy.
They will wake you up, and give you energy.
We started doing them to get high,
then before work for the extra boost.
Before we knew it, we were hooked."

## WHERE DO I START? 20

Chiara Stagliano

Where do I start? At the age of fifteen, I started to go to raves and got into the drug scene. I never saw it as an addiction. I was young and just having a good time, and it was only at parties. Then it started being more frequent. From doing it once in a while, I started going to parties more often. Then, before I knew it, I was getting high on ecstasy on a Wednesday night just because, and started snorting lines at 9 a.m. in the school bathroom. I still thought, "I'm young. It's okay. I'm a teenager. I'm allowed to be stupid."

A few years of this and I was starting to calculate my paycheques and how much drugs I could buy with them. I was working just to buy drugs and nothing else. At nineteen, I said, "I'm done. I don't need drugs anymore." In the past, I had thought, "If life gets rough, get high and forget about it all." Then I realized, "I don't want to depend on a drug to make life better." So, after four years of getting high, I was done.

Years later, I moved from my small hometown to a mid-sized city. I moved out of my Dad's house at around twenty-two years of age, and into my boyfriend's house. I continued to stay away from drugs, but my boyfriend was doing coke here and there. I didn't see it as an addiction. If we had a party once every few months, they would offer some to me, but I always said no, and just hung out. From once in a while, it turned into every weekend. Then, a few years after moving in together, my boyfriend got another girl pregnant. I felt so sad and empty and broken inside that, after seven years of not doing drugs, the next time they pulled out lines, I said I wanted some. I did lines all night and from that day onward every weekend.

As my boyfriend's business grew more successful, the parties and the coke became more frequent. He only wanted to be part of the child's life once it was born, and there was a lot of tension. With the increase in stress, we started to use drugs more often. Then we were introduced to Oxy. They will wake you up, and give you energy. We started doing them to get high, then before work for the extra boost. Before we knew it, we were hooked. We needed this terrible drug just to function every day, from one a day to five a day, and they were not cheap. Soon, he lost his office due to the drug use. When the office was gone, we got even more depressed. All we did was get high all day, every day, and the lines of coke turned into smoking crack, something I thought I would never do.

A year after that, we lost the house and slept on a friend's couch for a year. I did not want this life anymore. I knew I was better than this. We both went on methadone. I did not want those evil pills to take over my life anymore. I did stop the pills once I started the methadone program, but my boyfriend was still doing them. I may have stopped the pills but was still smoking crack. Now we didn't have our good friends anymore. All of a sudden, we were hanging out with people who have never worked a day in their lives, and lived off the government and scamming people. I didn't want to be around these people. I would get angry because when we were alone I told my boyfriend, "We deserve better than that. We don't belong here," and he would stick up for them and call them good people. I knew it wasn't him. It was the drugs talking.

I ended up starting a new job and renting out a room. He stopped coming home at night and was sleeping on crackheads' couches. After a few months of rarely seeing each other, as he stopped responding to my calls and messages, I got a call that he was in jail. He had been pulled over, and the police found crack pipes and needles in the car. The judge ordered him to go live with his parents, to get away from the people he was hanging out with. When I would visit him at his parents, he was sober and starting to act like the old person I loved again. I was so happy. He said he was ready to come home and go back to work, and be done with drugs. During the next court date, we fought to have his assurity changed from his parents to me.

He came home with me that day, about a week before Christmas. He would ask me for money. I would say, "No. I will leave you smokes and buy food, or whatever, but I can't give you money." We were supposed to go visit his family for Christmas, and the night before, I came home from work and found him passed out on the floor in the bathroom. I had seen him like this many times. I tripped over a needle. I was so upset. He was mumbling and talking gibberish. I said, "Tomorrow is Christmas. I'm not going to ruin everyone's Christmas by telling them what you did tonight. We will have a nice Christmas with your family. Come Boxing Day, I am telling them, and we'll be putting you into rehab."

Unfortunately, it was too late. He went to bed to sleep it off and be normal in the morning. To my horror, when I went to wake him up in the morning, he wouldn't wake up. I immediately called

9-1-1. I tried giving him CPR. When they arrived, they told me he had been gone a few hours. It's tragic because I know he wanted to be clean and stay clean so badly, but the demon was too overpowering. It was unfortunate that drugs won. He was an amazing person!

You think it's just once. It's just at a party. I won't get addicted. Then it ruins your life and, eventually, completely takes over. And the longer you wait to get help, the more it takes over. I was lucky. I went on methadone, and it took three years to get off the methadone. Now, four years later, there is no drug overpowering my life. We can only learn from our mistakes and the heartbreak and terrible things we experience.

"I have been struggling with
an addiction to opiates since the age of eighteen,
and it was my severe drug addiction
that led to my criminal convictions."

SETTING MYSELF
UP FOR SUCCESS

21

Andrew Carter

My name is Andrew Carter. I am thirty-one years old from St. John's, Newfoundland, serving my first federal sentence of five years for robbery, disguise with intent, and possession of a dangerous weapon. I have been struggling with an addiction to opiates since the age of eighteen, and it was my severe drug addiction that led to my criminal convictions. My addiction has interfered with all aspects of my life, including family relationships, education, and employment. I have tried several forms of intervention over the years, but have been unsuccessful until now.

When I was nine years old, my parents divorced, which led to feelings of anxiety, which also led to extreme OCD. I did not disclose these feelings to family and kept things to myself, resulting in these feelings going undiagnosed for several years. Due to the lack of medical intervention, the symptoms got increasingly worse over time. Throughout junior high, I started experimenting with marijuana and found this eased the symptoms and was a form of self- medicating. It was in high school that I started experimenting with other drugs such as ecstasy, cocaine, and alcohol. These provided short-term escape, but I was unable to function in daily life under the influence of these drugs. I quickly realized using drugs could provide an escape from the mental-health issues I was dealing with, but I had to find the right one which would allow me to self-medicate and live a "normal life." During this time, all my drug use was kept secret from my family. I was starting to associate with drug users and distanced myself from positive friendships.

At age twenty, I suffered a three-day-long panic attack while coming down off ecstasy. I reached out to my mother for help, and medical attention was sought. At this time, I was diagnosed with anxiety and depression and prescribed anti-depressants and Ativan. Once I discovered that Ativan provided the relief I was looking for, I stopped partying with friends and using ecstasy, cocaine, and alcohol, and turned to the street to find Ativan to self-medicate. It was through buying Ativan on the street that I was introduced to other drugs such as Percocet and OxyContin. After using Percocet, I would describe it as a "miracle drug." Every symptom of anxiety, depression, and Obsessive Compulsive Disorder (OCD) would be gone while using this. After becoming dependant on Percocet, I started on the methadone program. While on methadone, I was abusing Valium, and was removed from the methadone program after a short time. During this time in my life, I was able to maintain employment and relationships with family and friends.

After being removed from the methadone program, my addiction spiralled out of control. I started using morphine intravenously daily, hundreds of milligrams per day, and I was unable to function without it. I was receiving unemployment insurance at the time, and I would do small cash jobs to support my addiction. I was attending trade school, which was funded by unemployment insurance. I would lie to my family and ask for money for work supplies, bus passes, and other things necessary for school, as a way to get money to support my addiction. Over time, my grades started to slip and attendance was poor, and I knew I probably would not make it through the course. There was one specific time I received $1200 to pay for textbooks that my mother already paid for, and I was supposed to pay her back. Instead, I quit school and blew the money on drugs. It was at this time my mother became aware of my addiction, and I went to Humberwood Treatment Centre in Corner Brook, Newfoundland, for four weeks.

I was unsuccessful at that chance at recovery and was removed from the treatment centre one day prior to the end of the program due to a positive urinalysis test. I feel I was unsuccessful at this program because it was too short, and I was suffering withdrawals while I was there. I was unable to focus on the skills they were teaching. I also had difficulty opening up to the group about personal experiences and feelings. Upon returning to St. John's, my family did not want to enable me, and they could no longer trust me in their homes, so I ended up living at a homeless shelter. I was eventually set up in a bed-sitting room, by the homeless shelter, with four other drug addicts in an negative area of town. It was very difficult for me to focus on staying drug free while living in these conditions. During this time, I continued to use opiates and distance myself from all positive supports and family members in my life. I struggled to find ways to support the addiction and turned to crime as a last resort.

At the age of twenty-seven, I had a weeklong crime spree, which included five armed robberies at gas stations in the St. John's area. I knew this was wrong and did not harm anyone. I was called the "polite robber" in the news. My life had slipped out of control.

My father saw a video of one of the armed robberies, and he recognized me in the video. He convinced me to do the right thing and turn myself in. I realized I had reached rock bottom, and if I did not turn myself in, I would end up dead. I was sentenced to five years for the crimes and was able to avail of programming while incarcerated, which helped me with my addiction as well as other aspects of my life.

While incarcerated, I was able to experience a lengthy period of sobriety and participate in programming offered through Corrections Canada in relation to addiction. Due to good institutional behaviour, remaining drug free within the institution, and successful completion of required programing, I was granted a day parole release and resided at a halfway house. The recovery process proved more difficult back on the street where I could have contact with old friends and drugs were more available. It was also very overwhelming to be back on the street after being incarcerated for twenty months. The anxiety and stress started to build up again. I was not honest and open with my supports in reaching out for help when I felt my mental health was not in a good place. I had a relapse after being on the streets for approximately six months, which resulted in me being sent back to prison.

While incarcerated due to the parole violation, I was able to attend more intensive programming and have another lengthy period of sobriety. It was during this time I found out my girlfriend was pregnant and I realized the importance of dealing with my addiction, so I could be there for my child. Luckily, I was given another chance of a day parole release and went back to living at a halfway house. I continued with programming while in the community and took advantage of the positive supports I had around me, and used them to my advantage to make the most of my situation. I had a completely different mindset on this release due to the birth of my child, and used this as additional motivation to stay clean.

Shortly after returning to the street, I realized I would need help managing my cravings and addictions, and sought the help of medical professionals. I was prescribed Suboxone and have been compliant with all aspects of this program as outlined by my doctor, including urinalysis testing. I also was prescribed medication to help me with my anxiety, which has also helped me maintain my sobriety, as there is no longer a need for self-medication. I was able to maintain my sobriety and successfully complete my day parole, and was granted full parole. I am currently living with my girlfriend and child. I also secured full-time employment and completed courses to increase my chances of finding employment. As a young person with a criminal record, it is difficult to find employment, and this was a major source of stress upon returning to the street after being incarcerated. Despite maintaining sobriety for a long period of time, I still use skills every day to overcome stressful situations, which in the past would have led to drug use as a coping mechanism.

I have not been dependent on drugs now for four years. However, I had some slips along the way. It has been twenty-three months since I last used, and I now feel that I have the skills to stay drug free, and avoid any relapses in the future. Without the positive support from my family and the Suboxone program, I may not have been successful in my battle with addiction. There have been struggles along the way, and it took time to regain the trust of my family. I was lucky they supported me through this difficult part of my life. I have made the necessary changes in my life to set myself up for success, by changing the people I spend my time with and finding positive ways to use my time.

# DIGITAL ADDICTIONS:

## SEX, VIDEO GAMES, GAMBLING, AND SOCIAL MEDIA

"Drugs were a convenient way
to make it possible to feed this insatiable need
for external approval, for validation,
by having sex for days on end. I've started
to try changing this: to accept that
I am a worthwhile human being without
trading sex for validation."

## HOW SOON IS NOW?

Ricardo Villela

I was born in Sao Paulo, Brazil. My mother, if truth be told, was something of a "party girl." My father was her boyfriend at the time. They got married when they found out she was pregnant with me. My grandfather was rich, so they had a big, fancy wedding. He was so happy as he thought getting married and having a baby would fix her, settle her down. But it didn't. They split up after one year. My father married another woman. My mother went back to her party-girl ways, and there were lots of strange, sketchy characters constantly coming and going in my mother's house. I also spent time at the house of my father and his wife, who I confusingly also call my mother. I didn't want for material things. We were pretty well off and had nice houses, maids and so on. But my childhood was a constant state of being shuttled back and forth. A strange mix of affection and abandonment. When I was very little, I was close to my mother. But that changed over time. She drifted away from me as her attention seemed to grow more towards other things. She was always drinking, partying, busy with guys.

The maid and the handyman had a little one-bedroom house at the back of the garden. He was very nice to me and we got along really well. I liked being with him. I used to hang out with him while he was working, or in their cottage. I sometimes used to take a nap there in their bed. One warm summer day when I was about eight, I was dozing in the cottage. His wife was working in the house. He came in and lay down beside me. This was the beginning of him having sexual relations with me. It went on for about four years. It wasn't violent but I can see now that this was a kind of abuse. This was also the beginning of me thinking of my body, of sex, in a certain way. That doing certain things with sex would allow me to get things I wanted from people, even if it was only to feel less lonely. To feel wanted. I started playing like this with some of the other boys in the neighbourhood.

Then when I was twelve, it was decided it would be better for me to live with my father when they found that one of my real mother's boyfriends was a drug dealer. The sex with the handyman ended then, when I moved. My father's wife, my other mother now, used to listen to English rock music. She, we, didn't fully understand all the words, but it was a way of learning English. Music is global. One line from the song, "How Soon Is Now?" by The Smiths, sticks in my mind: "I am human and I need to be loved, just like everybody else does." Was I loved? I didn't always feel I was. Is sex love? I'm not sure, but for most people they seem pretty closely related. I'm not sure if that's really true though. Sex and love can be quite different, not really connected.

When I was eighteen, my parents figured out I was gay. Although my mother was totally on board and loved to go shopping with me, my father was not very happy about it at all. One night, when I was nineteen, I had been out drinking with a friend. I was still living with my parents. We went back home and just crashed on my bed. I'm not sure if we planned to make out or not, but we were so drunk we just fell asleep. In the morning, my father walked in on us. We were asleep in bed but kind of intertwined a bit, so he was shocked. Appalled, really. My aunt has a little travel agency, which arranges study-abroad placements for kids to go to other countries and learn English. I had worked there a bit and had previously expressed an interest in going abroad. My father said now would be a good time to go. Like, right now. He called my aunt that day, and we arranged it all for me to leave and go to Canada. I guess that was his way of dealing with my being gay.

One thing I should tell you, even though it makes me sound all arrogant and full of myself, is that I'm very good-looking. I have a pretty good body, too. Always did. Good genes, I guess. Guys fall in love with me all the time. A friend of mine once told me that going into a gay bar with me is like going into shark-infested waters and throwing slabs of bloody meat into the water. It only takes a few minutes before I'm surrounded by hot guys buying me drinks. So finding sex is pretty easy for me.

So I arrived in Toronto at nineteen. Studied English for a while. Made a little money in construction, cleaning, and other "under the table" jobs used by people on student visas not allowed to work. Went to a gay club and found a boyfriend. Found this cool, sketchy afterhours club with great dance music and where you could get any drugs you want. After I'd been going there every weekend for a while, I met this guy, Brian, and his group of friends. They were fun and we used to go to his place after the club to do drugs all weekend. Brian and some of the other guys seemed happy to buy drugs for me. We did a bit of everything: E, K, G, coke, meth. This went on for a while. It was exciting exploring the sensations of different drugs. I had done a little coke in Brazil, but not all this other stuff. But it got kind of weird when Brian started to fall madly in love with me. I started having sex with one of the other guys in the group, even though I didn't think he was very attractive, just to show Brian I wasn't into him. He went kind of crazy, and the group fell apart. So I found some other people to party with.

It went on like this for a couple of years. I went to community college, graduated, and got a decent job. I partied when I could on the weekends. Just social drug use, like everyone else seems to do. Nothing serious. Went through a few boyfriends.

Then my father told me he wanted me to go to university and get a degree so I could get a better job, a career even. I think this was his way of making up for more or less kicking me out a few years before? Our relationship got much closer then, as he seemed to make peace with the whole gay thing. I quit my job and got a part-time job so I could go back to school. This was kind of a strange time as I had just ended a pretty intense relationship. I had money my father was sending me for school. I took some continuing-education night courses I needed to get admitted. Did okay in some, flunked others. University was harder than community college, and studying all the time was a bit boring. Maybe I wasn't cut out for this? So I started using phone apps to have some sex as a diversion. Finding sex in the gay neighbourhood of a big city is so easy. Only takes a few minutes, really. Some guys want to chat endlessly or meet for coffee. Block them. What bullshit. When I'm online, I want to get fucked. Now. I don't want to get to know what kind of movies you like, or where you work, or what your name is. I want to see a dick pic and if it's big enough, then let's meet to fuck. Now.

That year at Pride, I met a couple of guys. Steve and Rodolfo. We went back to their hotel room. Steve lived in Toronto, but Rodolfo lived in London and was just here for Pride. We had fun doing some G and having sex and then went our separate ways. Didn't exchange numbers or anything. Normal Pride activities. A couple of weeks later, I ran into Steve at a bar, and he was very happy to see me. Steve was very good-looking, really nice, smart, successful, and keen to spend more time with me. We started dating. He had this job where he travelled a lot. Actually, he spent more time outside of Toronto than in town. Within a month of our starting to date, he was going to Paris for work and offered to take me along on his airline points. I went. It's hard not to have a romantic time in Paris, so we had a romantic time in Paris. Within a couple of months, I moved in with him.

I was still going to school and working part time. Not trying too hard, but hard enough to keep my father happy. So while Steve was out of town working, I had a lot of free time. Trying to study all the time was a bit boring. Steve tried so hard to look after me. He treated me like a king, really. He was a great cook, so he did all the cooking, and when he was going away, he would spend all day Sunday cooking stuff to put little containers of food in the fridge for me, so I wouldn't have to do anything myself while he was away. We even had a cleaning lady for our tiny little apartment so I didn't have to clean.

I was bored and lonely without him, so I used to go hang out with my friend, Pedro. Pedro liked to smoke meth. I used to go over, smoke with him, and we'd be up all night talking and laughing. Meth makes you feel smart and witty. We laughed a lot, had a great time. In the morning, he'd have to go to work, and I'd go home and maybe watch some porn. Meth does make you kind of horny. I never fooled around with Pedro. For a while, porn was good enough after these nights. I was trying to be a good boyfriend to Steve. But then I started chatting with guys on hook-up apps, and then I started meeting them. Sometimes they had more meth, and we'd smoke some more. Sex while high on meth is fantastic. The sensations are so much more intense. And it can go on for a long time. Often, usually, I would go to another guy's place after I'd finished with one. And then another and another. It was pretty easy to go through five or six or ten guys a day/night. You look for PnP in the profile. Party and Play. Sex and drugs.

Sometimes I'd feel guilty about cheating on Steve. But once I'd done the first guy, it kind of didn't matter anymore. Once you'd done one, you may as well do ten. What's the difference? Cheating is cheating, right? Besides, when you're high, those sorts of things seem like silly little details. Trivialities. Needless to say, Steve eventually found out. But he was so in love with me, we just went to couples counselling, and he paid for me to have my own therapist, too. Lots of talking. Blah, blah, blah. When we had some of these arguments, I would try to not do it on his next business trip. Try. That never really worked very well, though. It got to the point where, as soon as I saw the cab drive him off to the airport, I would head out to some guy's place. I had a few regulars to smoke some meth with and have sex. Sometimes, Steve would call me from the airport to say goodbye, and I'd say how much I missed him, while already high and naked with another guy.

Eventually, he ran out of patience. He called me up one day at work and told me we're not breaking up, we're broken up. He had packed all my things in my suitcases and had them by the door, and when I got home, he told me to leave. I took my bags and sat on them under the nearby freeway overpass while it rained, and I cried. I went back to Steve's in tears. That usually worked, made him feel sorry for me, but he made me sleep on the couch and texted one of my friends who had a nice house with a spare room, to see if I could stay there for a while. He agreed.

It was a nice place, newly renovated. I had helped him pick out some furniture and make design choices. I have a pretty good design sense. I had my own bedroom and bathroom. He lived in a different neighbourhood, so there was a whole new group of guys nearby to work through on hook-up apps. When I was with Steve, I had to stop and sober up for a few days when he was in town. Now there was no need to do that at all. So I could take the sex and meth thing into a higher gear. I started on PReP. I didn't like sex with condoms, and being high all the time doesn't exactly lead to careful, sensible choices. I had been put on PEP twice while with Steve.

Over the course of the next three months, I stopped even trying to pretend I did anything else outside of work besides hooking up with guys and getting high. I'd given up on school completely. Often I'd come home at 6 a.m., after being out all night, shower and change, and go to work for seven. Still high as a kite. If I had a day off, I often wouldn't go home at all. I'd spend it a friend's place downtown, smoking meth and hooking up. Sometimes there would be parties at guys' houses where you spend all weekend hanging out, smoking meth, and doing G, with different guys coming and going all the time. Dealers showing up with more drugs. Sometimes the sex would be in groups, sometimes individually. Some guys slammed it—that is, dissolved the meth in water and injected it into a vein. I never did that. I hate needles. I smoked it and sometimes hooped it—that's dissolving it in some water and shooting it up into your ass. A faster rush that way. But it was all great. Sometimes I'd leave straight from the drug/sex parties to go to work and then come right back to the party after my shift. I'd wear the same clothes to work two or three days in a row. I didn't care.

Every now and then, I'd have to come home and crash. Sleep and eat for a few days. Once I fell asleep in a bowl of cereal. My roommate had to pretty much carry me to my room. It didn't take long for him to figure out what was going on. He said I was an addict and tried to get me to go to rehab. I said I was totally in control and just having a good time. Why shouldn't I enjoy myself? I was young. Unattached. He said he was "enabling" me by buying me food—I never seemed to have any money—and giving me a place to live. So he kicked me out, but said I could come back if I went to rehab. If I'm so good-looking and everyone loves me so much, why do people keep kicking me out?

I went to live with another friend, sharing a junior one-bedroom apartment now. My accommodations had taken a big step down. I did go to some group sessions at a rehab place after he kicked me out. But I never really slowed down on the drugs. I was back downtown, so I could ratchet things up even more. More than once, I went to group at rehab while high. At first my roommate tried to be understanding and supportive, but that didn't last long. We started arguing a lot. He yelled and screamed at me. All that same stuff about being an addict needing rehab. It wasn't too long before he moved out to a nicer place on his own. After that, because I was living on my own now, it was non-stop. Some nights I wouldn't even close the door to my apartment. One guy after another would come and go.

It shouldn't be a big surprise that I often arrived late to work. When this happens, they put a letter in your personnel file. If it happens often enough, the manager talks to you, reprimands you, warns you. So after a bunch of these letters, and a stern talking to from my boss, they put me on medical leave and told me to clean up my act if I wanted to keep my job. Because addiction is a heath issue, they didn't fire me. So I tried to organize inpatient treatment at the rehab, not because I thought I needed it, but because that's what I had to do to keep my job. But all the rehab places covered by health insurance had a long waiting list. I tried to slow down the drugs a little. Just a little. It didn't really work. There is a program at one place for gay meth users, but there are a lot of us, and not too many spaces available, so the waiting list is pretty long. I would need to wait for a few months.

I decided to go to Brazil to visit my family. This forced me to be clean for a couple of weeks while there. I had to be. Not fun to come down with the family around, so I just ate and slept and drank a lot. My father had heard what was going on from Steve. He asked what he could do. Did I want to go to rehab in Brazil? He was very understanding and supportive. I convinced him that I had it all in hand, and was just waiting to get into rehab back in Toronto, which was all arranged, a little white lie, but close enough to the truth. I tried to stay clean after coming back, but you know how well that usually works.

Shortly after getting back, in August, I went to Montreal Pride with some friends. I went to a bathhouse and spent the whole time there. I didn't sleep for eight days. Who knows how much meth I smoked and G I took? A lot. Who knows how many guys I had sex with? Fifty? A hundred? Two hundred? Who knows? Who cares? It was one after another. I would go into the darkroom and have sex for hours with guys without ever seeing their faces. I felt I was free, that I was doing exactly what I wanted to do. I didn't want to miss out on anything, on any experience. I wanted to fulfill every desire. I wanted to do it all. A couple of times I saw people there that I knew, who weren't part of the same scene. With them, I was a bit embarrassed about how I looked, how skinny and sketchy I was. But that didn't bother me much. I wasn't there to socialize. I was there to lose myself in a sea of sensation, to dissolve myself in pleasure, and by doing so, to be free. I felt happy there. I saw my doctor back in Toronto after this, figuring I must have caught something requiring a shot, or a pill. He was shocked that I hadn't caught anything.

A month after this, a spot opened up in a rehab in town. Not the one I wanted, but rehab anyways. I was starting to get nervous about the length of time I'd been away from my job, so I went. They were mostly straight alcoholics. At one group session, I tried to explain how I would have sex for days on end, but people could not even grasp the mechanics of how this was physically possible. I only lasted three days there before I snuck out during a walk and went home.

I tried to stay clean after this while waiting to get into the gay program at the other rehab. That didn't work very well. Eventually, I got into the gay rehab program in the fall. It's a two-week inpatient program. It was good. The people there were like me, and we all shared the same experiences. I'd even had sex with a couple of them before. There were doctors and meds to manage the physical withdrawal. There is a lot of physical pain in stopping after using meth practically every day for a long time. It was good but not long enough. After I got out, I went back to work. I stayed clean for ten weeks in total. Then I had a little relapse. In no time at all, I was back to using every day with no let up. Not much sleep. Not much food. Meth kills your appetite. I had lost a lot of weight. I looked like shit. I used to drink Ensure just to make sure I didn't starve to death. I was supposed to go to Brazil to visit my father and the family for Christmas. He bought me a plane ticket. At the last minute, I told them I had to cancel due to work and would come in late January. That was a lie of course. I just didn't want to stop using and come down. I didn't want to feel the physical pain while trying to be smiley and happy at Christmas. I didn't want to feel the guilt and shame you feel when you come down and see what a mess your life has become. Best not to stop. Best to keep going.

At this point, it wasn't really fun anymore. It was a compulsion. A necessity. There was a part of me that didn't want it, that knew I shouldn't, but really there was no choice. That part that had to have it was much bigger and more powerful than the squeaky little voice saying I should stop. When the time to leave for Brazil in January came around, I made another excuse and just partied non-stop instead, since I had the week off work. I didn't sleep at all during that week, until the night before I had to go back to work. Then I crashed and took a couple of sleeping pills to make sure I could sleep. I slept through the alarm and was late to work. I got another reprimand in my personnel file. I went to my doctor to get another note from him, so work put me on disability again. My father rebooked my plane ticket for the next week. I missed that flight too. Couldn't stop. But I finally got on a plane the next day.

After taking four plane tickets to get me there, my father knew what he had to do and had already booked me into rehab. He gave me the choice of going in or not. My family was supportive, but I could see in their eyes how worried and disappointed they were. I went in without resisting. I was ready. I was just so tired of it all at that point. So tired of pretending I felt okay, that everything was okay. So tired.

I was in inpatient rehab in Brazil for four months. It was good. They managed the pain. They put me on a bunch of anti-anxiety, anti-depressant and anti-who-knows-what meds. I can't even pronounce the names of them. Sixteen pills a day. I guess it takes a lot of drugs to get you off drugs. There was a lot of food, a gym, a pool, a hot tub. Almost like a spa, really. Individual therapy and group sessions. I'm out now, living with my father. Still going to therapy and group every week. Still on some meds, though the doctor is talking about weaning me off. Clean and sober for over a year so far. The plan is to go back to Toronto soon and see if I can restart my life there. I'm feeling a lot healthier than I have for a long time and feeling much better about my life.

The therapy and counselling I've had have really helped me to understand the things that happened in my life and what an enormous effect they had on the things I've done. How the childhood abuse taught me that the approval of others and my own sense of self-worth came from sex. That I felt worthless without this sort of external validation, that sex and love were different and not really connected. That it was easy to have sex, but hard to feel loved. My addiction to sex preceded my addiction to drugs. Drugs were a convenient way to make it possible to feed this insatiable need for external approval, for validation, by having sex for days on end. I've started to try changing this: to accept that I am a worthwhile human being without trading sex for validation. To love myself. But it's hard to change the mindset of a lifetime. It's one thing to say something, but much harder to actually believe it and feel it in your bones.

I'm still working things out, but a year clean and sober is longer than I can remember being in that state for at least a decade—my entire adult life, really. I must admit I still miss the lifestyle sometimes. Being up all night just talking or hanging out, feeling connected with a group of friends. The sex and drug parties going on for days. Walking around the city at 4 a.m. en route to a hook up. A new guy, a new body, and some rough sex with someone whose name I would never know, and whom I would never see again. Does this seem appealing to me now because I was high on meth, and so all of this is associated with that euphoric feeling? Or is there something inside me that wants to feel like this, that thinks this is who and what I am? I've only just started on the path to accepting that I am worth more than this. I'm still a little bit scared about what will happen when I go back to Toronto and have that world at my doorstep again, a text message away. Recovery is a process, not a moment. That's where I am now, anyways.

"I am glad I stuck it out. Glad I worked through the social shaming, challenged myself to remain open and brutally honest, and to maintain some faith, if not in his capacity for change, then faith that anything is possible, if we are so willing, at any time."

# HE HAD MULTIPLE ADDICTIONS: SEX, GAMBLING, VIDEO GAMES, ALCOHOL, AND DRUGS

Damasya Wing

Healing society is like gardening—we must tend to our gardens and contend with the weeds. I am a social worker by profession, and I love to muck around in the garden. What we think of as weeds often have healing properties we would do well to rediscover. Think dandelions (a digestive aid) and plantain (an astringent, antibacterial, and anti-inflammatory aid). I have sought to rid myself of these weeds for years and to no avail. They seem to be nature's way of asserting itself to force a reckoning—*we are here, we are remedies, get used to it.*

We know people need nurturing to develop to their fullest. Yet we collectively treat some groups of people in society like weeds, like they don't belong and have nothing to contribute. What if "those people" hold properties we need, that will assist in healing our sickened world? Allow me to get personal.

The first time I fell in love with an apparent alcoholic (though not apparent to me at the time), the discouragement from my social network was swift. It mostly amounted to, "What are you? Stupid?"

I recall asking a close friend and social worker the question I was struggling with, "Don't alcoholics deserve to be loved too?"

"Yes but only by other alcoholics!" she replied with pointed anger. Both her parents were alcoholics. She felt they deserved each other, but didn't feel she deserved them. She wanted to spare me the pain.

By the way, the term "alcoholic" is considered "inappropriate" and no longer employed in most professional health fields. Instead, the term "substance user" or "substance abuser" is used, which is meant to be more benign. Still sounds judgy, if not even more offensive. Would you rather be called an alcoholic or a substance abuser? What substance? What abuse? I have here adopted the language my partner and clients themselves prefer to use.

So, when I fell in love a second time with another apparent alcoholic, I was in immediate existential crisis and truly questioned my sanity, for I knew better. I had gone through the devastation of building a family with the previous alcoholic, who struggled with multiple addictions, only to lose the battle. I found myself alone with three small children on social assistance for the first time ever, endeavouring to survive the consequent debilitating depression, while struggling to complete my master's thesis on my own; I also worked in a specialized mental-health field in the rehabilitation and recovery of individuals with co-occurring disorders (serious and persistent mental illness and addictions). Certainly, I knew not to get involved with an alcoholic. Yet, I was literally, magnetically, drawn to this human being. Why? What fucking lesson did God want me to learn now?

Let me explain the magnetism. From the moment I saw this enchanting creature-man, my gaze was transfixed. He reminded me of utterly magical personas I had encountered in my youth whilst in Paris. Here, the scene was a dingy, virtually empty Winnipeg gay bar that my dearest female friend and I occasionally attended during a weekday, for the solidarity, solitude, and absence of white-male harassment.

This mortal floated across the bar room in a long leather Matrix like a cape.

"Batman is in the house!" I thought.

His features were beautiful and manly. An Ernest Hemmingway type, a fedora covering his shaven head, a strong jaw-line and captivating profile, weathered ripped jeans, and black army boots wrapped in chains. He moved to the tune of his own drum as he swayed onto the dance floor alone. His foot movements were intoxicating.

Then, he walked towards me, and we simultaneously locked eyes. Instantly shot through the heart—tasered! The jolt was exhilarating and disturbing. What the fuck was that? Did he experience that too? Because I saw him jolt back. He stood beside me, eyes darting in my direction.

I initiated verbal contact, we proceeded outside, lit up, and I asked him upfront, "So, what are you, a skin-head?"

I liked that he answered calmly, wasn't offended by the question, and summarized what he was all about in two sentences. "I'm a salesman; I fix things. But I want to experience things, theater, travel; I want to live."

We danced. He was intoxicated.

I said, "I have to go."

He gave me his number. I left. Felt compelled to return. Moments later we danced again. Leaving him felt dreadful; staying longer felt scandalous. I thought about how any involvement with him was going to be painful; he's got a drinking problem, and I have a saviour complex. This would be disastrous to the fragile psychological equilibrium I had achieved for myself, let alone the harm it would bring to my children, the disrepute to my family and friends. But, by way of compelling attraction, dance, and his demeanour, something touched the deepest part of my yearnings for connection and meaning; I was simply drawn to him. I couldn't even wait a day. I called him in the middle of the night. No answer. He was passed out.

Investments of time, money, emotional work, and actual labour (side-by-side cleaning, teaching, coaching, and support) frequently seemed futile. He had multiple addictions (sex, gambling, video games, alcohol, and drugs), difficulty articulating thoughts and feelings, remarkably poor social skills, severe depression, and an anxiety disorder. The drugs, especially crack cocaine and methamphetamines, he actually kicked himself, with a little help from family who transplanted him one day from the Vancouver meth scene to a tiny town in Manitoba. But it was my hopes and dreams that were hammered on daily. I pounded back with my reality.

For two horrendous years, I demanded he stop lying (to me but mostly to himself) and demanded he keep trying. I openly hoped he could overcome his addicted brain. Secretly, I felt doubt and even shame because my friends and family would not hold to my faith. Some abandoned me, others distanced themselves for a while, co-workers pitied me, and some intervened to encourage clearing out my own closet "to make way for something better." Of course better was possible and probably around the bend. However, I tenaciously held his desire to come into the land of the living, to be sincere and worthwhile. Come what may, I wanted to save him and in turn be saved.

The rest is a long and instructive history (not provided here) on the first two wretched years of careless abandon of my career-track dreams, balancing motherhood responsibilities with this curious exploration of addiction up close and personal, followed by carefully calibrated love, and the ever-present struggle with a man in the grips of "demon rum." What began as a falling in love experience, for me, turned into more of a friendship, even a parental obligation, with the uncertain promise of someday partaking in a real relationship. He continued to make ongoing incremental changes, so we grew together. Then he would relapse, so at times we grew apart.

One day, he told me he researched a drug called Antabuse, discussed it with his family physician, secured a prescription, and announced he started taking it. Within a few days, he developed an allergy to alcohol. Just the smell of mouthwash would have him gaging. He was warned that if he drank while on this drug, he would land in hospital.

Well, he took Antabuse for three months without ever drinking a drop of alcohol (for the first time since he was twelve). During this time, his skin began to clear, his appetite returned, he began to put on weight, to look and feel good. Most of all, his mind began to clear, memories began to return (not always a great thing), and new habits had some time to form and displace the old ways of coping. In other words, new neural pathways developed in his brain. Positive feedback was swift and consistent from me, my kids, his workplace, friends, and family. He began to emerge as a sober man.

It's been two and half years since he took that faithful step. His life is marked by his own volition, his agency, this highly motivated turn towards transition. As he says, there was life before as Drunk-Man, and life now as Sober-Man. Fortunately, we all really like Sober-Man.

I am glad I stuck it out. Glad I worked through the social shaming, challenged myself to remain open and brutally honest, and to maintain some faith, if not in his capacity for change, then faith that anything is possible, if we are so willing, at any time. Also, I am pleased I shared the precarious nature of our relationship with my children, to instruct them in reality, and foster their empathy.

I often muse on how my lover was once like a social weed, a pariah, relegated to the margins of society, if not wholly written off, because of our collective moral failing, not his. But I have the pleasure of rediscovering his hidden value—a grateful, adventurous, hardworking, skilled, truthful, discreet, loyal, and good-looking fella (to name only a few qualities) who wanted a family, who in turn needed him to complete and heal their family, too.

"For example, being fired from work
for being absent due to continually
seeking sexual escapades, experiencing
relationship issues due to excessive porn use,
or contracting a STI due to excessive
unsafe sexual encounters are strong
indicators that one is struggling with a sexual
compulsion."

## SEXUAL COMPULSIONS

Kaila McAnulty

Sex addiction: this is an up-and-coming term that is being heard more and more frequently. But what is it, and is it actually an addiction? Let us commence with where the concept of sex addiction began. Before sex addiction had a better-suited label, being *hypersexual* was considered by many to be either a sin or a disease (Garcia and Thibaut, 2010). Historically, hypersexuality had been recognized since the late nineteenth century when it was labelled as *satyriasis* and *moral insanity* (Levine, 2010). Beginning in the twentieth century, and up until recently, being hypersexual was labelled as *Don Juanism* for men and as *Nymphomania* for women (Leiblum, 2007). Later in the twentieth century, hypersexuality carried with it a variety of labels such as compulsive sexual behaviour, hypersexual disorder, or simply out-of-control sexual behaviour (Kaplan and Krueger, 2010). Until recently, the term addiction was only used to describe chemical addictions, and the idea of becoming addicted to a behaviour, such as sex, was not considered possible (Hall, 2013). Then, in the 1960s and 1970s, forms of sexual behaviour and exploration became acceptable (Reay, Attwood, and Gooder, 2012). The primary factors in this making were an addiction discourse to sexual matters: a combination of conservative-Christian and radical-feminist social purity, and the initial impact of AIDS in the 1980s that so dramatically intensified sexual apprehensions (Reay, Attwood, and Gooder, 2012). Finally, in the 1980s, the term *sex addiction* began appearing in literature. In the 1990s, the media began to play a part in this new term we call sex addiction. Television, the tabloids, and the case histories of claimed celebrity victims all helped to popularize this newly invented term (Reay, Attwood, and Gooder, 2012). At this point in time, hypersexual disorder was proposed as a new *Diagnostic and Statistical Manual of Mental Disorders* (DSM-V) classification for the Sexual and Gender Identity Disorders category (Woody, 2011). Unfortunately, this disorder is intended to recognize only normal sexual activities or fantasies that have become problematic, caused distress in an individual, and interrupted their pattern of functioning. According to the DSM-V, sex is not yet perceived as a substance or behaviour one can develop an addiction to.

Sex addiction was recently denied entry into the DSM-V due to the fact that there was not enough empirical evidence to support the theory behind sex being an addiction. This doesn't change the fact that many sex therapists do believe that sex can be an addiction just like alcohol or gambling. Indeed, there is research out there that suggests sex addiction is similar to chemical addictions such as alcohol and cocaine.

Let us first look at the definition of addiction. The term *addiction* refers to the inability to consistently abstain from a behaviour, including difficulty in behavioural control, craving, and decreased recognition of significant issues with one's behaviours and inter-personal relations, leading to dysfunction in one's daily activities (Smith, 2012). So in laypersons' terms, you may be addicted if your relationship to the substance/behaviour is interfering with day-to-day functioning of finances, relationships, or health. For example, being fired from work for being absent due to continually seeking sexual escapades, experiencing relationship issues due to excessive porn use, or contracting a STI due to excessive unsafe sexual encounters are strong indicators that one is struggling with a sexual compulsion.

Like chemical addictions, some research suggests that hyper-sexuality consists of experiencing a recurrent failure to resist impulses to engage in a specific sexual behaviour, an increased sense of tension immediately prior to initiating the sexual behaviour, and pleasure or relief at the time of engaging in the sexual behaviour (Garcia and Thibaut, 2010). Similar to chemical addictions, hyper-sexuality also includes an escalation of sexual behaviours as the disorder progresses, withdrawal symptoms such as depression, anxiety, and guilt related to a reduction of sexual activities, as well as difficulty stopping or reducing the frequency of sexual behaviours (Garcia and Thibaut, 2010). Hypersexuality, like most other addictions, is also often used as a coping mechanism: a way to deal with stress. Those with sexual compulsions engage in these behaviours as a way of relieving stress and alleviating negative emotions with the goal of creating positive emotions just like any chemical addiction (Hall, 2013).

Treating sexual compulsions is similar to treating other addictions. One important difference is that when addressing hypersexuality, reducing shame is a major component. Most addictions entail some feelings of shame, but due to the stigma that still surrounds sexual compulsions, there appears to be more intense feelings around shame. As a sex therapist, I often combine Cognitive Behavioural Therapy (CBT), Prochaska and DiClemente's stages of change model, and Hall's cycle of sex addiction model which involves six treatment objectives (Hall, 2013). The treatment objectives I often use are: understand sex addiction, reduce shame, commit to recovery, understand and personalize the cycle of addiction, resolve under-lying issues, establish relapse prevention strategies, and develop a healthy lifestyle.

Firstly, it is important that patients are educated in what exactly hypersexuality is. Research supports the idea that, until the client is aware that this is a genuine health condition rather than a poor excuse for poor self-control, infidelity, or a heightened sex drive, they will be prevented from being able to move on to the next stage of treatment (Hall, 2013).

Secondly, we address shame. It is important to somewhat normalize hypersexuality by educating the patient on just how prevalent it is so they understand that they are not alone in this battle, and that it can be treated. If a patient is stuck feeling shamed, recovery will be unattainable and relapse is most often the result. It is also key that to ensure that the therapist uses genuine empathy and compassion when discussing shame, which is why the therapeutic alliance is essential.

The next objective is the commitment to recover. When patients attend therapy, they should already be at a point where they are willing to at least contemplate committing to treatment. The focus should not just be on what the patients need to give up, but what they want to gain (Hall, 2013).

Additionally, it is important that the patient is able to person-alize elements that make up their own unique sex-addiction cycle. This entails identifying triggers, recognizing cognitive distortions they may have, and understanding what works for them in regards to relapse prevention (Hall, 2013).

Another important objective in treatment is to look at any underlying issues. Relapse prevention strategies may be helpful to allow the patient to temporarily abstain from acting out, but until the deeper unmet needs and issues are addressed, recovery will be much more difficult (Hall, 2013).

The next objective is to establish relapse prevention strategies. Because relapse prevention stems from CBT, the relapse prevention work used in therapy not only needs to acknowledge the emotional and environmental triggers but also the automatic thought patterns that can lead to relapse (Hall, 2013).

The last objective is to develop a healthy lifestyle or a healthy relationship with sex. It is not just about learning to manage the sexual compulsion, but learning to manage life. Recovery often entails one to change their lifestyle (Hall, 2013). Patients are encouraged to develop a positive outlook on their sexuality and a healthy way to express and enjoy their sex life.

As a practicing sex therapist, I often encounter various sexual issues, which means that I have to approach each patient and each issue uniquely. I often adapt treatment plans so they best suit that particular patient. That being said, I must emphasize the importance of the therapeutic relationship. If the patient does not trust or feel comfortable with their therapist, the likelihood of a successful treatment outcome is slim. Building trust with the patient is optimal and a crucial first step. Next, I cannot stress enough the importance of normalizing particular sexual issues. It does not matter, in my opinion, if the sexual issue is morally wrong. The point is that they are coming to you for support. So normalizing even a socially unacceptable behaviour (as many of them do actually occur more often than people think), will encourage the person to feel at ease and more inclined to be open to treatment. Lastly, normalizing also decreases shame. This is imperative as shame often prevents people from accessing services. If they are sitting in your office, they are most likely vulnerable, so being empathic and compassionate is so important to whether or not they complete treatment.

Hypersexuality still has a great amount of stigma tied to it. It is imperative that we start talking about it in order to break down those barriers so treatment is more readily accessed. The more education there is surrounding sexuality and its concerns, the better the chance of increasing awareness and decreasing stigma.

REFERENCES

Garcia, F.D., and Thibaut, F. (2010). "Sexual Addictions." *The American Journal of Drug and Alcohol Abuse*, 36, 254-260. doi: 10.3109/00952990.2010.503823

Hall, P. (2013). *Understanding and Treating Sex Addiction*. New York: Routledge.

Kaplan, M.S., and Kreuger, R.B. (2010). "Diagnosis, Assessment, and Treatment of Hypersexuality." *Journal of Sex Research*, 47(2-3), 181-198. doi: 10.1080/00224491003592863

Leiblum, S.R. (2007). *Principles and Practice of Sex Therapy* (4th Ed.). New York: The Guilford Press.

Levine, S.B. (2010). "What is sexual addiction?" *Journal of Sex and Marital Therapy*, 36, 261-275. doi: 10.1080/00926231003719681

Reay, B., Attwood, N., and Gooder, C. (2012). "Inventing Sex: The Short History of Sex Addiction." *Sexuality and Culture.* 17. doi: 10.1007/s12119-012-9136-3

Smith, D.E. (2012). "Editor's Note: The Process Addictions and the New ASAM Definition of Addiction." *Journal of Psychoactive Drugs*, 44(1), 1-4.doi: 10.1080/02791072.2012.662105

Woody, J.D. (2011). "Sexual Addiction/Hypersexuality and the DSM: Update and Practice Guidance for Social Workers." *Journal of Social Work Practice in the Addictions*, 11, 301-320. doi: 10.1080/1533256X.2011.619926

"The pain that a sex addict inflicts
will be real and will be long lasting.
However, the road to recovery will likely not
be found in a courtroom, but rather with
the help of professional therapists,
supportive friends, and
empathetic family members."

# SEX ADDICTION AND EVIDENCE IN CANADIAN FAMILY LAW COURTS

David Frenkel

Accordig to *Newsweek* magazine and other sources, Harvey Weinstein is en route for sex addiction therapy. Mr. Weinstein is now part of a growing list of celebrities that have relied on this rational to explain the reason for their infidelities. Those other celebrities include Charlie Sheen, Rob Lowe, Tiger Woods, Anthony Weiner, Russell Brand and, ironically, Steve Jones of the Sex Pistols, among others.

As a family-law lawyer practicing for over ten years, I have met many clients that have suffered unimaginable pain and embarrassment from their spouse's infidelities, which included sexual addiction. My job as their counsel is to always ensure that their emotions are validated, but also to advise them how the law and the rules of evidence apply to their particular case.

It may be surprising to hear that the courts in Canada have rarely considered sexual addiction as a relevant factor in determining family-law issues. The reason is likely because the evidence required to substantiate such claims needs to be significant in nature. And, even when there is evidence of sex addiction, it likely may not be enough to influence a decision with respect to child custody or spousal-support entitlement.

For example, in a 2012 New Brunswick Court of Queen's Bench decision (*Green v. Reed*), the mother and father had marital issues in part due to the lack of a sex life and the father citing an erectile dysfunction. However, they ultimately separated when the mother found the father naked in the kitchen online with a woman having cybersex. During litigation, a psychologist determined that the father's sexually addictive behaviour was not good role modelling for the children. The court did order the father not to leave the children unsupervised and exposed directly or indirectly to sexual materials or any kind of pornography. However, the court still decided that both parents were entitled to have a shared custody arrangement.

Sometimes, the courts do take the claims of sexual addiction more seriously. In a 2012 Ontario Superior Court decision (*Santor v. Santor*), the court determined that the parties separated in part due to the father's sex addiction, soliciting the services of prostitutes and regularly watching Internet pornography. The mother was concerned that the father was unable to parent their ten-year-old son, that the father was unable to seek treatment for his sex addiction, and that he refused to properly address his psychiatric issues. The court suggested that for the father to be able to see his son unsupervised, he would need to provide a thorough report from a qualified mental-health professional along with any information regarding follow-up treatment and compliance.

In general, for an individual to have to produce psychiatric or psychological records that may contain information of sex addiction, there would need to be evidence that such records would be relevant to any of the issues of a matrimonial case, particularly issues of parenting.

For example, in a 2011 Ontario Superior Court decision (*Yunger v. Zolty*), the mother sought a court order for the father to produce his medical records relating to his sexual addictions. The father denied that he had sexual addictions. The mother claimed that the medical records would assist the court to determine whether the father had or has sexual addiction and why the marriage broke down. The court ultimately decided not to force the release of the records and held that the disclosure of medical records is highly intrusive and that there are compelling reasons for preserving the confidentiality of communications between the patient and his doctor or therapist.

When it comes to a person who admits having a sexual addiction, the way that such evidence gets entered into court is critical. This was highlighted in a 2016 Ontario Superior Court decision (*G.(J.M.) v. G.(L.D.)*) where the father had a preoccupation with sexual fantasies that negatively affected the marriage. During the marriage, the father entered therapeutic programs to deal with his issues. However, during his treatment, he kept a therapeutic diary which the mother improperly obtained and was so disturbed and devastated by its contents that it resulted in the marriage deteriorating. The mother was concerned that the children might be exposed to pornography or sexual remarks or jokes made by the father. At the trial, a psychologist recommend that the father obtain further therapy to address his issue of sexual related fantasies that led to poor judgment and inappropriate social behaviour in the past. However, the psychologist concluded that his therapeutic intervention was not a precondition to instituting a normalized parenting plan, and that there was little evidence to suggest that the father's issues with sexual fantasy negatively impacted his ability to appropriately parent the children.

Overall, the main concern for judges will be the best interests of the children and how a person's sexual deviations would affect those interests. Typically, the connection is hard to make and would need to be supported by a professional deemed to be an expert witness in the case.

For example, in a 1995 British Columbia decision (*Wilson v. Wilson*), it was the mother who was found to be guilty of adultery. The father claimed that the children were at risk by reason of the mother's "interest in her various sexual partners." The court ultimately held that there was no evidence to suggest that the mother's alleged "pre-occupation with sex and sexual partners" would take priority over the interests of her children.

As a final example, the 2017 Ontario Superior Court decision of *Shaikh v. Matin* shows how dangerous it could be to make a false claim against one's spouse. In this case, the mother attempted to slander the husband in order to gain an unfair advantage in a custody fight. Her attempts to do so seriously backfired. The mother attempted to abduct the children by claiming in part that the father assaulted her and was a "pornography and sex addict" without providing any evidence. The mother sent an email to the police of her claims. After a police investigation, it was found that her allegations were unsubstantiated. At trial, the court reversed custody from the mother to the father and required the mother to have supervised access. The court decided that the mother had no credibility, that her evidence could not be relied on, and that she was prepared to and had lied to the court. This was a painful reminder to litigants that a short win with the police or a temporary custody order may end up in a drastic turn of events once all the evidence (or lack thereof) is before the courts.

Consequently, it appears that a claim of your spouse being a sex addict will not be easy to make and will likely require substantial evidence supported by a professional opinion. Failing which, there is a risk that making such claims in court would be at best ignored and at worst result in cost consequences or even a custody reversal in the severest of cases. The pain that a sex addict inflicts will be real and will be long lasting. However, the road to recovery will likely not be found in a courtroom, but rather with the help of professional therapists, supportive friends, and empathetic family members.

This article was originally published by *Canadian Lawyer*, a Thomson Reuters business.

"In the fifth round, when all cards were
being dealt facedown, I found myself
    staring across at my neighbour-friend, and
his mountain of chips in contrast to my
    molehill. As each card came, I became
more assured that I had an unbeatable hand.
    I drew four jacks and the
            queen of hearts as kicker."

## A ROGUE ASTEROID

Blaine E. Hatt

I've always had a compulsive personality. In instances such as fidelity to my wife, love of family and friends, commitment to my work, and steadfastness in my faith, it's been a positive characteristic; in other areas, not so positive, actually tending toward the negative if not the destructive.

My teenage years were hell! I was neither fish nor fowl. I didn't seem to fit in anywhere, well at least not at home or at school. Grade seven, we were bused to the high school in town. Where I had excelled in leading the class from grade one to six, I now found myself a small fish in a large pond of smarter, more capable fish. I felt and was intimidated, and despite applying myself to my studies, my academic achievement was, at best, average and often mediocre. My drive to fit in, to be accepted beyond my acceptance at church, where I was the only one my age still attending, continued to grow and grow and grow.

I didn't belong academically in school, but I loved sports and directed my efforts to athletics and cross-country running, finishing sixth in the provincial championship in grade seven. After cross-country, it was basketball, volleyball, soccer, and finally, track and field. I was never the top athlete in team sports. I was more accomplished in individual performances. However, as a member of each team, I was proud to wear the uniform that visibly declared I belonged, and that I was able to contribute whenever given the opportunity to participate. We travelled to different towns and sometimes cities to play, and I came to realize a world outside the narrow one of my family and community.

In the summer of my thirteenth year, my life changed forever. I began to smoke. Crouched in the culvert under the highway just before you go up the long hill out of our village, it seemed like the thing to do. The first inhale nearly killed me. I gagged, choked, tears came to my eyes, and I nearly passed out. One of my friends just said, "You'll get use to it." And, I did. I reasoned it must be all right because my father, mother, grandfathers, uncles, some of my aunts, most of my cousins, and my best friends smoked, and they had invited me to smoke: it must be all right! Finally, I felt I belonged in my immediate and extended family and in my community.

I smoked through high school, through qualifications for Officer Cadet Training Program (OCTP) Air Force (which I didn't enter), through various jobs after high school, through teachers' college and, along the way, added drinking and gambling to my repertoire. I deceived myself into believing I was a social drinker and not a binge drinker. That's not to say I didn't tie a few on during my college years, but previous to that, I didn't have either the money or the opportunity to drink in any serious way. However, I did get sick one time on gin. My best friend stole a pint from his grand-father's stash and came out to my place and we slipped off into the woods and drained the bottle in record time. The effects were almost immediate: my head started spinning, my speech became slurred, I had difficulty walking, and my guts were churning. I became violently ill, and when it passed, I had a massive headache that lasted for two days.

Thereafter, my headaches became more severe, developing into classic migraines that were intensified by my use of alcohol. Even on a hot summer afternoon, a single beer would result in a pounding headache that could last for several hours or for several days.

In my college years, I paid attention to my health in respect to smoking, but not drinking. I had been successful in making the college basketball team, and our coach insisted that all players be non-smokers. Playing basketball became more important to me than smoking. So, I quit!

I quit for eighteen months until one evening, in the third year of my Bachelor's degree program, my fiancée and I were at a social club. We had ordered and received drinks when she declared that she needed a cigarette. I went to a friend, bummed a cigarette, some matches, and returned to our table. She lit her cigarette and immediately had to visit the ladies' room. The smoke from the cigarette billowed up into my face no matter where I placed the ashtray. Finally, I picked up the cigarette, held it in my hand and said, "I'll bet you taste like bullshit," and then took a drag. I wasn't disappointed; the taste was as I expected. I replaced the cigarette, took a stiff drink to rinse the taste from my mouth, and when she returned, enjoyed the rest of our evening. Later, while talking to her parents in their living room, I instinctively reached over and picked up her father's smokes, withdrew one and lit it. I had another from her mother's package before retiring, and the next morning I drove to the corner store and bought a pack. I continued to smoke, and to do so heavily (reaching a maximum of more than two full packs a day) for the next decade.

As I entered my second year of elementary teaching, I returned to full employment at the Student Union Building on campus. I taught elementary school during the day and managed the SUB during the evening and early morning hours six days a week. I met the day manager in the Social Club at 6:00 p.m., he coming off shift and me beginning my shift. He had a double to end his day, and I had a double to begin mine. From 7:00-9:00 p.m., I organized staff, provided resources, supervised events, and attended to office work. When in the office, I topped up my glass of coke, ginger ale, or ice with rum, rye, or scotch, depending on my evening preference. We had an endless supply of beer and spirits in our office cabinet paid for by patrons through previous special-occasion licensing permits that did not allow excess stock to be returned to the patron.

Each week day and Saturday, from 6:00 p.m. to 2:00 or 3:00 a.m., I fuelled my body with caffeine, nicotine, alcohol, and fatty foods. The nightly cycle repeated itself until mid-April.

Then one Thursday, at 2:00 a.m., I was compiling the cash-out and preparing the bank deposit. I reached into the lower drawer of my desk and withdrew the bottle of dark rum. It was a rum-and-coke night. I spun the cap and emptied the contents of the bottle into my cup. It was then that the drama of my life froze. Call it apocalyptic or whatever, but in that suspended state, a series of insights came to me with profound clarity and impactful force. I recognized that, since 6:00 p.m. the evening before, I had consumed fifty ounces of alcoholic beverages, and I was stone-cold sober! Shockingly, my actions were not a one-off; I had been engaged in similar pursuits for several months. My life-world was in danger of spinning out of control, and I knew that I could not, indeed dared not, continue the orbit that I was on. I desperately needed an exit plan.

The conditions for an exit strategy began almost immediately to materialize. I reasoned if I could teach school all day, coach afterschool sports programs without needing or requiring any booze to get me through, I could cut down, if not eliminate, my drinking. I submitted my letter of resignation from the SUB effective the end of June. In the intervening weeks, I reined in my drinking habits. My resignation from elementary teaching, which was filed at the end of April, was received and accepted, and within days, I was interviewed and re-hired to teach high-school English. My first child, a beautiful and healthy daughter, was born. I withdrew my application for the Masters programme and, I committed more of myself to my relationship with my wife and to being a dedicated father. All in my galaxy seemed to be aligning with the exception of the impending danger of a rogue asteroid.

I have always loved gambling. At first it was penny-ante stuff, but gradually the stakes got higher until I was playing earnestly. I mentioned my love of gambling to a neighbour-friend of mine. He worked with the police and said he might be able to get me into a serious poker game if I would promise not to reveal the identity of any players in attendance. I promised.

My first Thursday-night game in the basement lounge of the police station was an eye opener. All levels of the legal system were represented, including municipal, provincial, and federal agencies. I was blown away; I had no idea that such an event happened in our city every fortnight. The games started slowly, $25 bid entry, then as the evening progressed, $50 and maxing out at $100 per entry. I played cautiously that night while getting a lay of the land. I lost a respectable amount and again the second night. After a couple of months, I was comfortable with the patrons and they with me, and I began to play more seriously and to win more than I lost. Over the course of two years, I amassed thousands in winnings, which I squirreled away in a separate account for that special occasion.

I kept my use of alcohol to a minimum each night, preferring to have my wits about me as I played. One night, a court judge approached me and asked if I was up for a challenge and did I want to play in a more serious game. I accepted the invitation and was told the location, date, and time of the event. The buy-in was $1000 to a maximum of $5000 per round. A buy-in of that amount was high stakes for me, especially on a teacher's salary and more especially since I hadn't disclosed my poker playing to my close friends or family.

I was early for the game, anxious to get underway. I took the seat immediately to the dealer's left with a full view of the players at the table. The players entered, most were high-ranking legal officials, and took their preferred seats. I was surprised to see my neighbour-friend enter and take the last seat. He gave me a quick nod and settled in. We hadn't played against each other in the past, preferring to take someone else's money or lose to someone that we didn't need to drive home with after the game. I had come alone that night and so, obviously, had he.

I was uneasy from the get-go, but I shrugged off my anxiety as a sign of my desire to do well. And I did well during the first few hours of the game, but as the evening progressed, my cards went cold. I couldn't buy a round of good cards although I attempted to do so on more than one occasion, much to my chagrin. My stack of chips was depleting as we moved into the early-morning hours, and one by one the players either cashed out or lost out, and removed themselves from the game. In the fifth round, when all cards were being dealt facedown, I found myself staring across at my neighbour-friend, and his mountain of chips in contrast to my molehill. As the round progressed, I became more assured that I had an unbeatable hand. I drew four jacks and the queen of hearts as kicker.

With anticipation rising, I confidently pushed all my chips into the sizeable pot and jokingly added, "I'll throw in the new suit that I bought yesterday for our anniversary outing." To my amazement, my neighbour-friend called me and revealed a straight flush running from five to nine in spades. I was sunk; I had dug a hole for myself and had foolishly leapt in. All my neighbour-friend had to do was bury me, and he did so. In a few short hours, I lost several thousand dollars that had taken me a long time to accumulate, and lost the opportunity to share that special occasion with my wife and family. During the drive home, I felt hollowed out and, to add insult to injury, my neighbour-friend appeared at my door the next day and asked for his "new suit." I retrieved it and handed it to him still reeling from disbelief. Fortunately, my wife was not home. She never knew I had purchased and lost a suit to celebrate the occasion of our seventh anniversary.

I learned my lesson the hard way. I disassociated myself from my neighbour and no longer attended the fortnight poker games. But lottery tickets were the next big draw, and I was purchasing more and more each week to ensure the "big win." Around the same time, my wife decided, with me as a reluctant tag along, that our two daughters should be brought up in a faith so that they could one day choose for themselves. She had been raised Roman Catholic, I, Baptist, and we wanted to be a part of a church community that celebrated families. Over the course of several weeks, we visited Catholic and Protestant churches but did not find what we were looking for. I had given up on finding a family-centred church when, one August evening, two missionaries from The Church of Jesus Christ of Latter-day Saints knocked on our door to share a message with us.

We listened to their message, attended their church, agreed to take the investigator's discussions and in due time were baptized. As members, we agreed to obey the commandments of God including The Word of Wisdom. There are a number of dos and don'ts in The Word of Wisdom, each associated with developing and maintaining physical and spiritual health. We agreed to live this doctrine to the best of our abilities, which meant abstaining from drinking tea, coffee, and alcoholic beverages; avoiding using tobacco in any form; and not participating in games of chance—all that we might more fully keep our bodies clean and pure before the Lord.

Adherence to the teachings contained in The Word of Wisdom was the iron rod that I needed to grasp firmly, and I did so. I easily gave up tea, coffee, and alcohol. I struggled in my attempts to quit smoking before finally succeeding, and I abstained from participating in games of chance, including poker and lotto tickets. One of the immediate effects of so doing was that the classic migraines that I had suffered for many years ceased. I came to recognize and heed the warning signs my body emitted before a migraine, and I have not suffered one since I joined the church and committed myself to living the fullness of the gospel. For that, I am and will remain eternally grateful!

"I have the gambling addiction
        due to my like of taking calculated risks,
    the allure of easy money, and
                my competitive nature. I never like
to lose. I believe that I'm smarter
                than the game."

## IN ALL REALITY, EVERYTHING IN LIFE IS A GAMBLE: BORN TO WIN, TODAY, TOMORROW, AND EVERYDAY

Mark Tannous

Jackpot! Show me the money, monkey! Daddy needs a new car (Ferrari)!

Are all sayings that I've used when I've been gambling. I've been gambling my whole life. I used to gamble on snooker, darts, cards, and at the casino. The list goes on and on. I once asked myself, "Where did this start?"

Well, I learned from my father, his ups and downs. At a very young age, I used to see my dad go to his weekly poker games. I used to hear of all the vacations he went on with my mother, and they would gamble thousands of dollars. Dad's game was craps, and my mom's was slots. My mom would normally lose, and my dad would recuperate her losses.

I've always tried to figure out what hooked me in to take so many chances. I guess that I have an attitude that thinks I can always win. Truth be told, I figure that my whole life is a gamble between the girls I date, "Will it work out or waste my time?" to the job I have, "Will I make money selling goods from my store, or will I be like the rest of the businesses in my neighborhood, struggling to make a profit or gain, just a little, after putting in so much hard work?"

In part, I have the gambling addiction due to my like of taking calculated risks, the allure of easy money, and my competitive nature. I never like to lose. I believe that I'm smarter than the game. I had confidence that I would always win, but I was schooled hard. I used to play online poker and slots. That site absolutely crushed me financially. When I paid for it by credit card, I got charged extra fees and massive interest charges. Eventually, I hit rock bottom.

My father came to my rescue. He offered to move my debt into their house mortgage, but that didn't stop me. I stopped playing on that site. For a while, I stopped gambling, and tried to pay all my debts with my hard work from my store, but it wasn't enough. I found another site and started gambling again.

Now I only bet on sports, and I am doing very well at it. I study stats, player injuries, win/losses, records, etc., which helps me, but of course, the favourites may lose. I like knowing the details about a game before I bet. Overall, I believe I've lost money gambling, but my ego says, "Born to win, today, tomorrow, and everyday."

I think the main reason I gamble is that I have very high expenses, and I like to take risks to make my ends meet. I often lose betting on sports, but I love taking the chance. When I win, normally, I win multiple games in a row, which builds a nice bankroll. However, when I lose, I look at the things I could have done with all the money, and the time wasted producing nothing.

In some element, I think my losses push me harder to produce and chase after the shortfalls of my addiction. My best friend never wants to hear of my winnings. He totally disagrees with taking such high-dollar risks. However, I explained to him that even buying a house is a high risk, a gamble. There are lots of variables that can jeopardize your safe gamble, even something as simple as losing your job; then the mortgage can't be paid. Maybe the housing market might crash, or your house may depreciate in value.

I'm a gambler with boundaries. I never use my companies' money to repay any of my losses before I go to gamble hard again. Everyone I know is looking for easy money, but in all reality, it's hard money. It's stressful getting a few games called right, but to me, it's always been an adrenaline rush. One day, I'll pull off the ultimate dream, and win the lotto, or get easy money for my simple dollar risk.

« Je ne le savais pas mais cette
décision de m'éloigner
du monde de rêve qu'est
le jeu est encore à ce jour
la plus grande décision et le point
tournant de ma vie. »

## MA PLANCHE DE SALUT

Richard Morin

Le 6 mai est et sera toujours une journée digne d'être conservée dans ma mémoire car, sans le savoir, à ce moment précis de mon existence, je débutais une nouvelle vie loin du monde du gambling, cette vie que je poursuis toujours aujourd'hui dix-huit ans plus tard. Le 6 mai 2000 fût ma toute première journée d'abstinence de toute forme de gambling. Si quelqu'un m'avait dit cette journée là que je ne placerais aucun pari pour les dix-huit prochaines années, je ne l'aurais sûrement pas cru.

Pour la première fois de ma vie, j'ai été honnête envers moi-même. Je me suis finalement admis après un long parcours tortueux que j'avais un sérieux problème de jeu, et que j'étais résolument décidé à cesser toute forme de gambling et prêt à prendre tous les moyens nécessaires pour y arriver. Le soir même, j'ai assisté à une première réunion des Gamblers Anonymes à Montréal, cette même fraternité que mon père m'avait fortement suggérée une dizaine d'années auparavant…lors de cette réunion et les suivantes, j'ai parlé honnêtement de mon histoire d'horreur, du sentiment de honte qui m'habitait comme un locataire qui ne veut pas quitter, de mes dettes, mes énormes pertes financières, ma rupture familiale et, surtout, mon quotidien de joueur compulsif devenu manipulateur, menteur, insolvable, non digne de confiance. Avec de la patience et ce grand remède qu'est le temps, ce très désagréable sentiment de honte a fait place à des sentiments plus nobles que je n'avais pas encore connus réellement dans ma vie: fierté, dignité, honorable et digne de confiance. Tout en poursuivant ce que j'appelle aujourd'hui ma nouvelle vie, j'ai partagé mon histoire et mon message d'espoir avec d'autres personnes prises avec le même problème. Je tiens à dire qu'heureusement ici au Québec, il y a beaucoup d'aide disponible pour aider les personnes qui développent un problème de jeu compulsif. Je doute fortement que je m'en serais sortie seul sans cette précieuse aide car, le fait de pouvoir me réunir avec des semblables pour discuter et surtout de rencontrer d'autres personnes qui se sont sorties de l'enfer du jeu, est une grande source de motivation et d'espoir car s'il n'y a plus d'espoir, il n'y a plus rien…

À cette époque, j'avais trente-cinq ans. Je ne le savais pas mais cette décision de m'éloigner du monde de rêve qu'est le jeu est encore à ce jour la plus grande décision et le point tournant de ma vie. Au début, ce fût très difficile de me relever car, les dommages que m'a causés le jeu ont étés très éprouvants financièrement et moralement. Avec le temps, je me suis remis sur pied, j'ai commencé à activer du mieux que je peux les plus belles qualités de l'esprit qui m'habite, en commençant par celle que je crois la plus importante de toutes, c'est-à-dire l'honnêteté et d'autres telles que, l'indulgence, la tolérance, la patience, la persévérance, et le don de soi.

Je crois que mon expérience désagréable dans l'enfer du jeu devait être vécue pour me permettre de croître en tant qu'individu; ce fût pour moi un espèce de passage obligé, une souffrance temporaire qui finalement m'a permis de sublimer et de m'élever vers des valeurs morales un peu plus élevées que celles que j'exprimais lorsque je jouais.

Depuis l'automne 2014, je fais un retour à temps partiel sur les bancs d'école à l'université où j'ai entamé dans le cadre de ce que j'appelle affectueusement mon projet académique, un BAC multidisciplinaire. J'ai complété un premier certificat en toxicomanie et présentement, je fais un deuxième certificat en santé mentale. J'aimerais amorcer prochainement pour compléter mon BAC, un troisième certificat en psychologie. Le but de ce retour en classe est d'accéder aux études de deuxième cycle pour faire une maîtrise en intervention en toxicomanie. Une fois les études de deuxième cycle terminées, je veux travailler dans le domaine des dépendances, en particulier dans tout ce qui concerne les addictions dîtes comportementales, surtout le gambling et les jeux vidéo en ligne qui sont de toutes évidences des dépendances émergentes actuellement.

En terminant, je veux mentionner que j'ai un bon boulot actuellement. Par contre, je ne suis pas tout à fait heureux dans ce que je fais. J'ai juste une vie à vivre et je crois qu'il est important que je m'accomplisse dans un travail que j'aime et mes études vont me permettre de le faire dans un avenir rapproché. J'aimerais avoir ou du moins diriger une maison de thérapie spécialisée dans les addictions comportementales pour ainsi donner un vrai sens à ma vie pour que mon expérience dans le monde du jeu n'ait pas été vaine.

Everything happens for a reason…

> "At my absolute worst,
> I played video games sixty-four of
> seventy-two hours;
> the rest was spent passed out in my bed beside
> my computer or directly on
> the keyboard."

# SAVED FROM DROWNING
# IN VIDEO GAME ADDICTION

Ian Young

I was fully addicted to video games for about five years. By "fully addicted" I mean I was completely lost in the throes of my addiction and was apathetic to its affects on my life. Prior to that I was building into my addiction for about three years. What started as a fun past time with friends slowly became more consuming and demanding of both my time and focus. As my parents divorced, my love of video games went from a pastime that I was distracted by to an escape. As I progressed further through my preteen and teen years, and the abuse and neglect at school escalated further and further, I sunk further and further into my addiction. I 'peaked' in my addiction as my relationship with my family was rent in half, and I was kicked out by my father. Several years of agonizing rapid spirals downwards followed this. At my absolute worst, I played video games sixty-four of seventy-two hours; the rest was spent passed out in my bed beside my computer, or directly on the keyboard.

Video games gave me a community of like-minded individuals who didn't care for the things I was mocked for in my real life. Their expectations were laid firmly out in the games we played, and by improving myself in the game I earned their respect and friendship. I found people I could trust, and people that found value in me as a person. Progression and achievements in video games, which are meticulously calculated by developers now, kept me locked into a cycle of dopamine and validation, followed by deprival and destitution until my "next hit."

My escape from addiction was more thanks to those around me than myself. I had my epiphany regarding my life after a psychotic episode from a mental breakdown at the hands of legitimate use of an expired prescription and the stress of my life. If it wasn't for my father reaching out, I am very unsure I would have fully recovered. He sought an addictions counsellor for me, and I was able to get help. Thanks to the combination of my father's sacrifice, the diligence of close friends, and the stoic help of my addictions counsellor, I was supported out of my addiction into a new life. A life free of the horror from the heavy breaking waves of isolation and fear smashing me into the rocky cliff face of addiction.

Addiction, in my personal experience, is not a switch that happens or a defining moment where I found myself tossed over the precipice control into chaos. Addiction is a symptom, the pulsing sore of a decrepit malignance festering inside yourself. Much like physical illness, an addiction is not just instantly inflicted upon ourselves, but is a constant slide down a steeper and steeper slope until freefall. My experience with addiction started as a young child. My addiction grew slowly over years, corrupting my life and personality with unnerving thoroughness. At one point it was a complete consumption of myself, and my only survival thanks to the buoyance of family and friends. Much like the tides along the shore, the drowning waters of addiction crept steadily up the beachhead of my life until it was submersed and obscured from view. However, the tale does not end as terribly as it starts, and over time the tide of addiction retreated from my life as the root causes were orbited away from my existence, and again my true self could see the light of day.

The barriers I faced prior to the realization of the power of my addiction were primarily stigma and a lack of proactive programs. Through high school, I saw a dietitian for my ADHD until I out aged his practise, and I was the patient of child psychologists before this. Despite the growing signs, and serious unrest in my family, I never dared reach out for help due to fear of both exposing myself to others and fear of a lack of support if I did. A counsellor for psychological issues saw me briefly in my mid-teens, but this amounted to a dismissive report because I was not actively suicidal and not a threat to others. When I saw a full psychologist for a diagnosis, I was told that I simply was troubled and was clearly suffering from ADHD and mild depression, but that there was little to do besides medication and steady visitation with a profes-sional. I had no way to monetarily support this, and my employers at the time did not provide the benefits for me to seek treatment. I am incredibly lucky that my father's family was wealthy enough that I was able to secure a professional counsellor in my mid-adult years, and once I was ready for addictions counselling, my father again paid for my treatment. Had I not had access to these private funds, I can not make any fair estimate of where I would be today, and how much of a recovery I would have made from my addictions.

I was incredibly fortunate to be provided with excellent services by both a private counsellor and the services from Richmond Addiction Services Society (RASS), when I finally did gain access to support programs in Canada. RASS provided me with a personal counsellor who had experience and interest in those suffering as I was. Over the span of several years, I was aided in re-orientating my life, and distanced myself from the behaviours that enabled my addictive behaviours. Outside of professional services, I am uniquely gifted with an infinitely patient father, and close family relatives who took the time to be understanding, forgiving, and supportive through my recovery. My aunt, in the frank and loving way that is so iconic of my family, is to be quoted as saying, "You never escape it, you are always in recovery, but we will be here." Buoyed by a supportive family and having garnered access to thorough programs with educated and skilled providers of care, I was able to overcome my addiction and succeed despite it. Once I had managed to access treatment, I had little struggle returning to it when necessary. My private counsellor was an email away, and my addictions counsellor remained in touch despite the official closing of my file. Understanding employers who provided accommodation and assistance where possible enabled me to succeed in my career despite challenges presented by both my diagnosis and my history with addiction.

The truest struggle of my addiction was not remaining in treatment or lacking support during a relapse. The challenge was accessing treatment and braving the social stigma of addiction and mental-health challenges. Fortunately for me, being a citizen of Canada enables me access to some of the best physiological healthcare around the world. However, our mental-health programs, while improving, were definitively lackluster when I sought treatment. Major challenges were getting approved referrals to psychiatric professionals, due to a lack of supply and long waiting lists. When I initially was admitted to an emergency ward and I sought follow-up treatments, I was given no solid timeframe of treatment, and was left to essentially fend for myself while I waited in an extensive list of names also seeking succour from our torments. This in and of itself is the greatest failing, in my opinion, of our mental-heath care provisions in Canada. Not the fact that our programs lack for quality, or support, but that access is increasingly gated by a lack of supply that is absolutely outstripped by a growing demand. Provincial and Federal initiatives act as band-aids for what is clearly becoming recognised as an arterial bleed in the health of many Canadians. I personally experienced this as I was flippantly handed between professionals and given no long-term solutions or support. Only recently, after several years of hunting and pursuing contacts through my general practitioner and my mother's own psychologist, was I able to find a psychiatrist willing to take on another client and provide me with mental-health support. Families that lack the financial support, or who must enter the system afresh in their adult years, would clearly have a far more challenging time than I in accessing skilled treatment.

The enormous social stigma of addiction and my diagnosis of ADHD created a solid set of obstacles that I would not have been able to cross myself without the guidance and support of family, friends, and skilled professionals. The struggle to attain these provisions was the hardest part of my recovery process to date. It is a perilous and challenging road that disables many from being able to seek help, and as such hampers our programs terribly, leaving Canadians helpless, afraid, and alone when they need it the most.

"Therapy aspires to manage
the gamer's use and assist him or her
with employing computers in
a productive and healthy manner.
Moreover, teaching gamers to live
in the reality of the present,
rather than in a virtual reality
setting, is paramount."

# USING COGNITIVE BEHAVIOURAL THERAPY TO TREAT VIDEO-GAME ADDICTION

Grace R. Vitale AND John L. Vitale

Cognitive Behavioural Therapy (CBT) is a successful therapeutic approach that combines both dialogue and behavioural-based treatment. Essentially, CBT is a form of psychotherapy where clients alter negative thinking patterns into positive thoughts (Gleissner, 2016). Positive thoughts ultimately lead to positive actions and behaviours in moments of stress and difficult situations.

CBT is empirically based, deals with serious problems, and

examines the origins of problems (Leahy, 2011). Moreover, CBT is often viewed as the psychotherapy treatment of choice when treating clinical depression and anxiety, but is also an effective and successful form of therapy for treating addictions. In fact, depression and anxiety can cause addiction, and likewise, addiction can cause depression and anxiety (Ahmadi et al., 2014; Jang, Hwang and Choi, 2008). Regardless, CBT is an ideal form of therapy for all of these diagnoses.

While CBT as a treatment protocol is generally beneficial, what works for one client may not be so beneficial with another. It is helpful, therefore, to analyze CBT treatment and determine what specific aspects of CBT are most successful, which is the principal purpose of this chapter. As a framework for such an analysis, we have chosen to explore video-game addictions among school-aged youth, which is essentially a "persistent and maladaptive pattern of video game playing behaviour" (King, Delfabbro, and Griffiths, 2013) that can negatively alter physical and mental health, as well as social behaviour patterns. Specifically, we will explore how video-game addictions among school-aged youth were diversely treated through a series of three case studies, namely, Mark, Aaron, and Joseph. Although all cases studies presented in this chapter are based on actual events, all names and situational circumstances (age, educational settings, and ancillary surroundings) have been altered in order to guard and protect actual identities. Before we begin with the three case studies, we need to first identify the critical components of CBT, and second, explore the nature of video-game addictions.

## CRITICAL COMPONENTS TO COGNITIVE BEHAVIOURAL THERAPY

Like all forms of therapy, CBT involves a high level of commitment between the therapist and client (including parents/guardians of a client who is a minor). Although CBT does not work for all clients, success can be fostered with the presence of four key elements. First, clients must maintain regular appointments to ensure that any gains are cultivated and sustained. When clients are unable to keep regular appointments, the success of treatment is adversely affected. Second, CBT requires a treatment plan that involves establishing a clear set of goals and objectives (in writing) that the client wants to achieve. This usually starts with discussing the client's purpose for engaging in therapy. It is also important for the therapist and client to periodically (once a month) revisit the goals and objectives to make sure that (a) they are staying on course, (b) tracking progress, and (c) knowing when to terminate treatment. Thirdly, a client's success is determined by his/her motivation to succeed and desire to actively participate in the process.

CBT is not unidirectional and transmissive, but rather a bidirectional and transactional dialogue where both therapist and client participate. Finally, the therapist should try to cultivate a support network for the client. In some cases, such a network is readily available through family members and friends. In other cases, the therapist needs to be creative in helping the client establish a support network when family members and friends are not readily available. For example, the workplace, an important hobby or spiritual practice, and even a pet, can provide a tangible and sustainable support network. When working with minors, there is indeed a fifth key to CBT–parents/guardians. Specifically, parents/guardians must be encouraged to monitor crucial behaviour patterns. For instance, does their child engage in unusual behaviours that are linked to specific events? For example, is their child showing physical symptoms (e.g., headaches and stomach pains) before going to school; having a tantrum while doing homework; or engaging in an outburst when told to stop playing a video game? Lack of monitoring affects treatment outcomes because these records are used to discuss successes and ongoing areas of difficulty during the therapy hour. In sum, there is much more to CBT than just regularly scheduled appointments. Rather, CBT involves an ongoing commitment and effort by both parties over and above the traditional therapy hour to ensure success.

## THE NATURE OF VIDEO GAME ADDICTIONS

*It's very difficult for people who don't play video games to understand their power simply by watching, and it's very difficult for people who aren't close to technology to understand how rapidly it can change whatever it touches.*

BING GORDON, Video Game Executive and Technology Venture Capitalist

Although video games were primarily arcade based in the 1970s and 1980s, addictive behaviour started taking root when video games became readily available for home use. Douglas Gentile, a psychologist at Iowa State University, has been studying video-game addictions for years and claims that nearly one in ten gamers around the USA are addicted to video games, with similar results around the world (Bresnahan and Worley, 2016).

Since there are two principal types of video games, there are naturally two types of video game addictions. The first category usually involves a single player, where s/he must complete some sort of mission. Hence, the addiction is often related to completing the mission as well as surpassing a previous high score or standard. The second category is connected to online multiplayer games, which are particularly addictive as they generally have no ending. In essence, the addictive appeal is based on the ability to play with and against opponents online in real time, which includes synchronous voice communication. Moreover, gamers in this second category enjoy vicariously living through an online character and building relationships with other online players.

Further evidence that supports addiction to video games can be found based on the sheer statistics of the gaming industry. In 2017, there was an estimated 2.2 billion gamers worldwide, generating an estimated 108.9 billion U.S. dollars in revenues. Even as far back as 2010, the screen time stats are staggering. By the age of twenty-one, the average young person racks up 10,000 hours of gaming, which is twenty-four hours less than they spend in a classroom for all of middle and high school if they have perfect attendance. Moreover, there are over five million gamers in the U.S. that spend more than forty hours a week playing video games, which is the equivalent of a full-time job (McGonigal, 2010). With even more access to video games over the last eight years, these numbers have surely increased.

From a psychiatric perspective, Section III of the DSM-5, the principal manual of the American Psychiatric Association that classifies mental disorders, shows Internet Gaming Disorder as "a condition warranting more clinical research and experience before it might be considered for inclusion in the main book as a formal disorder" (American Psychiatric Association, 2013, pp. 795-798). Moreover, addiction to video games has a high correlation with young males (Wittek et al, 2016). In fact, Smith (2017) maintains that we are losing an entire generation of men who use video games as a substitute for living. According to van den Eijnden (2016), girls are less likely to be addicted to video games based on the fact that girls spend an average of 4.5 hours per week playing video games, while boys spend an average of sixteen hours per week.

## CASE SYUDY #1: MARK

### Set of Circumstances

Mark was a young boy in grade eight who was addicted to video games, particularly warfare games. Mark engaged in about thrity-two hours per week of video-game play—about six hours of play on non-school days, and four hours of play on school days. Mark's parents were not initially concerned as Mark did very well in school and was a popular student with many friends. About midway through his grade-eight year, Mark started showing a number of symptoms that concerned his parents. Mark became easily irritated, aggravated, and complained of headaches when not gaming. He even showed signs of poor personal hygiene. Relationally, Mark's interest in friends and the social aspects of school showed a notice-able decline, as did his normally high grades. Behaviourally, Mark started to show aggression towards his parents when they tried to limit his gaming play. This concerning set of physical, relational, and behavioural symptoms compelled Mark's parents to contact a therapist for treatment of suspected video-game addiction.

### CBT Treatment

Sometimes, young people appear to have video-game addictions when there are actually signs of other underlying disorders. Through extensive data collection, what came to light was that Mark was always socially apprehensive. Throughout elementary school, he had many friends, but never developed deep, meaningful relationships with any of them. This persisted into later elementary school. As social demands increased, his deficits became more apparent. He was actually presenting with a social anxiety disorder, which made it difficult and uncomfortable for Mark to be in a large school setting. More and more, he retreated to a more comfortable world of online gaming. Mark benefitted from treatment for social anxiety, and particularly his fear of being evaluated and judged harshly by others. As he felt more comfortable in social settings, and was willing to take more risks by being out of the home, his need for online gaming waned. Over time, while he still enjoyed gaming, the time he spent was much more reasonable and acceptable to parents.

CASE SYUDY #2: AARON

**Set of Circumstances**

Aaron was a grade-eleven student who always enjoyed the social aspects of school. He had many friends and was a very popular boy at his high school. Although Aaron had always played video games a few hours a day, he always made time for social outings and playing sports with his friends. Near the beginning of his junior year of high school, Aaron's parents noticed that his on-screen time had increased significantly, while his social outings decreased commensurately. Moreover, Aaron's parents became overly concerned when Aaron showed a considerable decrease in appetite and consistently talked about his virtual friends. It was at this point when Aaron's parents sought treatment for their son.

**CBT Treatment**

After meeting with Aaron and his parents, it was clear that he had maladaptive cognitions about himself, including low self-esteem and negative self-evaluation that may have stemmed from long-standing difficulties with academics. The Internet (online gaming) was the only place he felt competent and valued. Aaron's gaming was clearly meeting his self-esteem needs (that he was unable to fill elsewhere). As part of a comprehensive treatment plan, we developed a detailed list of Aaron's antecedents and triggers, which increased his need for the Internet. We also incorporated a self-monitoring component in addition to CBT work around challenging his cognitive distortions.

CASE SYUDY #3: JOSEPH

## Set of Circumstances

Joseph was a competent and bright young man who recently completed his freshman year of high school with good grades. As a reward for a stellar report card, Joseph's parents purchased a new and upgraded gaming system with a series of new games. Over the summer, Joseph engaged in video-game play all day long while his parents were at work, and Joseph neglected to complete basic chores that his parents gave him from day-to-day. Moreover, Joseph's parents noticed that Joseph lost all interest in other activities he once enjoyed, such as playing hockey and soccer, and was obsessed with gaming. It was at this time that Joseph's parents sought treatment for their son.

## CBT Treatment

At the time of the initial intake, Joseph's parents revealed that the family history was positive for drug and alcohol addiction. Joseph's father, Samuel, also recalled that his dad had struggled with periods of gambling addiction when Samuel was a child. Joseph also had addictive personality traits. Joseph reportedly struggled between game play, and gaming took on almost an obsessive quality. He was quite obsessed with Internet gaming, and would constantly plan and anticipate the next gaming session. He rushed through any activities that he had to accomplish in order to be able to game. Eventually, delaying the gratification became too difficult and he stopped attending school. He was consumed with reaching certain levels, beating opponents, and gaining virtual currency.

In therapy, we worked on teaching impulse control techniques (reflection, delay, and distraction). With someone who has a family history of addiction, moderate use of gaming is difficult. Hence, his parents were encouraged to remove all gaming equipment to the chagrin and disapproval of Joseph. As part of the therapy, Joseph took part in a gaming support group for youth, and was guided toward more productive uses of his time. Frequent relapses occurred, and these were sometimes met with resistance and feelings of failure by Joseph's parents. Despite such relapses, commitment to therapy eventually proved successful, as Joseph was able to effectively withdraw from gaming. He has since cultivated many meaningful friendships with other members of the support group.

## CONCLUSION

Gaming addiction has become a serious problem in recent years, leading to the creation of many residential centres for gaming-addiction treatment, including digital detox programs. Such programs are aimed at assisting individuals to cope during the withdrawal stage of treatment, which often includes feelings of anxiety, irritability, petulance, and depression. Eventually, treatment programs focus on minimizing, and in some cases eliminating, gaming through positive social behaviour and life skills.

CBT is by far the most commonly used therapeutic approach for gaming disorders. In sum, therapy concentrates on questioning and changing negative and/or unproductive attitudes and feelings in order to stop the causes, behaviours, and underlying emotions that encourage and ultimately lead to a pathological gaming disorder. Therapy aspires to manage the gamer's use and assist him or her with employing computers in a productive and healthy manner. Moreover, teaching gamers to live in the reality of the present, rather than in a virtual reality setting, is paramount. Finally, counselling can also assist with addressing impulse control issues as well as any underlying mental-health concerns. In conjunction with a medical doctor, antidepressants may at times be used to supplement and enhance the treatment protocol.

REFERENCES

Ahmadi, J., Amiri, A., Ghanizadeh, A., Khademalhosseini, M., Khademalhosseini, Z., Gholami, Z., and Sharifian, M. (2014). "Prevalence of Addiction to the Internet, Computer Games, DVD, and Video and Its Relationship to Anxiety and Depression in a Sample of Iranian High School Students." *Iranian Journal of Psychiatry and Behavioral Sciences*, 8(2), 75–80.

American Psychiatric Association. (2013). *Diagnostic and Statistical Manual of Mental Disorders* (5th ed.). Arlington, VA: American Psychiatric Publishing.

Bresnahan, S. and Worley, W. (2016). "When video games become an addiction." Retrieved from https://www.cnn.com/2016/01/06/health/video-games-addiction-gentile-feat/index.html.

Gleissner, G. (2016). "What Is CBT? How CBT Can Be Useful in Eating Disorder Recovery." *Psychology Today*. Retrieved from https://www.psychologytoday.com/blog/bottoms/201611/what-is-cbt

Jang, K. S., Hwang, S. Y. and Choi, J. Y. (2008), "Internet Addiction and Psychiatric Symptoms Among Korean Adolescents." *Journal of School Health*, 78, 165-171. doi:10.1111/j.1746-1561.2007.00279.x

King, D. and Delfabbro, P. (2014). "The Cognitive Psychology of Internet Gaming and Disorder." *Clinical Psychology Review* 34(4), 298-308.

King, D., Delfabbro, P. and Griffiths, M., (2013). "Video Game Addiction" in *Principles of Addiction*, Peter M. Miller (editor). Cambridge, MA: Academic Press.

Leahy, R. (2011). "Cognitive-Behavioral Therapy: Proven Effectiveness. CBT Is the Treatment of Choice." *Psychology*

*Today*. Retrieved from https://www.psychologytoday.com/blog/anxiety-files/201111/cognitive-behavioral-therapy-proven-effectiveness

McGonigal, J (2010). "Gaming Can Make a Better World." TedTalk retrieved from https://www.google.ca/search?q=TED+Speaker+Jane+McGonigalandhl=enandsource=lnmsandsa=Xandved=0ahUKEwjj26Cuk_vZAhXOq1MKHXOKBNIQ_AUICSgAandbiw=1164andbih=620anddpr=1.1

Smith, Kyle (2017). "We're Losing a Whole Generation of Young Men to Video Games." Retrieved from https://nypost.com/2017/07/08/were-losing-a-whole-generation-of-young-men-to-video-games/

Van den Eijnden, R. (2016). "Almost 10 Percent of Boys who Play Video Games is Addicted to Gaming." Retrieved at https://www.uu.nl/en/news/almost-10-percent-of-boys-who-play-video-games-is-addicted-to-gaming

Wittek, C. T., Finserås, T. R., Pallesen, S., Mentzoni, R. A., Hanss, D., Griffiths, M. D., and Molde, H. (2016). "Prevalence and Predictors of Video Game Addiction: A Study Based on a National Representative Sample of Gamers." *International Journal of Mental Health and Addiction*, 14(5), 672–686. http://doi.org/10.1007/s11469-015-9592-8

"Currently, young people are
sleeping less than they ever have,
and I think it is no coincidence
that we sleep within an arm's
length of our phones, and are using
them as alarm clocks."

# CAN PEOPLE BE ADDICTED TO TECHNOLOGY?

## 10

Lisa Pont

These days, it seems everyone is glued to their tablet or smartphone. If people can be addicted to technology, does that mean that most of us would meet the criteria for that diagnosis? How many hours each day do you have to use technology to be considered addicted? As a clinical social worker providing treatment and education in the area of problem technology use, I am asked these questions frequently, and I will address them in this essay.

Technology is part of our everyday lives, and most of us use it to work, study, play and stay connected to friends and loved ones. It is hard for many of us to imagine our lives before the Internet and smartphones. For those born after a certain time, they have never known life without Google or Facebook. This provides particular challenges for people who develop problems with technology use because it is impossible to avoid it completely. In a position statement, The Canadian Paediatric Society recommends no more than two hours per day of screen time for children between five to seventeen years of age (see Ponti et al., 2017). For most of us, regardless of age, this is not realistic. Many schools are using technology in the classrooms, and most of us are using it at work, so it would not be unusual for people to surpass that guideline by lunchtime!

Millennials, also known as Generation Y, those born since 1980 and coming to maturity towards the end of the twentieth century, and the "iGeneration" (Rosen, 2010), those born in the new millennium, are the focus of the debate surrounding technology addiction. It can be challenging to distinguish problem technology use amongst young people because frequent use is more common in this age group and holds a different meaning for them. There is often a generation gap between how we use technology and how we interpret its use. For example, older generations not born into a world with the Internet or smartphones may think it is rude to look at your phone when in the company of other people. For younger generations, this is normal behaviour, and texting is their preferred way to communicate. This generation gap results in different values and can impact how we label behaviour, and whether or not it is considered a problem. However, the more one uses technology, the more likely they are to develop a problem; and since most mental-health issues develop in our youth, it is prudent to evaluate use among young people and promote balance with technology.

To further complicate matters, there is a recent phenomenon related to the advent of technology that youth may be particularly susceptible to, and to which adults are not immune. This is known as "FOMO" or the *fear of missing out*. FOMO can cause us to be online at the expense of other activities. I have worked with some clients who say that if they are not online when their friends are, they will miss being invited to social events or they "won't know what's going on." Peers become increasingly important to youth, so the thought of being excluded in any way can be distressing.

In addition to new phenomenon, there are other themes related to the heavy use of technology, including fear of boredom, sleep deprivation, and social comparison. Boredom has become an intolerable state for people, given that we have hand-held entertainment in the form of smartphones to get through any dull experience, from line-ups at the grocery store to classroom lectures. Currently, young people are sleeping less than they ever have, and I think it is no coincidence that we sleep within an arm's length of our phones, and are using them as alarm clocks. Using these devices may keep us up longer at night because we become stimulated by these devices as we play games, read, text, or watch videos before bed. The Internet allows social comparison to occur on a global level now that we can look at the curated lives of others on social media and compare our realities with theirs. In a recent survey of Ontario high-school students (Boak et al, 2016), higher rates of social-media use were correlated to increased psychological distress.

Prior to the release of the latest volume of the *Diagnostic and Statistical Manual of Mental Disorders* (DSM-5), there was much debate about whether Internet Gaming Disorder should be included as an official diagnosis. This widely used reference for diagnosing addiction and mental-health issues determined that, while the problem is significant, there was still not enough research to substantiate its inclusion as an official diagnosis. Does this mean that if it is not an official diagnosis, it is not a real problem? It often takes time for research to catch up with clinical observation, so while researchers do their important but painstaking work, healthcare providers need to respond to the clients who are suffering. Gambling is a good example of a behavioural addiction or non-substance use addiction that was only included in the most recent version of the

DSM-5 as an addictive disorder (APA, 2013). People with gambling problems and gambling counsellors would have confirmed that gambling was an addiction long before the research did. But we need to have rigour, and we need to be cautious around labels. There is weight to these labels that results in stigma, and that can be damaging to people.

Many people wonder how you can become addicted to something that is not an addictive substance. Research on gambling and problem technology use—including the Internet, smartphones, social networking and gaming—indicates an increase in dopamine when thinking about and/or engaging in these behaviours. Games, "apps," and smartphones are created to reinforce use by offering intermittent rewards to the user, whether it is achieving a new level in a game, getting a "like" on an Instagram post, or hearing a text alert on your phone (King et al., 2010; Shaw and Black, 2008). This is similar to other addictions, which typically involve rituals or behaviours like "scoring" the drug, pre-paring the drug, or going to the place where you typically use the substance, all of which create an increase in dopamine before you have even taken the substance. Furthermore, just as not everyone that uses drugs or alcohol becomes addicted, the same is true for technology. Gabor Maté (2009, p. 129), a medical doctor, writer, and speaker in the area of addiction, states:

> All addictions—whether to drugs or to non-drug behaviours—share the same brain circuits and brain chemicals. On the biochemical level the purpose of all addictions is to create an altered physiological state in the brain. This can be achieved in many ways, drug taking being the most direct. So an addiction is never purely "psychological"; all addictions have a biological dimension.

There are many people in the field of addiction that believe that certain life experiences such as trauma, can make a person vulnerable to developing an addiction. Gabor Maté (2009, p. 36) also says:

> Not all addictions are rooted in abuse or trauma, but I do believe they can all be traced to painful experience. A hurt is at the centre of all addictive behaviours. It is present in the gambler, the Internet addict, the compulsive shopper and the workaholic. The wound may not be as deep and the ache not as excruciating, and it may even be entirely hidden—but it's there. As we'll see, the effects of early stress or adverse experiences directly shape both the psychology and the neurobiology of addiction in the brain.

I think it is not merely the substance or behaviour that predicts addiction; rather, it is the combination of the characteristics, life experiences, and temperament of the person that increases the likelihood of a problem.

There are critics who warn that by classifying a wider range of activities as addictions, we are diluting the term and rendering it less meaningful. I do not like engaging in comparison when it comes to suffering, but I concede that in all likelihood someone who is "addicted to chocolate" will not suffer the same severity of consequences as someone with a cocaine addiction, even if the chemical processes in the brain are similar. I also understand that many of us co-opt certain words and dilute their meaning by saying things like, "I am depressed" when you are not clinically depressed, or "I love that show" when you merely enjoy watching it. Yes, we probably should use language the way it was intended to keep the meaning pure and universally understood, but that is an ideal. I think that when we are referring to something as an addiction, we need to keep in mind the criteria for addiction: a pattern of behaviour that includes preoccupation, a loss of control, withdrawal, tolerance, and negative consequences. I think we *do* need to spend time observing, researching, and discussing the reason for identifying something as an addiction, but in the meantime, many people are suffering with problems related to their use of technology.

Ever since the word addiction has become more frequently used to describe different types of behaviours, from shopping to sex, some people have asked, "Then can't you be addicted to anything?" The simple answer is yes, if you like the activity or substance, if it serves an emotional purpose for you, and if it is causing negative consequences. Some people get addicted to socially reinforced behaviours such as running or working, and the addiction remains neglected or misinterpreted.

Technology addiction can be hard to detect because many of us use computers and phones for our jobs or school, particularly if working or studying in the field of technology. So how do you determine whether you have an Internet Addiction or another technology-related addiction (gaming, social media, smartphone, etc.)? One method is to ask yourself, "Is this causing me problems?" If you are not sure of the answer, you might question, "Would those close to me think I have a problem with technology?" Then you can ask yourself (and those closest to you) more specific questions to determine the nature and scope of the problem. The amount of time you spend online is one criteria of Internet Addiction, but there are some people who spend a lot of time online and do not meet any of the other criteria, such as experiencing negative consequences.

The latest version of the *Diagnostic and Statistical Manual* conceptualizes addictive disorders as mild, moderate, or severe (APA, 2013). I think this is a useful way to think about addictions. In regards to technology use, it is not like you either have a problem or you do not. You can have a minor problem with technology, where you experience some loss of control over time that results in ongoing negative consequences or a major problem that results in negative effects in every area of your life. Consequences do not always have to be dramatic or extreme to be considered a problem. Someone who regularly games well into the night might not think of themselves as having an addiction, but if they wake up tired and are not performing well at work, their gaming is clearly causing problems.

The extent and variety of things that you can do online is vast, and includes gaming, gambling, shopping, viewing pornography, blogging, watching/posting videos, file sharing, instant messaging, using social media, and more. This begs the question of whether you are addicted to technology itself or to the activity you are using the technology for, or both. Interestingly, some activities are ones that only exist online via technology such as file sharing or social media. They are often the kinds of activities that are classified under the umbrella term Internet Addiction. I am inclined to think that it is both the activity and the technology that facilitates the activity, by providing ease, access, and sometimes anonymity that result in addiction.

One of the big research questions that is being debated at the moment is whether Internet and gaming addictions are standalone diagnoses, or symptomatic of other primary issues such as depression, anxiety, Attention Deficit Disorder, Autism Spectrum Disorder, and/or Obsessive Compulsive Disorder. All of these issues commonly co-occur with Internet/gaming addiction (Brezing et al., 2010; Chen et al., 2015). In my experience, most addictions are not standalone conditions but rather an attempt to reduce suffering caused by another factor, whether it is related to poverty, trauma, or serious relationship issues. Regardless of whether it is a primary or secondary issue, the behaviour needs to be addressed as well as any issues that drive the behaviour. If a client comes to treatment with Obsessive Compulsive Disorder and it is underlying the problem echnology use, the disorder would need to be addressed in order to recover effectively. It is often hard to know with certainty what came first, "the chicken or the egg" with co-occurring issues. Often, there is a well-established relationship between the co-occurring issues that keep people in a vicious cycle of trying to relieve symptoms in the short-term but ultimately worsening them over the long-term.

It is virtually impossible to avoid technology completely in the twenty-first century, and there is no reason to. It can enrich our lives in many ways and make many tasks more efficient. Our access to information is unprecedented as is our ability to connect with people at all ends of the earth. People that have mobility issues or live in remote communities can connect with people and even get treatment online. So while most people could not, and would not, abstain from technology, it is possible to avoid or reduce the amount of use, especially if there is a specific activity that has become problematic. I think it would benefit all of us to reflect on our technology use and weigh the added value it offers to our lives or detracts from it. It is particularly important to reflect on which new technology you introduce into your life and your home, and how you intend to use it. What we do know is that technology and many online activities are not benign; they have addictive features that, when used by people with particular vulnerabilities, may cause harm and/or result in an addiction.

REFERENCES

American Psychiatric Association. (2013). *Diagnostic and Statistical Manual of Mental Disorders* (5th ed.). Arlington, VA: American Psychiatric Publishing.

Boak, A., Hamilton, H. A., Adlaf, E. M., Henderson, J. L., and Mann, R. E. (2016). "The Mental Health and Well-being of Ontario Students, 1991–2015: Detailed OSDUHS Findings," (CAMH Research Document Series No. 43). Toronto, ON: Centre for Addiction and Mental Health. Retrieved from: http://www.camh.ca/en/research/news_and_publications/ ontario-student-drug-use-and-healthsurvey/Documents/

2015%20OSDUHS%20Documents/2015OSDUHS_
Detailed_MentalHealthReport.pdf

Brezing, C., Derevensky, J.L., and Potenza, M.N. (2010). "Non-substance-addictive behaviors in youth: Pathological gambling and problematic internet use." *Child and Adolescent Psychiatric Clinics of North America.* 19(3), 625-641.

Chen, Y.L., Chen, S.H. & Gau, S.S.-F. (2015). "ADHD and autistic traits, family function, parenting style, and social adjustment for Internet addiction among children and adolescents in Taiwan: A longitudinal study." *Research in Developmental Disabilities,* 39, 20-31.

King, D., Delfabbro, P. & Griffith, M. (2010). "Video game structural characteristics: A new psychological taxonomy." *International Journal of Mental Health and Addiction,* 8(1), 90-106. DOI: 10.1007/s11469-009-9206-4

Ponti, M., Bélanger, S., Grimes, R., Heard, J., Johnson, M., Moreau, E., Norris, M., Shaw, A., Stanwick, R., Van Lankveld, J., and Williams, R. (2017). "Screen Time and Young Children: Promoting Health and Development in a Digital World," *Paediatrics and Child Health,* 22(8), 461-478. Retrieved from The Canadian Paediatric Society https://www.cps.ca/en/documents/position/screen-time-and-young-children

Maté, G. (2009). *In the Realm of Hungry Ghosts: Close Encounters with Addiction.* Canada: Vintage Canada.

Rosen, L. D. (2010, March 27). "Welcome to the iGeneration!" *Psychology Today.* Retrieved from: https://www.psychology-today.com/us/blog/rewired-the-psychology-technology/201003/welcome-the-igeneration.

Shaw, M., & Black, D. W. (2008). "Internet addiction." *CNS drugs,* 22(5), 353-365.

"Cyber-bullying, online sexual misconduct,
      and the overuse of technology towards
a compulsive need for instant gratification and
      stimulation are some of the concerns
that can emerge. Furthermore, video gaming is
      not the only form of digital activity
      to become problematic.
Clients seeking help have clinically
      presented problems related to online
      gambling, shopping, pornography,
and social-media misuse."

# FROM "VITAL ADDITION" TO FATAL DISTRACTION

Benjamin Shing Pan Wong

The scenario is becoming all too common among twenty-first-century teenagers. The week before spring break, we witness fourteen-year-old Perry, who aced his way through elementary and middle school, dreading receipt of the second report card in his current ninth-grade year. His parents attest that it all began when

Perry went to summer camp the previous August and befriended others who would spend as much, if not more, time on their desktops, tablet computers, and/or gaming consoles. They have since observed Perry's increasing preoccupation with online activities— mainly chat and MMORPG (massive multiplayer online role-playing games), often both simultaneously—to the expense of hockey practice, chess-club meets, tenor-saxophone recitals, and trips to the local library to helm that next best-in-his-class assignment, activities in which he used to, yet now fails to, find enjoyment. Perry's mother became concerned at the very first instance he skipped dinner at home, offering the excuse he was actively in an online discussion on a school project. Perry's father, however, reasoned that the family computer was there for Perry to learn to make good use of and that computer literacy was not a mere asset but a necessity these days. Neither parent could honestly cherish the benefits that a personal computer might bring when looking at Perry's current report card with two failing grades and none above C+.

If labels such as "Technology Addiction" or "Video-Game Addiction" catch your attention, chances are you have already come across people who are or whom others have seen to be spending an excessive amount of time, energy, and other tangible resources in order to remain "plugged-in" to their smart devices. Texting on smartphones, gaming on consoles the likes of Xbox and Nintendo Switch, browsing social-media platforms, and "random Googling" are all popular activities among many. Engagement in the aforementioned can become less than healthy preoccupations, particularly in the younger generations, yet not limited to them. Whether technology addiction should be understood as having comparable mechanisms as addiction to alcohol, marijuana, cocaine, or gambling remains a hot topic of debate in academia. Nevertheless, when behaviours associated with the use of digital technology become part of one's life so much that they begin to pose risks and problems affecting important aspects of daily living, such behaviours warrant concern. Doing so through the lens of addiction, from a decade and a half of clinical experience, may not only be a helpful perspective, but also a platform on which to begin recovery and healing.

The reality that parents face nowadays is quite a dilemma. Technology promises to improve our daily lives with convenience and efficiency. While computer technology has facilitated elementary and secondary education in significant ways, it has also presented our generation of children with unprecedented access to information, learning, and activities that are not appropriate for their age and developmental stages. Cyber-bullying, online sexual misconduct, and the overuse of technology towards a compulsive need for instant gratification and stimulation, are some of the concerns that can emerge. Furthermore, video gaming is not the only form of digital activity to become problematic. Clients seeking help have clinically presented problems related to online gambling, shopping, pornography, and social-media misuse.

Under the various labels of what is essentially the same condition, I've chosen (early in my work) to use the term *problem video gaming*. The primary reason is the idea that video gaming has the potential to create problems in the user's life, especially in those areas the user did not believe would be affected. Such has been how the condition of pathological gambling is understood, studied, and tackled by academia and mental-health professionals.

This essay aims to include for readers observations made in clinical work with individuals and families affected by problem video gaming and other related digital dependencies, tips on where to begin in order that a child's experience of information technology becomes a pleasant and constructive one, and strategies to minimize potential, and realistic, harm.

## WHY IS THE DIGITAL WORLD ATTRACTIVE?

A fair question to begin with is, "Why is the digital world so attractive?" In other words, what is it about electronic screens that makes us glue to them at the expense of physical health, mental health, and more?

Consider the features in our electronic-screen culture that renders itself attractive, especially to our young ones, whose brains, as neuroscience nowadays confirms over and over again, constantly increase in capacity through unceasing development of novel neural connections in response to external stimuli. Observable, from clinical conversations, are at least six such distinct elements, including *autonomy, anonymity, reward mechanism, preference for low-effort high-reward, realism, and preoccupation.*

Our current electronic environment has not only given us unprecedented access to large quantities of information, but also unprecedented *autonomy*, which is one's ability and authority to decide how, what, when, where, and with or without whom to execute certain actions on any digital platform. This feature offers the user a strong, unshakeable sense of control, which is particularly appealing to individuals who often find themselves in situations where they tend not to have control at all.

The virtual world is a platform on which no one needs to present their full/entire/true self in their relational transactions with other online users. *Anonymity* is a feature of the online world that draws many into it. Building on the feature of autonomy, anonymity further solidifies, in the user, a sense of control, to the extent of not needing to take responsibility for one's actions, as well as statements expressed. Even for users who opt to include in their online and/or social-media profile, photos of their actual selves, they continue to maintain control over much of the rest of their true self (names, ages, ethnicities, etc.), determining whether or not to disclose such personal information. This feature is such a cornerstone aspect of the online experience that an overwhelming majority of activities can be conducted anonymously.

Digital content, whether in the form of video games, social media, or webpages, is frequently designed using sound psychological principles to thimblerig our brains into wanting more of the experience. Such a strategy utilizing the brain's reward mechanism is made possible by brain scientists' understanding of the dopaminergic circuit, where the neurological chemistry of pleasure, elation, and motivation happens in our brains (Hoeft et al., 2008). When dazzling colours, sights, and sounds are choreographed in a fashion that manipulates the user's anticipation and experience of reward (and the lack thereof), we then have a situation in which a user is hooked. To Facebook users' surprise, or to some their chagrin, they began observing videos on "auto play" since two years ago. Another perhaps more frequently used dynamic is known as adverse impact effect, a procedure by which the user faces unannounced penalties for leaving their video game or other activities prematurely, such as the loss of points, ranking, or status.

Related to reward mechanism ingrained in digital activities is the preference for low-effort, high-reward experiences on the user's part. Long-term exposure to the electronic screen contributes to the passive, egoistic poise of not only a "serve me" mentality, but also development of an attitude that prefers activities demanding minimal efforts, yet perceived as rewarding. No wonder conflict arises when the thirteen-year-old gamer is told, at 11:00 p.m., to shut the Xbox game off. Angry yelling ensues between parents and child as the evening takes an extremely wrong turn.

For decades, *realism* has been the guiding standard in the advancement of computer-generated imagery. Long gone are the days when pixelated graphics were considered adequate and acceptable. The more real the graphics are in video games and websites, the better and the more appealing. The quest for realism, however, does not cease at that which appeals to the human eye. Over the past two decades, we've witnessed increasingly vigorous efforts in and meticulous attention paid to experiential dynamics directed at senses other than sight.

*Preoccupation* (or busyness) is yet another feature of the digital world to consider. A platform on which the user exercises autonomy can very well be one where they experience an overwhelming sense of accomplishment and adequacy. When this is the case, the mere act of being preoccupied and busy with the smart device takes on an emotional quality, triggering the dopaminergic circuit. Multitasking becomes an end in the user's mind rather than a means to one, gradually becoming a habit, and perhaps, down the road, a sort of virtue (Ophir et al., 2009).

## WHAT AMOUNT OF SCREEN TIME IS APPROPRIATE? WHAT AMOUNT IS TOO MUCH?

More often than not, troubled parents and loved ones reach out for professional help when alarmed by the amount of time the gamer puts into their video gaming. A long-held assumption is that time spent on gaming is indicative of addiction. However, studies have shown that the mere investment of time, albeit disproportionate, problematic, and mindless, does not necessarily predict negative health and/or psychological outcomes (Ferguson et al., 2012). Sixty hours a week spent on an online strategy game could be beneficial and even sustaining for the user whose livelihood (a career in video-game development, for instance) depends on such levels of screen time while detrimental to another user's well-being where such gaming only exhausts their physical, emotional, and mental resources.

So how much screen time is "too much?" To the child in possession of a precious, young, fragile, highly malleable/plastic brain in which neuronal circuits (based on genetically pre-wired blueprints the operation and existence of which can still barely be explained by science even in 2018) are forming at the speed of light in manners highly sensitive to environmental stimuli received through all six senses (sight, smell, touch, taste, sound, and proprioception), who still has yet to develop mindfulness, integrity, sense of responsibility, curiosity, and empathy in his/her core attitude towards mature global citizenship? Responses to questions that follow shall further strengthen this position of mine.

## CAN VIDEO GAMING BECOME AN ADDICTIVE BEHAVIOUR?

An addictive behaviour, by definition, is one that can affect the user's mood, adversely affect normal functioning, be used to cope with emotional or psychological issues, and result in neurological changes. Over the years, mental-health professionals have seen increasing incidence of such resulting from engagement with video gaming.

Comorbid conditions have also been reported, often confusing the user and the professionals who treat them as opposed to the crux of their problems. Gamers concurrently suffering from diagnosable severity of mood disorders, substance use disorders, anxiety disorders, impulse-control disorders (Cutler et al., 2003), attention deficit hyperactive disorder (Lemona et al., 2011), poor school performance, insomnia, financial difficulties, relational problems (Gentile et al., 2013), and conduct problems (Holtz and Appel, 2011) have been reported and studied.

## WHAT ARE THE EFFECTS, BOTH POSITIVE AND NEGATIVE, OF DIGITAL PLAY? WHAT CONCLUSIONS CAN BE DRAWN FROM THEM?

Let us survey the negative effects of video gaming, and perhaps of other digital dependencies, too. Whether graphic violence in video games is harmful or not has long been a controversial topic in academia. Research that evaluates the connection between video-game violence and violent criminal behaviours has yet to yield conclusive correlational results, let alone causal. Such is the observation on which critics base their arguments against the notion that engagement with violent video games produces antisocial behaviours. Nevertheless, long-term violent video gaming was found to have the ability to confuse one's critical thinking and decision-making ability, thereby affecting behaviours negatively (Ferguson et al., 2012). Furthermore, desensitization to violence on the gamer's part was observed to be significant as well as diminished empathy and likelihood of prosocial behaviour (Bushman and Anderson, 2009). In other words, even if violence found in video games is not linked to physically aggressive behaviours, there is the possibility of it influencing aggression in gamers. Can this aggression be that which drives bullying (and/or cyberbullying), which is an increasing concern in our society?

Concern in the prevalence of attention problems and executive functioning is growing. A number of studies over the last decade established causal effect between video-game play and greater attention problems, as well as several other abilities related to learning and social functioning, including impulsivity, self-control, executive function, and cognitive control (Gentile et al., 2012). Games, when violent content is featured, are particularly disruptive to attentiveness in children (Hastings et al., 2009).

Time spent in front of electronic screens is not time spent on school activities related to productive learning (acquisition of skills and knowledge). The finding of a significant negative association between the amounts of time spent on screens and school performance should not surprise anyone (Sharif and Sargent, 2006).

Emotional development also takes a toll when children are exposed to digital play at young ages. Higher levels of early childhood electronic-media use are associated with children being at risk for poorer outcomes with indicators of well-being (Hinkley et al., 2014). Skills with nonverbal emotional cues in preteens are undermined by electronic-screen usage.

Video games are often marketed as platforms that make possible creative play. However, such claims are quite far from the truth. Multiple studies point to how video gaming spaces out time and energy which would otherwise be available to allow children hands-on, creative play (Vandewater et al., 2006). Screen time has also been observed to space out children's interactions with caring adults (Mendelsohn et al., 2008) and interferes with parent-child conversations (Kirkorian et al., 2009).

Turning to effects of video gaming on physical health, we cannot but recognize it as a risk factor for obesity (Oliver, 2017). Some studies (Harrison et al., 2011) established correlation between video gaming and consumption of junk food, while others found video gaming's link to increased food intake and being overweight in gamers. Contrary to popular belief, exergames do not always increase the level of physical activity the user actually experiences (Baranowski et al., 2012). Other than obesity, sleep disturbance as a result of electronic usage is also well-documented (Barlett et al., 2012). If a gamer's habit of regular exercise, diet, and sleep quality can be undermined, to assert that problem video gaming poses threat to one's physical health is no exaggeration.

Positive effects of video gaming are also extensively documented. They include benefits in visual-spatial skill development—i.e., the fine-tuning of hand-eye coordination (Feng, Spence, and Pratt, 2007); educational games as augmentation to pedagogical methods in the traditional classroom (Gentile, 2008); encouragement of physical activities in the form of exergames (Rosenberg et al., 2010); as well as games that promote prosocial behaviours such as kindness, respect, and empathy (Anderson et al. 2012). Although deemed scientifically significant, the aforementioned "benefits" surveyed are not true benefits in the strictest sense. Were we, as a people, devoid of reliable means to develop skills in adequate hand-eye coordination, the acquisition of knowledge, exercising, and building sound relationships before Samuel Finlay Breese Morse launched humanity into our current electronic environment? The answer, when giving the issue more than two minutes of thought, is a resounding "no." If electronic means are chosen to develop any of the aforementioned skills, or any skill at all, the reason is because we can, and never because we need to.

## WHEN "VITAL ADDITION" BECOMES FATAL ATTRACTION (OR DISTRACTION)

Consider the formation of addiction. Any addiction. An addictive behaviour forms in an emotional environment laden with conditions that enable the user (i.e., that which fuels the user's engagement in the addiction), along with unaddressed psychological vulnerability in the user, as well as their access to any addictive medium (e.g., alcohol, drugs, video games, pornography, casinos etc.). When loved ones of problem gamers seek help, they tend to focus efforts on tackling the last of the aforementioned trio. Statements from parents include, "Perry would have been fine if he did not make friends with those online gamers", "We're giving serious thoughts to removing Jenny from her school where dealers and addicts hang out" and, "Better screen time management on our part would do the trick so Perry would learn how to coexist healthily with his electronics." However, clinical outcomes tend to be most positive when interventions focus on addressing the environment that currently enables addiction, and building up the user who suffers from vulnerabilities rendering them defenceless against the draw of addictive media.

Having worked with more than 350 individuals/families affected by problem video gaming and related digital dependencies, has taught that clinical modalities (cognitive-behavioural therapy, acceptance and commitment therapy, motivational interviewing, reality therapy and existential theory are those most often employed) do not by themselves account for positive treatment outcomes, if at all. Two other foci have proven to be of higher significance when dealing with such a socially-acceptable behaviour which is now deemed addictive and destructive. The first is therapeutic rapport, the building of which between clinician and client stands paramount in determining the trajectory of potential recovery. Feedback Informed Therapy (previously, rather aptly, termed client-directed, outcome-informed treatment) is a realistic encapsulation of the version of rapport necessary for client recovery and growth. The second, which deserves discussion well beyond the scope of this chapter, is the need for *technophilia* to be addressed in some fashion, if not as comprehensively and thoroughly by the typical, dedicated communications scholar. Clients, who present addiction to, obsession with, and/or compulsion for behaviours made possible by the most advanced of communicative technologies accessible to the average citizen, all suffer from a blind love of technology, unconsciously attributing it the status of godhead. That is to say, psychological work needs to be done to untangle the problem gamer's emotions, aspirations, and existential outlook from the potentials, promises, and possibilities that technology professes and has been conditioning them to believe in, rely on, and live by. Works by Marshall McLuhan and Neil Postman are highly recommended as reference if the reader is so inclined to dive deeper into the topic; we can all equip ourselves better in mindfully and intelligently negotiating with technology.

BOYS AND VIDEO GAMES

Pew Research Center, based in Washington, DC, reported in 2015 that fully seventy-two percent of teens play video games on a regular basis on a computer, game console, or portable device like a cellphone. A closer analysis of these teens reveals that boys "are substantially more likely than girls to report access to a game console (ninety-one percent, compared with seventy percent of girls) and to play games (eighty-four percent of boys, compared with fifty-nine percent of girls)." Such discrepancies between the genders are hardly surprising. Haven't we all observed that boys seem to be drawn into video gaming more frequently and intensely that do girls? An overwhelming majority of clinical cases I've dealt with involved boys. Not that girls never struggle with problem video gaming (I've worked with a small number of them who do), yet more of them experience problems related to social media use or television viewing than video gaming (Lenhart, 2015).

Researchers at Stanford University gathered evidence supporting a neurological explanation regarding the apparently stronger appeal, and hook, that video games have on boys than on girls (Hoeft et al., 2008). Using fMRI to monitor brain activity of subjects on video games, they observed that "males showed greater activation and functional connectivity compared to females in the mesocorticolimbic system." That is to say, males are biologically more responsive to the digital stimuli video games offer, with the reward circuit in the brain generating stronger dopamine release and response compared that in females.

Psychologist Leonard Sax (2007) observes that boys are driven to video gaming largely due to boys' innate *need to conquer* and *will to power*, which are typically most obvious during adolescence Boys' need to conquer speaks to their desire to be impactful in what they do, whereas their will to power demonstrates adequacy, which seems consistent with the elements foundational to the teenage boy's sense of self. When gender differences in game activity preferences were quantitatively evaluated in a 2008 study, the attempt of which was to develop video games that appeal to both boys and girls (Kinzie and Joseph, 2008), more light was shed on the unique appeal of certain types of games towards boys. Among the six game play activity modes identified in the market, boys were observed to strongly prefer games that fall under Active play (e.g. first-person shooter games, Mindcraft, etc.) and Strategic play (e.g. role-playing games) (the other 4 types being Explorative, Problem-solving, Social, and Creative) compared to that of girls' (who overwhelmingly preferred Explorative and Creative). As defined, the Strategic mode of play is consistent with boys' need to conquer, with conditions demanding that boys create and solve problems in order to attain victory within bounds by rules the game itself sets forth. The Active more of play, furthermore, is relevant to boys' will to power, having opportunities to exercise autonomy given the design of the game.

A more recent study, one that looks at motivational components of tolerance in internet gaming disorder in 480 adult male participants (and 150 female participants), identified three factors relevant to tolerance-like processes (King et al., 2018). They include wealth (the need to accumulate in-game rewards of increasing rarity, novelty, or quantity), achievement (the need to pursue goal-driven activities of increasing complexity, difficulty, or uniqueness), and inadequacy (the need to rectify perceived insufficiencies in gaming capability of progress) Such observations lend further support to video games' appeal to male gamers. In contrast, female gamers gravitate towards gaming activities involving, to broader extents, social and creative elements, e.g., games that promote prosocial behaviours, drawing and/or painting games).

## PREVENTION OF PATHOLOGICAL DIGITAL DEPENDENCIES

The most advanced of neuroscience has shed substantial light on how addiction develops at the neurological level. Stressful emotional environments in childhood render reward pathways underdeveloped, and therefore less than normal levels of dopamine and opiate receptors are produced (signs of an undermined stress-response circuit). The body, in turn, compensates by seeking external surges in dopamine through addiction. Since the job of elation, motivation and pleasure is now "outsourced" to internal mechanism (drug use, gambling, video games etc.), the brain's natural capacity to produce dopamine learns to shut down, thus forming a biochemical reliance on addiction. Thus, stress reduction, development of emotional intelligence/resilience, and maintenance of healthy diets, exercising and nutrition all contribute to prevention.

For parents and caregivers, maintaining a channel of communication over computer use, among other things, is crucial. Teenagers can be prone to peer and media influence. The ideal is for parents to foster and maintain an atmosphere of open communication at home that allows dialogue over teenagers' questions, concerns and curiosities. When done with trust, honesty, understanding and permission of mistakes, such an atmosphere stands the best chance to make the home a place that invites the youngsters' input and ideas, a place where they would gradually value and receive, if not agree to, parents' advice around the use and misuse of the computer.

Having agreements on some limits around computer use is one important factor. It is best to begin by allotting shorter sessions of use as necessary and having some ongoing awareness of how much time is being spent using technology and in what way. Furthermore, we urge parents to guide in exploring uses of the personal computer that are relevant to the child's daily engagements (e.g., school, other extra-curricular activities etc.). Enjoying entertainment on the computer, such as games, online chat, video and audio clips, also makes a wonderful family time with adult guidance.

Parents report that children frequently claim to need the computer for school, and hence it becomes challenging to set time limits in computer use as it can be hard for parents to gauge the amount of time necessary to complete assignments on the computer in a timely manner. Gaining firsthand knowledge of the need of computer use for schoolwork purposes from teachers and school administrators therefore is a must. How else other than to be aware of the actual expectations on teachers' part regarding computer use necessary for homework completion can parents set boundaries on responsible computer use? Only if communication over this issue are parents able to set realistic and agreeable parameters around daily screen time allowance, thus limiting opportunities for teenagers to use homework as an excuse to be online not being appropriately productive.

Being well-informed of the benefits, risks and dangers that our young technology users face enables parents to be effective guides to keeping a healthy balance. Particularly, getting to know what it is that your child gets out of their tech activities is helpful. Many who play on-line role playing games such as League of Legends receive exciting visual stimulation, the power to explore virtual worlds, feeling a sense of belonging with other live game players in ways that they might have a harder time getting in the "real world." Understanding the needs a behaviour fulfills can help parents encourage alternative activities and involvements that satisfy those important developmental needs.

In closing, readers are urged to keep their eyes out for the 3 Cs of addiction: losing *control* over their use of technology, acting out of *compulsion* regarding any activity on the PC, and experiencing negative *consequences* as a result of excessive "screen time." Do not lose hope! A helpful resource, which is available at your local library, is Kimberly Young's *Caught in the Net* (1998). It provides practical measures that family members may take to support the excessive technology user in changing their behaviour. Discussing the issue with teachers and school counsellors can also prove to be helpful in the long term since computer misuse inevitably affects school performance and interpersonal relations.

REFERENCES

Anderson, C. A., and Warburton, W. A. (2012). "The impact of violent video games: An overview." In W. Warburton and D. Braunstein (Eds.) *Growing Up Fast and Furious: Reviewing the Impacts of Violent and Sexualised Media on Children*, 56-84. Annandale, NSW, Australia: The Federation Press.

Baranowski, T., Abdelsamad, D., Baranowski, J., O'Connor, T. M., Thompson, D., Barnett, A., Chen, T. (2012). "Impact of an active video game on healthy children's physical activity." *Pediatrics*, 129(3).

Barlett, N. D., Gentile, D. A., Barlett, C. P., Eisenmann, J. C., and Walsh, D. (2012). "Sleep as a mediator of screen time effects on children's health outcomes." *Journal of Children and Media*, 6(1), 37-50.

Bushman, B.J., Anderson, C.A. (2009). "Desensitizing Effects of Violent Media on Helping Others." *Psychological Science*, 20(3), 273-277.

Cutler, D., Glaeser, E. and Shapiro, J. (2003). "Why have Americans become more obese?" *Journal of Economic Perspectives* 17(3), 93-118.

Feng, J., Spence, I., and Pratt, J. (2007). "Playing an Action Video Game Reduces Gender Differences in Spatial Cognition." *Psychological Science*, 18(10), 850-855.

Ferguson, C. J., San Miguel, C., Garza, A., and Jerabeck, J. M. (2012). "A longitudinal test of video game violence influences on dating and aggression: A 3 -year longitudinal study of adolescents." *Journal of Psychiatric Research*, 46(2), 141–146.

Gentile, D. A., Gentile, J. R. (2008). "Violent Video Games as Exemplary Teachers: A Conceptual Analysis." *Journal of Youth Adolescence*, 37, 127-141.

Gentile, D.A., Swing, E.L., Lim, C.G. and Khoo, A. (2012) "Video Game Playing, Attention Problems, and Impulsiveness: Evidence of Bidirectional Causality." *Psychology of Popular Media Culture*, 1, 62-70.

Gentile, D. A., Coyne, S. M., and Bricolo, F. (2013). "Pathological technology addictions: What is scientifically known and what remains to be learned." In K. E. Dill (Ed.), *Oxford Handbook of Media Psychology* (382-402). New York: Oxford University Press.

Harrison, K., Liechty, J., and The Strong Kids Program (2011). "U.S. preschoolers' media exposure and dietary habits: The primacy of television and time limits of parental mediation." *Journal of Children and Media*, 6(1), 18-36.

Hastings, E.C., Karas, T.L., Winsler, A., Way, E., Madigan, A., Tyler, S. (2009) "Young Children's Video/Computer Game Use: Relations with School Performance and Behavior." *Issues in Mental Health Nursing*, 30(10), 638-649.

Hinkley, T., Verbestel, V., Ahrens, W., Lissner, L., Molnár, D., Moreno, L.A., Pigeot, I., Pohlabeln, H., Reisch, L.A., Russo, P., Veidebaum, T., Tornaritis, M., Williams, G., De Henauw, S., De Bourdeaudhuij, I., (2014). "Early Childhood Electronic Media Use as a Predictor of Poorer Well-being A Prospective Cohort Study." *JAMA Pediatr.* 168(5), 485–492.

Hoeft, F., Watson, C., Kesler, S., Bettinger, K., and Reiss, A.L. (2008). "Gender differences in the mesocorticolimbic system during game-play." *Journal of Psychiatric Research.* 42, 253-8.

Holtz, P., Appel, M. (2011). "Internet use and video gaming predict problem behavior in early adolescence." *Journal of Adolescence*, 34(1), 49-58.

King, D. L., Herd, M. C. E., Delfabbro, P. H. (2018). "Movitational components of tolerance in Internet gaming disorder." *Computers in Human Behavior*, 78, 133-141.

Kinzie, M. B., Joseph, D. R. D. (2008). "Gender differences in game activity preferences of middle school children: implications for educational game design." *Education Tech Research Dev*, 56, 643-663.

Kirkorian, H. L., Pempek, T. A., Murphy, L. A., Schmidt, M. E., and Anderson, D. R. (2009). "The impact of background television on parent-child interaction." *Child Development*, 80(5), 1350-1359.

Lenhart, A (2015). "Video games are key elements in friendships in many boys." *Teens, Technology and Friendships.* Retrieved March 16, 2018, from: http://www.pewinternet.

org/2015/08/06/chapter-3-video-games-are-key-elements-in-friendships-for-many-boys/

Lemona S., Brand S., Vogler N., Perkinson-Gloor N., Allemand M., Grob A. (2011) "Habitual computer game playing at night is related to depressive symptoms." *Personality and Individual Differences.* 51, 117–122.

Mendelsohn, A. L., Berkule, S. B., Tomopoulos, S., Tamis-LeMonda, C. S., Huberman, H. S., Alvir, J., and Dreyer, B. P. (2008). "Infant television and video exposure associated with limited parent-child verbal interactions in low socioeconomic status households." *Archives of Pediatric and Adolescent Medicine*, 162(5), 411-417.

Oliver, C. S. (2017). *A Review of the Relationship between Screen Time and Low Levels of Physical Activity with Obesity and Sedentary Behaviors in Children and Adolescents.* Georgia State University from: https://scholarworks.gsu.edu/cgi/viewcontent.cgi?article=1062andcontext=iph_capstone

Ophir, E., Nass, C., Wagner, A.D. (2009). "Cognitive Control in Media Multitaskers." *Proceedings of the National Academy of Sciences*, 106 (37), 15583-15587.

Rosenberg, D., Depp, C. A., Vahia, I. V., Reichstadt, J., Palmer, B. W., Kerr, J., Norman, G., and Jeste, D. V. (2010). "Exergames for subsyndromal depression in older adults: A pilot study of a novel intervention." *American Journal of Geriatric Psychiatry*, 18, 221–226.

Sax, L. (2007). *Boys Adrift*. New York: Basic Books.

Schor, J. (2004). *Born to Buy*. New York: Scribner.

Sharif, I., and Sargent, J. D. (2006)."Association between television, movie, and video game exposure and school performance." *Pediatrics*, 118(4), e1061–1070.

Twenge, J. M., Joiner, T. E., Rogers, M. L., and Martin, G. N.
(2018). "Increases in depressive symptoms, suicide-related
outcomes, and suicide rates among US adolescents after
2010 and links to increased new media screen time."
*Clinical Psychological Science*, 6(1), 3-17.

Vandewater, E. A., Bickham, D. S., and Lee, J. H. (2006). "Time
well spent? Relating television use to children's free-time
activities." *Pediatrics*, 117(2), 181-191.

Young, K. (1998). *Caught in the Net*. New York: John Wiley and
Sons.

# FOOD ADDICTION,

# BODY DYSMORPHIA,

## AND

# EATING DISORDERS

"I started to spiral when it came to eating.
Food was the only thing that numbed
the pain I was feeling all the time. I knew
I didn't need the things I was putting inside my
mouth, but it helped me feel better—loved."

## MY FOOD ADDICTION

Hazel Mills

Walking down the street was not an easy thing for me to do. Low self-esteem was one of the biggest problems. Then there was the 585 pounds I was carrying around on my five-foot, one-inch frame that made it more difficult. Plus, there was the guilt I felt when some of the young children on the street came running out calling names after me like, "Fatty!" or "Ugly!" Then the real clincher came when I was told, "Mom said to tell you to stop walking 'cause you're making the dishes shake in the cupboard, and she don't want them to break."

I was overweight for most of my life. Looking back now, I can nearly pinpoint the exact time the weight gain started. Although it wasn't acknowledged for years, my mother suffered from depression. One particular day, when Dad was home from work (he used to work three months on and ten days off at that time), she was having a particularly difficult day; she was in bed and crying. I know I pestered Dad that day until I am sure he was ready to scream.

Instead, when I asked for the umpteenth time why she was in bed and crying, he picked me up, plunked me on the couch next to him and said, "Your mother is crying because she is sad because you are getting fat. If you really love her, you'll stop eating so much. Maybe have a cracker instead of reaching for sweets all the time?"

Well that was the first time I experienced wobbly knees. I stood there, not quite four years old, taking in what he had told me. I felt embarrassed that he had to tell me, but I felt pure devastation that the woman who had created me could be so hurt by me. From that time on, I convinced myself that if my own mother couldn't love me, I might as well forget it because nobody else could love me either. Well, except maybe my father because he loved me enough to be honest, and tell me what was really going on.

I started to spiral when it came to eating. Food was the only thing that numbed the pain I was feeling all the time. I knew I didn't need the things I was putting inside my mouth, but it helped me feel better—loved. I think it was also a way for me to get back at my mother because the more I ate, the fatter I got. If she didn't love me at forty pounds, let's see if she would actually admit that she didn't love me at 400 or 500 pounds.

When I was a teenager, I was weighing in at about 170 pounds, and I guess Mom was seeing how sad and miserable I was. So she encouraged me to lose weight, go on a diet, or eat healthier. Of course, that was just more proof, in my mind, of how she felt. However, I did try at that time, thinking that if I could lose weight, she might be able to at least like me. Unfortunately, I was not losing weight the right way. I cut myself down to about 500 calories a day, walked nearly two hours, and exercised when I could.

Most teens fight with their parents, but with Dad working away, and my siblings all left home, I realize now our fights were entirely different than most mother-daughter fights. She would say something that would rub me the wrong way. Instead of saying, "I hate you," and then stomping off, I would tell her, "It's okay for you to tell me you don't love me. I already know."

My food addiction got worse as I finished school, moved away from home, and eventually got married and started my family. Because I had essentially starved myself, when I started to eat anything after my child was born, I packed on pounds. The couple of new dresses I bought for returning to work in November were too small in December. It was a vicious cycle, and I kept eating. It was the only thing that gave me any peace, but then it was followed by guilt that consumed me, for example, when I had finished a big bag of chips. I sometimes lied about what I had eaten, and that only made me feel bad. So to make me feel better, I would eat more.

I had just turned forty when children were hurling insults at me as I walked by. I was heading out to take care of my elderly parents for two weeks and needed to pick up a few things at the mall. Now I am amazed that I could actually walk. I guess nobody told me I shouldn't be able to, so I did. I dreaded going out to stay with my parents. I felt uncomfortable about my size and even worse if I ate. Most of the time, it was a struggle between eating and not eating as I fought to maintain control.

We had a situation when Dad was sick with a serious illness and Mom was suffering from dementia. I had to stay for two weeks and, as usual, the days dragged by. The day before I was scheduled to leave, I got up with Mom and started to make breakfast. She was sitting at the table, and I tried to make conversation about the nice day it was, but when I turned around to bring her meal to her, she was crying.

I sat down and said, "Mom, I'm sorry I have to be here. I know it makes you sad to see me like this, so big and trying to get around, but I will be leaving tomorrow, so hang in until then."

It was as if, all of a sudden, something clicked for her, and she looked at me and said, "I'm not crying because you are here. I like having you here. I'm crying because it's what I do."

This was the second time in my life I had the wobbly knees feeling. It was like my life had changed—I felt free. I told her she had just given me the best belated birthday gift ever. When I returned home, I had a good talk with my overweight daughter about how we had to work together to start eating healthy.

At first, we made very subtle changes, like not eating after 8 p.m. Then we got brave about using more fruits, vegetables, and ground flaxseed meal in lots of different ways. We stopped using iodized table salt and used sea salt instead. Within weeks, there were small changes. Over the next ten years, we have carefully worked together on the biggest and best challenge of our lives. Together we have lost more than 400 pounds!

There are times when the weight loss stalls, but at least not a lot of it is going back on. Finally, we have worked through all the hurt and pain and issues that existed because of those very ill-placed words of my father. I have made peace with the fact that he had no idea what to tell me when I asked why my mother cried. It was not as acceptable to have a mental illness back then, and the stigma attached to it would have been crippling for them both.

I am still not skinny, and my bones ache trying to carry around the excess weight I still have. Yet I am alive, and I am free from the hurt that encompassed me for so long. I am so grateful for my mother's words. She loved me just as any mother loves her child, but I was blind to that love for too long. I am also grateful for my daughter, who has been right there with me every step of this journey. Life is good because of her.

"I become obsessed with food:
clean food, non-GMO food, organic food,
fair-trade food. I still eat too
much of it. Eating good food does not
mean you can eat as much as you want."

## IS FOOD ADDICTION REAL?

Margaret Scott

Addiction, in the strictest terms, involves the development of tolerance to a specific substance. Withdrawal symptoms occur when the substance is removed. "Food addiction" is not universally accepted as a true addiction, although some behavioural characteristics of true addiction may be present. Effective management bears some similarities to effective management for alcoholics (Cassell and Gleaves, 2006).

I am six years old. I am in the back seat of my parents' car with my brother and sister. On this Sunday in early June, my dad wants to drive by neighbours' farms to see how their crops are doing. I have not felt well for a few days, and my mom suggests we all go for the ride so I can get some fresh air. I feel terrible—I just want to go home to bed. Suddenly, I am vomiting—violently—I can't stop— it is awful—I am going to choke. Mom feels my forehead, "This kid is really sick. We have to get her to the hospital right away." Dad drops

Mom and me at the hospital and takes the younger kids home. The doctor declares, "Appendicitis. When is the last time she ate?" Mom tells him I haven't really eaten in a couple of days and anything I might have eaten has all come up. The doctor tells Mom, "We don't want a ruptured appendix on our hands—let's get this kid into surgery!"

I remember being prepared for surgery. I remember counting backwards as the anesthetic took effect. I remember waking up in my hospital room and being told I would have to have three needles a day, in the large muscle of my rear end. Of course, at six years old, I did not understand the significance of those penicillin injections. Years later, my mother told me that my appendix had been normal but my abdominal cavity was full of infection. The doctor looked for a perforation in my intestines and could not find one. He concluded that there had been a perforation and it had healed, after leaking material that started the infection. What he did find was that my intestines were all distended, from eating too much he said.

I am six years old and I have returned home from the hospital. My mother tells me, "We have been very foolish with you. We let you eat as much as you wanted. The doctor said your insides are stretched out from all the food you have been eating. Now you have to eat less." I am puzzled. I just eat because I like it.

And so starts my lifelong battle with food. While living at home, my mother tries to control my eating. She puts my food on my plate or watches as the bowls are passed around the table at meal times. She tells me what I can eat, what I cannot eat. She is trying to follow doctor's orders. At six years old, I am not fat, but I am not thin either. My mother is very concerned that I will become overweight, a natural and predictable outcome of my love of food. I think about food a lot, I love it, especially foods laden with fat, sugar, and salt.

The pantry in our home is always stocked with home baking. In our rural community, neighbours and relatives drop in unannounced on a regular basis, as we drop in on them. My mother believes it is important to offer home-baked goods along with the requisite cup of coffee. Our pantry usually has two types of cookies, coffee cake, muffins, and tarts. My mother is famous for her pies and cakes. I cannot stop thinking of them. I am not supposed to eat them between meals, and I am supposed to have a small serving at mealtime if desserts are offered. I take every opportunity to get into that pantry and grab a handful of treats. I have to be careful since I can be discovered if I take too many. I have to pace myself a little, but often I fail and am questioned about the falling stores of baked goods.

I am ten years old. It is Christmas and we are at my aunt's home for dinner. We never eat in restaurants, and we rarely eat a meal in someone else's home. Family dinners with aunts and uncles are the exception a few times a year. On these occasions, everyone contributes to the meal and the typical contribution is a dessert. The tables are laden with food, and we help ourselves. I always eat so much that I end up vomiting. I eat beyond the capacity of my stomach, and it rebels. But this Christmas is different. While I eat lots of shortbread cookies, my favourite, I don't eat so much that I vomit. On the way home, my mother tells me she is proud of me. I realize she is embarrassed that, at every family dinner, her daughter pigs out and then makes a spectacle of herself, barfing in the bathroom and needing to be cleaned up. I am not bulimic. I don't provoke the vomiting. My body just can't handle that much food. The desserts are my downfall.

I am twelve years old, and I am in my bedroom doing homework. My mother comes in with a bottle of pills. "Here," she says, "take these. They will help control your appetite." Maybe because I am entering my rebellious years, and maybe because the eating wars with my mother have escalated, I refuse to take them. I put them on a shelf in my closet and I never open them.

My mother has become desperate because, of course, I have start-ed to put on weight and she does not know what to do with me, for me. I am grateful that I resisted the pills because a year later, my mother asks about the pills and whether I ever took them. I think she knows I didn't take them. I get them from the closet, unopened, and unused. She takes them away, saying, "These are really bad. I should not have given them to you." They are amphetamines. She has been reading about the side effects of these pills: serious addictions, insomnia, restlessness, tremors, paranoid psychoses, and hallucinations.

I am now fourteen years old. My mother tries a new tactic. I will not have breakfast before I go to school. My bagged lunch will consist of half a sandwich, made of one slice of bread and half a slice of ham, along with an apple. By the afternoon, I am so hungry, all I can think about is food. I fantasize about it. I dream about it. I can't concentrate on my schoolwork. When I get home, I make a mad dash for the pantry and cram as much food into my mouth as I can without getting caught. And so it goes, all through high school. I am starving and binging, but now I am doing it myself. My mother is no longer involved.

I wish for an easy solution to my problems. I look at other kids and wonder how it is that they stay at a normal weight without seeming to worry about it. I see that they eat cookies, cake, in their lunches and don't seem obsessed with it. I watch what everyone eats. I dream of an easy solution to my increasing weight problem, one that involves me being able to eat what I want without putting on weight. I never dream of being able to control my eating.

Carlisle, Buser, and Carlisle (2012), in their review of the literature, conclude that the children of mothers who pressure their children to eat, or who restrict and control what their children eat, are more likely to have overweight children, or children with problematic eating habits. The eating patterns established in childhood are likely to persist into adulthood because of disruption of the children's hunger and satiety signals; the children lose touch with their internal cues. Parental models are a powerful influence on the eating habits of their children and this influence persists into adulthood.

I am in my first year of university and living in a women's residence. I am one of the first to be awake each day. Another student on my floor is also an early riser. She invites me to come to her room for tea when I get up, as we are usually the only ones awake for a couple hours. We both drink it clear, no sugar, and no milk. We get into a routine of drinking tea at 6 a.m. and chatting about our courses and daily events in the residence and on campus. It is such a pleasant way to start the day. She is an upper-year student from out of province, and she offers me good advice on studying and living on campus. I have noticed that she is very thin, and I have also noticed that I never see her at mealtime. Eventually, I share with her that I should lose a few pounds. She tells me she lost seventy-five pounds by drinking tea and restricting herself to six soda biscuits a day. She says she weighs eighty-five pounds but thinks she should lose another five pounds as she still has a potbelly. I am astonished! She is tall and skeletal in appearance, but it never occurred to me that she was starving herself. I don't know about anorexia. I learn about it later in a psychology course. I have no interest in restricting my food intake like that. I tell her I enjoy food too much to eat so little. She is angry with me and, gradually, we discontinue taking tea together. A year later, I hear from some of the other students that she has died. Starved to death. I am not an anorexic.

I am in my final year of university, and I am about thirty pounds overweight. I see an advertisement for Weight Watchers. I decide to try it. I go to meetings, and I hear people tell stories like mine, of eating half a three-layer cake in one sitting, of getting up to eat in the night when no one will see them, of feeling out of control. I am given a plan to follow, and I follow it. I have never given any thought to what I was eating before; I just ate what I wanted to eat. I am following a healthy food plan, and I lose weight, and I feel good. I know what to do now! I am free of my bad eating habits and gluttonous ways!

I am not free. I find my old ways creeping back. I don't want to deny myself those foods that have been my friends for so long. So begins a cycle of going to Weight Watchers, losing ten, twenty, thirty pounds, falling off the wagon, gaining the weight back, starting all over and so on and so on. I eat standing at the counter because that doesn't count. I eat in the night because that doesn't count. I eat off other peoples' plates because that doesn't count. I eat on special occasions because that doesn't count. I play many mind games with myself. And I cycle in and out of Weight Watchers. My adolescent rebellion kicks in. To heck with Weight Watchers, I am going to try something else. I try fad diets. I join other weight loss programs where I buy food or supplements. I get injections from my doctor. I am so messed up because all these programs have different ideas about food and I really become confused about what I should eat. I become obsessed with food: clean food, non-GMO food, organic food, and fair-trade food. I still eat too much of it. Eating good food does not mean you can eat as much as you want. I accept that I have to stay with Weight Watchers. I read an article in a medical journal that says Weight Watchers is the most successful of the major weight-loss programs and, as it is healthy eating plan, a person can follow it indefinitely.

I learn not to tell many people about my struggles with controlling my eating. If I do, I get all kinds of advice. Some people can't resist being sanctimonious. It is simple: calories in, calories out. You have to do more exercise. It is a matter of will power. You just have to decide. One tastes as good as two. I feel embarrassed and ashamed. Gluttony is one of the seven deadly sins.

I wonder where this problem comes from. I am like a homing beacon around food. I confide in a friend who has been a member of Alcoholics Anonymous for years. He says my problems with food sound similar to his problems with alcohol. "But", he says, "I think it must be very hard with food. For me, I have removed alcohol from my life. I don't have it in the house. I don't go to bars. I don't hang out with people who drink a lot. But we have to have food. We can't cut it out of our lives." Certainly, I have learned to avoid situations that are difficult. I don't keep problem foods in my home, and I try to avoid them in social situations. I am still learning to live with this problem.

My mother comes to visit. I go to work during the day, and my kids go to school. In the evening, I am making my kids' lunches for school. I buy one bag of cookies each week so I can put two cookies in each lunch. I don't bake because that exposes me to temptation. I can reach into a bag of commercially produced cookies, take out the ones needed for the lunches, close it, and put it into the back of the cupboard—out of sight, out of mind. I reach for the bag. It is empty. I don't understand what has happened. My mother sees me looking at the empty bag. "I ate them," she says. I now understand why she tried so hard to control my eating. She was living with the same problem and she was trying to protect me. So are my eating behaviours learned and modelled?

I read *Salt Sugar Fat: How the Food Giants Hooked Us* by Michael Moss (2013). I read about the billions of dollars spent each year on advertising foods to us, making us believe we need those products that are making us sick and even killing us. I learn about the billions of dollars spent on making the perfect flavours that will induce us to eat them and to eat more of them. Mere mortals don't stand a chance. Coupled with the billions of dollars spent on the weight-loss and health industries, it seems those of us living in affluent countries are immobilized by these competing forces—eat, don't eat. We fight against a survival instinct that has been honed through millions of years of evolution in environments that gave up nourishment only after the expenditure of great effort, and required us to eat when we could.

I find the *Yale Food Addiction Scale* online (Gearhardt, Corbin, and Brownell, 2009). I complete the instrument and score it. I score zero on seven of the eight subscales, meaning I do not have a food addiction. On one subscale, *Persistent desire or repeated unsuccessful attempts to quit,* I score on two of the four items. How much of this behaviour is learned? What actually happened when I was six years old? Was I actually eating too much, or did the doctor interpret my symptoms incorrectly? Maybe the distended intestines were a reaction to the infection, whose origin was unknown. Did my maladaptive eating patterns occur *because* my mother was trying to control my eating, being a good mom and following the doctor's advice? I will never know.

REFERENCES

Carlisle, K. L., Buser, J. K., and Carlisle, R. M. (2012). "Childhood food addiction and the family." *The Family Journal: Counseling and Therapy for Couples and Families.* 20(3). 332-9.

Cassell, D. and Gleaves, D. H. (2006). *The Encyclopedia of Obesity and Eating Disorders, 3rd Ed.* New York: Facts on File.

Gearhardt, A. N., Corbin, W. R., and Brownell, K. D. (2009). *Yale Food Addiction Scale* http://www.midss.org/content/ale-food-addiction-scale-yfas. Retrieved: February 20, 2018.

Moss, M. (2013). *Salt Sugar Fat: How the Food Giants Hooked Us.* New York: Random House.

"I grew adept at evading eating,
addicted to the sense of achievement and secret
pride it gave me. I passed food to
the dog when no one was looking,
declined whenever possible,
surreptitiously spat mouthfuls into tissues, or
rearranged the contents of my plate to
make it look as though I'd eaten."

## VANISHING POINT

Aisha Ashraf

When people think of anorexia, they think of concentration-camp figures with skin stretched tight over protruding bones, people with heads too heavy for their reedy frames. Anorexia's striking physicality steals the show, and few realize it's a disease that also consumes the mind.

Growing up, I had what's known as an athletic build. A child of the outdoors, I lived for dog walking and horse riding, but by age seventeen I disliked my strength and solidity, yearning for willowy grace instead. It seemed to me fragility evoked gentleness and protection in people, rare qualities in my home environment.

Somewhere along the way, what started as a desire to lose weight became an intoxicating feeling of control I was unwilling to surrender.

A lot had happened to make me feel helpless–parental abuse, divorce, homelessness, depression, self-harm, a salacious step-father, work-place sexual harassment; they all took their toll. Combined with my high-achieving personality, they formed a recipe for obsessive and controlling behaviour, not towards others or in any obvious way, but with my environment and myself. I vacuumed my tiny bedroom almost daily and limited my intake of food.

I grew adept at evading eating, addicted to the sense of achieve-ment and secret pride it gave me. I passed food to the dog when no one was looking, declined whenever possible, surreptitiously spat mouthfuls into tissues, or rearranged the contents of my plate to make it look as though I'd eaten. When serving myself, I placed food so that it covered maximum surface area and looked more than it was.

As the weight dropped off, my sense of identity became fused with my clandestine purpose. Christmas came and went, and I congratulated myself on having lost weight over the festive season. But the rigid grip of compulsion was tightening. I started to exercise in my room at night before sleeping. I couldn't stand the thought of any leftover calories melting into my body to become fat. Every evening and morning, before sleeping and upon waking, my fingertips would find my protruding hipbones and lovingly stroke the concave curve of my empty belly. I welcomed the comforting pangs of hunger, confirmation I was succeeding. As time passed, I felt them less and less, but thought about food more and more.

I bought a thick doorstop of a book that listed the calories in every food known to man so I could never be knowingly overfed, and I always rounded up my calculations so I had a margin for error. The daily limit I allowed myself was one thousand calories. I'd read somewhere that was close to the figure calculated by the Nazis as the minimum requirement to keep concentration-camp prisoners alive. After dinner, I cycled for miles to burn my meagre meal off. If something prevented me, I was consumed by inescapable panic, imagining the food sitting like a lead lump in my stomach. Slowly, the voiceless torturer that is Anorexia Nervosa engulfed my mind.

The sole inhabitant of my private world, I marvelled at my self-control and iron will and despised those ruled by their gluttonous appetites. Food was the *enemy*. Anorexics are notorious for their arrogance; I felt superior, supercilious, but I kept my secret close to my heart. I hadn't yet realized I wasn't the one in control—my behaviour controlled me. I was at constant war with myself; the last remaining rational part of me said eating was normal and necessary, but the authoritative voice of my illness argued I was one of the few who could see humanity's greed for what it was—that we actually needed a lot less to survive. Everyone was part of the mass conspiracy of the food industry. No one could be trusted.

By now my jeans and jumpers hung on me like laundry on a clotheshorse. When winter rolled around again, I wore in excess of seven layers and took hot baths to stay warm. Like most anorexics, I was obsessive about tracking my progress, weighing myself daily (often more than once), recording the data in graph form, and always, always searching for the compass-points of those hipbones in the dark, to be sure I was still moving in the right direction. They were the landmarks of success on my solo expedition.

Two years after I'd taken this path, my quest for control meant the stakes were constantly raised. As my body adapted to a lower food intake I had to work harder to keep losing weight. Any increase on the scales led to tears and anguish: a self-loathing and revulsion so powerful I couldn't leave the house. I felt as if my disgusting gluttony, my shameful greed was visible for the entire world to see. You cannot imagine the depths of my self-hate. I couldn't face college, couldn't bear my friends seeing me. I vacillated between listless melancholia and railing against my self-created, self-imposed entrapment.

In truth, I had lost almost a third of my body weight, going from

144 pounds to 100. My goal was ninety pounds. Standing at just under five foot eight, I was already skeletal. My periods became intermittent, and my starvation diet of a piece of fruit for breakfast and a tuna or ham salad for dinner was no longer enough to effect weight loss. But just as a master craftsman isn't content with knowing only the basics of his trade, I had acquired other tricks.

The panic after allowing myself a donut led me to use laxatives to rid my system of the calorie-laden blip in self-control. I rejoiced in the latest weapon in my arsenal; I could now occasionally give in to my desires. I experimented with different brands and studied the active ingredients to find the ones that were most effective for me, but over time, my body grew immune to the drugs, and I had to ingest larger and larger amounts to get the desired effect. Eventually, I was forcing down twelve to fifteen of the little red pills at a time (the recommended dose was 1-2). The abdominal cramps they brought the following day I viewed as punishment for my greed.

Looking back, I have no idea how I withstood the things I did to myself. Like a mad scientist, I conducted experiments, constantly pushing my boundaries. I remember not eating for three whole days, surviving entirely on black coffee and cigarettes. And throughout all this, I continued my studies. I do remember, once, leaving the college smoking room to re-enter the cafeteria and feeling dizzy. A ringing sound filled my ears then receded, and the chatter of diners sounded tinny and distant as though heard over a badly tuned radio. I think I came close to fainting.

Some people believe anorexics are "starving for attention," but that wasn't true in my case. I was striving for invisibility. I wanted to occupy as little space as possible in this world. One thing that is indisputable is that anorexics are stubborn, and I was no different, but one evening, through a sudden break in the clouds of my body dysmorphia, my boyfriend succeeded in showing me how terrible I looked. As he stood behind me, holding my arms aloft so I could see my naked, skeletal frame in the bathroom mirror, for a minute I could see what he saw–just a moment. And that's when I finally agreed to end my fade-out to vanishing point and take my first faltering steps on a barely discernible path to recovery. I weighed ninety-one pounds, but the burden of anorexia was incalculable.

"For years, I was addicted to the seemingly superhuman power of anorexia. I felt exhilarated when pushing my body, excelling at my studies, beating out all the guys, taking care of my family."

# SHRINKING BODY, SHRINKING VOICE: ONE PERSON'S JOURNEY THROUGH ANOREXIA

Angela Rinaldis

The silence is killing us. People are suffering from eating disorders—dying, even—because of our silence.

People tell me I'm courageous because I recovered from nine years of life-threatening anorexia. Today, I'm a successful litigation lawyer, a fierce, hockey-playing athlete, and a national spokesperson for fellow eating-disorder (ED) sufferers.

And yet…the silence still pulls me in. The other day, after yoga class, a guy came up to me and talked openly about his depression. He said he really gets how hard it is for people to break the silence around mental illness.

What do you think this kick-ass litigation lawyer and eating-disorder activist said to him about *her* mental illness? Nothing. Not a word.

Why didn't I speak up? Because he sees me as strong and athletic. If I told him about the anorexia, he might dismiss my athletic drive as a product of my ED. So, out of fear, I kept my mouth shut.

I also kept silent about my anorexia at my first job, at a preeminent Canadian law firm, not telling a soul that I was dashing over to the hospital each day for the lunchtime eating-disorders program.

And I definitely didn't tell *anyone* when, working in Toronto, I got caught shoplifting grapes. Grapes I wouldn't even eat, but felt compelled to steal and hoard, only to have them rot in my fridge. (And yes, I will be forever grateful for that moment of compassion from a supermarket employee.)

## WHY ANOREXIA? WHY ME?

I always wanted to know why. Was anorexia in my genes? Was it gender or culture? The stress of caring for my clinically depressed mother when I was just a kid? Are type-A perfectionists like me more vulnerable? All of the above?

I just don't know. What I *do* know is how my recovery started: I broke my silence and asked for help. (And then I spent a ton of money and worked hard at it. But that's getting ahead of the story.)

My story of mental illness doesn't start with me. I was seven when my mother fell into a deep clinical depression, swinging from manic to barely peeling herself off the couch to take a shower. I'll never forget the ratty housecoat she wore in her down periods; I hated that thing and wanted to burn it. Years later, I did.

In my teen years, when my older sister moved away, I *became* the mom. I cooked and cleaned, and my dad and I did the grocery shopping, paid the bills, dragged Mom to the doctor and counsellors, hounded her to take her meds. At age fifteen, I started working full time to help out at home.

I did not share this world with anyone, not even my best friend. From the outside, we were the perfect family. Friends and extended family saw an honour-roll student holding down a full-time job. But on the inside, I started to disappear. Gradually, over the next couple of years, I grew more strict with what I would and would not eat and developed a million and one food rules. And I started to exercise like a maniac.

## ENTER ANOREXIC ANNIE (WHO WON'T SHUT UP)

I knew I had a problem early on. There was this voice in my head— I called her Anorexic Annie. "No food for you today!" Her voice was overwhelming, and I couldn't make it stop. "Keep going just another thirty minutes on the treadmill, and then another thirty after that!" Some days, eating anything seemed like too much. Anorexic Annie became my worst best friend.

There's a stereotype of anorexic girls trying to look like the skinny models in fashion magazines. That was never me. I knew I was too skinny. I wore baggy clothing to hide my skeletal figure and ward off the perpetual cold caused by dangerously low body fat. Yet, at the same time, being able to count all my ribs gave me comfort and made me feel like I would have a "good" day. I got pleasure from the pain of being thin because it meant I was in control and no one could stop me.

While I appeared active and engaged, my secret life made me increasingly suspicious of friends and family. Would they disown me if they knew what I was really up to? I isolated myself, immersing myself in school, work, and taking care of the household, with frequent trips to different gyms to feel that sense of abandon I got from pushing my body to its limits and beyond.

When I graduated from high school with honours and a full scholarship to the University of British Columbia, my worried parents, not knowing how to help me, sent me to my grandmother in Italy for what turned out to be an anorexic cure from the eighteenth century. My grandmother force-fed me olive oil, ice cream, and other fatty foods. She yelled at me constantly, called me a slut, made me confess at church on my hands and knees, and locked me in the attic. While everyone slept in the afternoons, I crawled from the attic into my cousin's house next door and rode their exercise bike for hours. In spite of the force-feeding, I lost even more weight. Not surprisingly, I also had a minor nervous breakdown.

I returned home with a fear of olive oil and ice cream. When I later caught my mom sneaking butter into my food, I grew even more distrustful—and more restrictive in my eating. (Note: If someone you love has ED, sneaking stuff into their food is NOT a good recovery plan!)

Despite this secret suffering, I started at UBC and continued achieving at a furious pace. I got my degree in sociology and psychology and entered law school. Meanwhile, my food rules grew increasingly irrational, my exercise more intense.

## THE SEEDS OF MY RECOVERY

For years, I was addicted to the seemingly superhuman power of anorexia. I felt exhilarated when pushing my body, excelling at my studies, beating out all the guys, taking care of my family. I was terrified that if I slowed down, I'd end up like my mom, collapsed on the couch in a ratty housecoat.

I was willing to pay the price of losing my menstrual cycle, my hair falling out, unwanted hair growing all over my body to protect me from the cold, organs deteriorating, muscles getting eaten away, avoiding social situations where food was central, feeling lonely in crowds, and hiding my skeletal figure under layers of clothes. That anorexic superpower made it all worthwhile.

Until it didn't.

Friends and family never gave up on me. Even though I'd get angry at them for their "presumptions," they'd speak up in ways that sewed the seeds of my recovery.

Like the time my best friend said, "Ang, I just can't watch you kill yourself," and told me she had to step away.

Their collective concern started to affect me. I know the exact moment I hit rock bottom. I was twenty-six, at the end of my last year of law school, 5'8" and eighty-eight pounds—and dying. I didn't want to die, and I didn't believe I would, but I was too scared to eat, too scared to rest. I couldn't get Anorexic Annie to shut up, and I was just so tired.

Tired of hurting when I sat on my boney bum, tired of the bruises along my spine from my backpack, tired of the endless sit-ups and hours at the gym, tired of scrubbing pans to death to protect myself from the calories in whatever residue was left on the pan after it had already gone through the dishwasher.

I finished my Property Law exam and took the bus to the eating-disorder clinic at St. Paul's Hospital. For the first time, I broke my silence and asked for help.

## THE BUMPY ROAD TO RECOVERY

I finished law school while admitted to the eating-disorder clinic. I requested a deferment for writing my final exams from the dean and associate dean, but they turned me down. (To this day I marvel: what does it say about the stigmatization of mental illness if two educated feminist women, one teaching health law, don't consider ED a valid illness?)

I recovered from most of the physical symptoms of starvation at the hospital. What I needed now was outpatient options to help me find a new way to live. No small task, for which there were (and still are) few publicly funded resources.

I had to hunt down private counsellors, dietitians, hypno-therapists, and physicians. I found counsellors who had no ED experience, therapy groups where no one showed up, and clueless nutritionists with suspect qualifications. Eventually, I found the help I needed, but not until I had spent over $60,000 out of my own pocket. Good thing I went to law school!.

## BUILDING A NEW LIFE

When my ED was at its worst, I longed to be diagnosed with a different disease—something more respectable, a disease that wasn't my fault. Some other real disease like MS or cancer, one I didn't have to be ashamed of.

And nothing fed that shame like silence. For a long time I kept my eating disorder a secret. After all, what would clients think if they knew their lawyer had to wear a glove to move the butter for fear that she would absorb the fat through her fingers? Only over time did I see that silence leads back to the same dark place.

So, I took a chance. I started telling people about my ED. To my amazement, this new openness led not to broken connections, but to deeper ones. I even found a life partner who loves me for exactly who I am (other than not allowing me to scrub the Teflon-coated pans).

Eventually, I was able to open my own law practice so I could set my own hours and start Project True. This not-for-profit organization breaks the silence around disordered eating and gives cash-strapped ED sufferers funding for the outpatient resources they so desperately need.

As an anorexic, I strived for endless achievement. In recovery, my goal has shifted to reaching out to others and developing real connections. Sure, I'll always have ED. I'll always have to watch how much I exercise for fear of slipping into old patterns. But, my priorities have changed.

I was honoured a few years back with a nomination for a Courage To Come Back award. Honestly, though? I'm not sure it's courage. Maybe it's just my stubborn refusal to quit. Through a ton of hard work, I've reversed my osteopenia, rebuilt my body, and birthed a beautiful baby girl I was told I'd never have. I'm an athlete, a mother, a wife, an activist. None of it is what I planned, but I have found that life steps in with the best solutions when my plans step out.

To all of you who know someone with an eating disorder, I thank you for your compassion and caring. Mental illness thrives in silence and isolation; healing takes a community. We need your loving support.

If you've got an eating disorder, please don't suffer in silence. Your ED is a disease. It's not your fault. Speak up, ask for help. Get into recovery and be patient with yourself as you muddle through. Recovery can be a messy business that often doesn't go according to plan. But as long as you're talking, you're on the winding road to recovery. And, in my experience, that road leads to some pretty amazing places—places you can't even imagine until you get there.

"To let go of my hunger blanket
would be scary. I still don't feel like I can
        manage without it. However,
I know there are days that I do. In fact,
        there are more days this year than last year
that I managed; more social events
            that I attended, more food items
that I've added to my *safe* repertoire."

# LIVING BEYOND THE SYMPTOMS OF SEVERE AND PERSISTENT ANOREXIA NERVOSA

Erika Hunzinger

Monday, 7:13 a.m. My mind racing, I'm walking with intention, to burn as many calories as possible, and get to my job as a mental-health specialist in incredible time. I'm really hungry. I should have eaten breakfast. But I ate my overnight oats at 3 a.m. because I couldn't sleep (probably due to hunger and intense anxiety about work) and then decided at 6 a.m. that another meal would be gluttonous, absolutely in excess. Yet the thought that I didn't eat breakfast calms me like a warm blanket and shades the bright lights of the demands of the "real" world. Distracting myself with thoughts about food and weight makes me feel like I still have control. I can do this. I am *strong*. I pick up my pace, with focus, and start to wonder about what my work day will hold

I arrive at my new office with a growling, bouncy stomach. Clinical specialist. Mental health. Right. I'm supposed to be an expert on recovery from mental illness...then, I'm suddenly distracted by toast that is being made for an individual in the kitchen. My heart sinks because I'm reminded of my obsession about food. I am engulfed by a wave of shame and self-disgust regarding my twelve-year history of eating-disordered thoughts, rituals, and pre-occupations, and the stigma of being "mentally ill." My old record player starts to spin: "I can't do this," "Imposter!" "Fake!" and "You're a *patient*, not a professional!"

You see, I am a failure in my recovery from my psychiatric symptoms. I continue to meet diagnostic criteria for Anorexia Nervosa from the *Diagnostic and Statistical Manual of Mental Disorders*, 5th edition (DSM-V; American Psychiatric Association, 2013). Though I have improved my ability to manage my behaviours and symptoms of chronic anorexia (restriction of intake, intense fear and persistent thoughts about weight gain, and compulsive exercising), they still "pop up" in times of stress, transition, or crisis.

In the DSM's eyes, I'm "sick," have been for twelve years, and am likely to always be "sick" because I fit in this diagnostic box. I've been to treatment on five occasions, though for over six years I have managed without inpatient care.

Yet, I don't *look* as "sick" (i.e., thin) as before. Not on the outside, nor functionally. I work. I smile. I've gained (some) weight. I go to doctors' appointments. I go to an outpatient group, and I work on my recovery every day. People comment all the time on my "success." Then I go home, to my own apartment, and complete my eating-disorder rituals as a way to calm myself, and

obsess about what I have eaten as a means to distract my racing mind.
I am not sure these thoughts or behaviours will ever be completely
gone. The existence of these obsessions, though still serving me a
purpose, paradoxically leads to me feeling like an "imposter," a sick
mind in a body that everyone else believes is healed, recovered with
a period at the end. Done. Fixed. Some days, I find myself absolutely
horrified that my workplace does not know the *real* me, this eating-
disorder monster that lives under this skin of lies and pretending,
poisoning their organization. Some days I just want to scream, want
to be seen and heard, let the monster out that only I know is inside
of me.

I also feel like an imposter because I love food. I'm obsessed
with it, and it's difficult to concentrate when I'm around it. I am,
ironically, weak to it, especially after years of starvation. The years
of starving have trained my body to eat with such drive that the
eating disorder lags behind. My body eats when I'm trying to sleep.
Before I even realize what I'm doing, I have found myself awake at
3 a.m., in front of the freezer, putting frozen French fries in my mouth
with no recollection of getting out of my bed. My body is fighting
to save my life. But even that makes me ashamed; I'm not even "good"
at my eating disorder anymore.

Wanna know the truth? Some days I want to go back to the time
I didn't function. I want to go back to when I looked as messy and
vulnerable as I felt. So people wouldn't expect success of me, so I
wouldn't disappoint, so I wouldn't always have to feel I was hiding
this big secret. So when I showed up to work or school with
dead, hazy eyes and the same oversized clothes I wore yesterday,
I'd just get sent home, "take care of yourself." I'd be comforted, I'd
be validated.

So you may be wondering how anorexia nervosa continues to
serve me now? It's an addiction, an obsession, and a means of
coping. I can't stop, yet. But I'm trying.

Without my hunger blanket, every day feels like a precarious balance and racing thoughts of *should I or shouldn't I*? It's exhausting. In starvation, the pace of my thoughts feels a little slower, the lights and sounds just a little less sharp and abrasive, my emotions are blunted and less severe. The numbness of hunger is my lorazepam in this harsh reality; the world of self-criticizing is the sand I stick my head in when I need a break from the chaos around me, the ritual of eating the same dinner every night is just that thing I do that gives me a false sense of control of this life that moves too fast for me.

I have a set routine when I get home that calms and comforts me. I rarely stray from it, I get anxious if I do. It consists of eating the same foods, prepared in the same order, changing into certain clothes, eating out of certain dishes, and always listening to a podcast from Hidden Brain. Every night. Kinda like a "night cap" or a sleeping pill someone may have before they can sleep.

When I wake up in the morning, I'm often sad and disappointed in myself that I, again, succumbed to eating-disordered behaviours rather than my "approved" coping strategies. I'm sad I chose my isolating evening routine over my friends and family. Maybe I even lied to get out of a social event. So I don't eat, and then I feel a little less sad, a little less disappointed in myself because my emotions, on the whole, are moderated by the "brain fuzz" of starvation. The cycle begins again.

To let go of my hunger blanket would be scary. Without my obsessive thoughts distracting my anxious mind, I still don't feel like I can manage "real life." However, I know there are days that I do manage "real life." In fact, there are more days this year than last year that I managed, more social events that I attended, more food items that I've added to my "safe" repertoire.

This thought of being both a person of lived experience and a "professional" stirs this ethical stew within me that makes me nauseated the more I think about it. Perhaps it's the lack of confidence in my clinical skills (imposter syndrome), perhaps it's the precariousness of my self-managed partial recovery, perhaps it's the vulnerability I feel, perhaps I'm just hungry. I also feel terribly ashamed that I am not living to my "potential," as per my family. Likely it is a combination of all of the above.

What I *do* have, however, is a solid recovery from the *impact* of my mental illness. I have a job, and I am good at it. I live independently and have a few social connections. I am, well, WELL.

I haven't quite figured out how to live with the shame of my story yet, but I've figured out how to live with my addiction to my symptoms. But this duality I take with me. I live both sides of recovery and severe and persistent mental illness. In fact, I would go so far as to suggest it is what makes me fantastic at my job working in mental health.

This is what I have learned so far.

*Find the silver lining.* I was taught in recovery there would be a silver lining, and to look for meaning in my experiences. Things are not black and white. I don't have to be "ill" or "recovered." I'm somewhere in between, in progress. Every battle (every meal time!) is a teacher and an opportunity. I get these opportunities all the time. So I'm lucky in that sense. I can relate to the individuals that come to me for mental-health/addictions help—I feel the same stigma, imposter syndrome, shame, loneliness, and disappointment in self, and I understand why people have addictions and the purpose they serve.

*Meaning and purpose.* I'm not fully sure what mine is, but I'm learning and growing and advocating for mental-health and addiction services. I provide suggestions and education to other clinicians and meet with individuals with difficult behaviour patterns (including addictions and personality disorders). I understand and can appreciate fully why people drink or use substances to cope with anxiety and stress. I understand how ritual and routine can calm and comfort. We are all seeking and use various degrees of these coping strategies. The only real difference is whether you control it, or it begins to control you.

*Make making mistakes the goal.* Maybe not an intentional goal, but the process of making errors and changes yields novelty, excitement, living. Agility and adaptability have served me well, even though it is really hard.

*Releasing shame regarding "failures."* Shame is poison. Nothing feels so good as to show someone your weaknesses and still find acceptance. I have, on occasion, shared with others because it just felt right. I remember the first time I disclosed to another individual that I have food addiction, and I still can't "use my DBT skills" every time. I still struggle. She cried and softened, her eyes met mine, she knew I understood, and I felt whole just for a moment, like the years of pain and shame were worth it. Sharing my story made sense. I am not alone, and neither was she.

*Locate your hope.* The aorta of recovery. Where does it come from? What's it made of? Stories of rising from failure? No, I don't think so. It's having someone believe in you. To the point that maybe, just a little, you begin to see that you can believe in yourself. It's the belief that God is there, also believing in me, and that I'm on this journey for His reason. It's looking at life with a new lens—a lens of acceptance. Rather than focusing on having a "perfect recovery"; allowing myself permission to have setbacks, and celebrating the times in which I move forward. And celebrating again when you move forward more steps than the previous day. Accepting myself as I am, (maybe eighty percent better?) is still hard for me to do... especially when the work day is over and there's no distractions or tasks, just me and my slowly dissolving shame. By choosing to believe in myself and celebrating positive moments, my hope continues to blossom. It is also contagious. I truly believe the people I work with can feel my hope for myself, and for them.

So I get up with my alarm clock, come to work, make small chat, and read my emails. My secret addiction takes a back seat to my functional life for the work day. But it still calls out like the backseat driver that is not capable of taking the wheel. The backseat driver that wants to keep going in circles. Never getting anywhere, but comfortably and predictably existing in a haze of semi-conscious pseudo-life, with the sole focus of weight control and being numb. When nothing else matters to you but controlling your diet, life becomes so easy. Satisfying, hardly, but easy. The temptation remains.

God willing, I will remain in the driver's seat, but I know I have to work hard everyday to stay there. My addiction has taken so much but also given so much. I think I am afraid to let go of it, at least for now. So I continue to live in this psuedo-land of ironic expertise of my own addiction, the land of the "RecoverED," living beyond my symptoms, living with my symptoms, living for the future, living with hope, and living for God.

REFERENCES

American Psychiatric Association. (2013). *Diagnostic and Statistical Manual of Mental Disorders* (5th ed.). Arlington, VA: American Psychiatric Publishing.

"I continued hiding in plain sight.
Doing well in school. Avoiding other people,
and avoiding friends who might
verbally attack you when your guard is down.
Avoiding, avoiding,
avoiding everything. Hiding."

6

## CONCAVE MAN

Andrew Drechsler

I was a shy, skinny, bookish boy. Not athletic. Bad at sports. Like in those bad movies, I was always picked last for the teams. During a softball game, my brother once intentionally threw a softball at my head when I wasn't looking. He said I wasn't trying hard enough. Hit me right in the nose. That pretty much encapsulates the nature of our relationship.

I wasn't just skinny. I was extremely skinny. As I got older, it just got worse. I never seemed to "fill out," like the adults said I would. In fact, my chest looked caved in, and it didn't get better, only worse as I grew older. I thought this was just an extreme form of skinniness. My parents had WWII books, including photos of concentration camp detainees. I looked like them, only I seemed worse. Kids, boys, especially, are always looking for weaknesses, differences, to pick on in a *Lord of the Flies* kind of way. My sunken chest was the subject of much mockery and ridicule by the other boys. Fortunately, we lived in a relatively cool climate, so summers were mercifully short. Once when I went to the beach with my friends, they all laughed and made fun of my physique. Said I looked worse than the pictures on TV of the starving children in Africa. They were supposedly my "best friends." I didn't go to the beach anymore after that. I never learned to swim. I avoided any situations which required taking my shirt off in public, in front of any other people. Avoided any sports other than the minimum required by compulsory gym classes. In locker rooms, I changed quickly and furtively, hiding in corners as other boys paraded around showing off their flat chests and burgeoning muscles. I perfected the art of being present but invisible.

In high school, I found books on weightlifting and bought a set of Weider weights and installed them in the basement. The ads on the backs of comic books promised this would stop the other boys kicking sand in my face, metaphorically, of course, as I never went to any beaches anymore. My parents and brother ridiculed this weightlifting undertaking. I did put some weight and muscle on. A bit. But the dent in my chest never seemed to get any better. In fact, it only looked worse. As the pectoral muscles grew around it, the dent only looked deeper. There was no muscle in there. Only an eternal abyss of emptiness. Of shame.

Any sort of dating or sexual exploration was simply out of the question. At some point, one's shirt would have to come off and then...who knows? Some sort of galactic cataclysm might ensue.

I continued hiding in plain sight. Doing well in school. Avoiding other people, and avoiding friends who might verbally attack you when your guard is down. Avoiding, avoiding, avoiding everything. Hiding. Except in class. My teachers liked me, but in the days before nerds were cool billionaires-to-be, this just made me even more unpopular with all the other kids.

My marks meant I was accepted at, and offered scholarships to a couple of prestigious out-of-town universities. But as much as I wanted to go, the idea of a roommate or communal showers filled me with such horror that I stayed at home and went to the local university. I liked it a lot more than high school. It was better in terms of social structure, as doing well there was not a source of shame and mockery, as it had been in the past. I made a few friends. I still tried to work out periodically, but it never seemed to improve the look of my chest. I met another skinny guy at university, and we became friends. We had a lot of the same classes. He started working out, and as he gained a few pounds and put on some muscle, he looked great. He went from skinny guy to lean muscular guy in no time at all. I was frustrated about why I couldn't do that. The things that seemed to work for other people didn't seem to work for me at all. I was different than everyone else.

Upon graduation, I moved to Halifax to a good job. Worked hard. Made career progress. One Saturday, I went to the university medical library and looked through books on anatomy (this was in the ancient times before the Internet and Google delivered everything you wanted to know in seconds in the comfort and privacy of your own home). After some searching around in medical textbooks, I found my odd chest had a name. It was a "congenital deformity of the anterior thoracic wall" called Pectus Excavatum. It affects one in 300-400 live births with a three to one ratio of boys to girls. The cause is unknown. So I won a lottery that I had ¼ percent chance of winning. Lucky me. The pictures looked exactly like me. No smiling kids in any of the photos. And like me, this affliction gets worse and worse as you get older as a teenager—your bones continue to grow in this perverse way. For some reason, your ribs just keep on growing, instead of stopping where they're supposed to. So they grow inwards. This continues until your bones stop growing at around eighteen. There are usually psychological consequences for people so afflicted, including depression, low self-esteem, and poor body image. There is a surgery to fix it involving cutting the chest open, chopping up the ribs in question and sewing everything back together again in a more normal state.

I brooded on this for a while. A year or two later, I talked to a friend about it. He told me about a redheaded boy in his high school who had red pubic hair. He said that of course all of the other boys made fun of him in that hellish place called the gym locker room. My friend said it wasn't a big deal, it didn't matter, and I should just forget about it and "get over it" like his redheaded friend did. Easy for him to say, as he was a star athlete in high school. His parents' basement was full of his track-and-field trophies and medals.

But I tried to follow his advice and just forget about it. Although the "avoid and hide anything to do with my body" strategy still stayed in full force. I had brought my weightlifting set with me to the big city and still worked out when I wasn't too busy at work. Despite my medical research, I still maintained the now obviously irrational hope that it would change something. There was an episode of Star Trek, the original series, where there is a planet where beings existed as pure thought with no physical manifestation at all. I wished I were that kind of alien.

With a promotion at work came a compulsory physical exam. I didn't normally see doctors as I was still in my twenties and otherwise healthy. I asked this doctor about my chest and the possibility of corrective surgery. He could not have been more rude and insulting. He said I was an idiot if I ever considered such a thing. He said it was major surgery, and this issue was a "cosmetic" one. He practically spat out those words with the most derision and condescension he could muster. It was like I was fourteen again, and he was one of the boys at the beach laughing at me. So it seemed like the medical profession was not going to be particularly helpful either.

Years passed. I got into a relationship with a woman. She didn't seem to notice or care. We occasionally went on beach vacations. Now and then people would look at me a bit too long. Once I saw another of "me" on a beach carrying on as if nothing was amiss. Perhaps I was "over" it?

Then I came out as gay. And now the deformed chest became more of an issue again. Once, I met someone at a bar, and we went back to my place. Things progressed. But as soon as I took my shirt off, he quickly made up an excuse about somewhere else he had to be, and left. On another occasion someone exclaimed in shock and disbelief, "Oh my God! What happened to you? Were you in an accident? Does it hurt?" A bit of a mood killer, that. Going to dance clubs was a popular pastime then. As it would get hot and sweaty, shirts would come off. Well, except for mine. I would have two shirts. A very tight T-shirt, plus another shirt on top. If you only had one loose shirt then it may bend inwards in a way that would shatter the illusion of normalcy as one moved about.

It was strange. There were times I met and dated guys, and when the shirts came off, nothing happened. Not a word was said as though nothing was amiss. Then things progressed smoothly in the way one expects in these situations. I had somehow inexplicably managed to "pass" as a normal person. I always wondered what they thought, but didn't say. Then there were those other times when the reaction was shock and awe, and they ran away screaming into the night. I could never tell what awaited me when the moment of truth came, and the clothes started to come off. I suppose for others, this moment of taking clothes off, was a simple part of the thrill of sex. For me, it was always a moment of terror. What will the reaction be? Will this be a moment of thrilling excitement? Or an embarrassing moment of despondency, defeat, and despair.

It went on like this for a few years, but in the end, it was no good. It was pointless. The profound sense of incompleteness and brokenness and worthlessness was inescapable. The embarrassing moments of shame and sadness and rejection counted for more than the fleeting moments of happiness. Whatever progress I had made in "getting over it" was dead and gone.

Eventually I got the courage to ask my family doctor about it. He was kinder and more understanding than the—Yes, I'm going to be blunt and tell it like it is–the "asshole" doctor I saw in my twenties. He tried to talk me out of it, but I insisted, and so he referred me to a thoracic surgeon. I saw him a few months later, and he said yes, he did this procedure called the open repair or Ravitch surgery invented in the 1950s. It was usually done on younger people but he would do it on me if I wanted. He occasionally did this as a sideline as he normally did lung transplants, so cracking someone's chest open was not a big deal for him. He brought in a group of residents. They oohed and ahhhed and poked and prodded at me, as if I were not a conscious and sentient being, the way that doctors on their rounds do. You could see them trying hard not to look too shocked, but the eyes gave it away. Obviously, none of them had ever seen one of "us" before.

So we did the surgery and it was a success and I was elated. For a while. I started going to the gym religiously. Putting on weight. Bulking up. The "high" lasted for about a year. As is often the case with a Ravitch repair, my chest sunk back in again. The bones do what they want to do as if they have mind of their own. Back to square one.

Online I read about another surgery called the Nuss, or minimally invasive repair. Invented by Dr. Nuss in the 1980s, it was based on his observation of how malleable the chests of children were when the cartilage connecting the ribs to the sternum was still soft. He stuck a couple of u-shaped bars in from the sides and flipped them around, popping the chest right out. He left the bars in for a couple of years, until bone growth was done, sort of like braces on your teeth. Optimally done at fifteen and the bars left in until eighteen when the bone growth was done. The result was an almost entirely normal looking chest, and a more enduring result. The only problem for me was that now I was in my late thirties, and no one would do such a thing on such old bones. In Canada that is. There were surgeons in the United States who had started doing this on older patients. But it would cost cash. Lots of it. There was another surgeon in Berlin who had done a number of surgeries successfully on adults. Cheaper than the U.S. It was a harder surgery, with a longer recovery and more pain than with a teenager's supple cartilage, but possible, he said.

So, two years after my failed Ravitch in Toronto, I went to Berlin to get a Nuss. As predicted, it was difficult and painful with a lot of post-op pain medication. But ultimately it was successful. After eight weeks I was allowed to go to the gym and started working out. With a trainer and a rigorous workout regime and appropriate diet, I finally started to get the body I wanted. The body I had always dreamed of. I was normal. In fact, now, I was in considerably better shape than the typical person my age. People complimented me instead of laughing at me. I started dating a younger guy who I met at a party, and when he saw some shirtless selfies I had posted on Facebook, he was in love. Or what passes for love for a twenty-something. The relationship only lasted a few months before he moved away, but it started to make me feel better about myself.

Yet oddly enough, in my mind, I still did not feel fully normal. In my mind, I was still deformed. I could see the little imperfections, even if no one else said anything. The mind is harder to cure than the body. But I was in a better place.

Then two years later came time to take the bars out. This did not go as well. There was a post-op infection. The scars did not heal well. The German surgeon did not take as much care this time around. The scars are noticeably indented. So I am back to feeling abnormal again. Some obvious imperfections, abnormalities. To me, my chest looks like a chopped up mess. I go to the gym. I eat a healthy diet. My body wants to be skinny, but I try to gain weight. I had two years where I liked my body. Not anymore. Is that enough? Is that all I get? All I am allowed? It looks like it.

I still have low self-esteem. No enduring relationship with a significant other. I have dated a couple of guys since the last surgery. No one seems to notice or care about the flaws I see so clearly. If I start to date someone, I usually soon find fault with them, a reason to break up with them. After an initial thrill of excitement, I eventually become cold and distant, to reject them before they reject me. As they ultimately, obviously will. It hurts when people reject me. Abandon me. The truth is I still see myself as ugly, deformed, broken, inadequate. Not like everyone else. Unloved and unlovable Not *worthy* of love. All these things seem to come so easily to other people. "I hear the mermaids singing each to each. I do not think they will sing to me," wrote Eliot. I look in the mirror and honestly can't tell whether I am still ugly and deformed. In my mind, I am, but to others? Who knows?

One of my friends says I may have body dysmorphia. That I am addicted to my body, to working out. Is it an addiction to want to make myself better, normal? *Acceptable*? Will I ever be able to get there? Or is it impossible? An unfillable hole. The gym is full of people in pursuit of a perfect body. Some casual. Some serious. Some very serious. You see big guys with huge muscles that practically live at the gym. Follow special diets. Some do steroids. Are they all addicts? Or are they merely passionate about something. Where is the line between addiction and being passionate about, and intently focussed on achieving a goal? No one would ever achieve anything significant if they weren't passionate about it. Dysmorphia comes from the Greek for bad form. I think I once had body dysmorphia. But maybe now we need a new word: *dysorasi*—bad eyesight or bad vision. I can't seem to see myself the way others do. Who is that in the mirror? Do I see the same person others see?

If this is an obsession, perhaps I should take my friend's advice to forget about it and do something more "meaningful" with my life. Fix climate change? Solve the P versus NP problem? Help the poor?

But, I go to the gym. If three days a week is not enough, then maybe four. Or six? There is no end, no stopping. Do I, like Jay Gatsby, believe in the green light that recedes before me, but has so far eluded me? It doesn't matter. Tomorrow I will run faster and faster, stretch out my arms farther... I may never reach it, but I have to keep trying.

The great Oz would say the thing I was searching for was always there, inside me all along. If that's true, I'm not sure why it proves to be so elusive. I've tried clicking my heels three times. Nothing happens. I don't think it's so bad to want to look normal. To *be* normal. To have what other people have, what other people take for granted. But is it too late now? Maybe it was simply the case that I was always to be denied the ordinary life, the normalcy, the love that other people have. Or maybe it was there for the taking all along. Perhaps I will never know.

"The road to recovery is often hard to find, especially for men. Traditionally, men have not been taught to talk about their emotions and certainly to never show weakness."

## MALES AND BODY DYSMORPHIC DISORDER: FROM MEDIA IMAGES TO ANOREXIA AND BIGAREXIA

Naomi Perks

*"We live in an empire ruled not by kings or even presidents, but by images."* –Susan Bordo

And oh. how those images can be harmful.

In 1985, I was unhappy. Like many young girls, I struggled with puberty, hormonal changes, and a growing realization that a body type...*my* body type...which was once considered "cute," was now something much less endearing, veering towards "unhealthy" or, dare I say, "fat."

By the time I was fifteen, I realized I would never be a ballet dancer and, really, even acting was likely out of my reach; talent aside, it was my body. Not only was I short, but also I was "chubby." Diets? Oh, I tried those. Exercise? Yep. I flirted with bulimia. I took up smoking and drinking coffee to curb my appetite. I've tried nearly all the fad diets and tricks to lose weight and be "thin." As a teenager and young adult, I never found peace with my body. But I am female. It's not a surprise that at one point in my life I struggled with body-image issues and an eating disorder. According to the Canadian Mental Health Association, forty percent of nine-year-old girls have dieted to lose weight. When we think about eating and body-image disorders, we tend think of this being primarily a women's issue and not a men's issue. Yet although it's been suggested that "If eating disorders were a disease associated with men, rather than women, they would be taken more seriously, and treatment would be funded properly" (Penney, 2018), men *are* at risk.

REAL MEN DON'T HAVE BODY IMAGE ISSUES

But they do. It's estimated that men represent twenty-five percent of those affected by anorexia, and they are the most at risk because the disorder will often go untreated from being overlooked (National Eating Disorder Association). And perhaps this should not come as a surprise. Following the rise of the feminist movement, there have been cries of a crisis or destabilization of masculinity and what it means to be 'masculine.'

This destabilization can perhaps best be illustrated in the story about the transformation of Mr. Gwilym Pugh, an Englishman who transformed himself from a slightly overweight, yet successful young businessman into a GQ model because, even though at the age of twenty-one and having launched a successful insurance business, he still felt he "Needed to get [his] life in order and wanted to get healthy again" (Larbi, 2018). While I can't fault Mr. Pugh for wanting to get healthy, I was struck by the comment that he felt he needed to get his life in order. It doesn't seem that long ago that being a successful businessman was the measure of masculine success. However, it appears this is no longer an indicator of having one's life "in order." Instead, men must now, as women have for years, also fit into a socially defined concept of physical "beauty" in order to feel valued.

## HOW DID WE GET HERE?

In a nutshell, the same way we got here with women. The transformation of G.I. Joe is a great way to illustrate the changes in the representation of masculinity in popular culture over the last fifty years. In 1964, when G.I. Joe was first introduced, the action figure was muscular, but within the realm of something that was achievable by many men, albeit with a bit of dedication, hard work, and sweat at the gym. However, by "1994 [the] figure displays the sharply rippled abdominals of an advanced bodybuilder. The modern figure also displays distinct serratus muscles along his ribs — a feature readily seen in bodybuilders but less often visible in ordinary men" (Pope et al, 1999).

And it's not just G.I. Joe sporting washboard abs and biceps larger than Barbie's legs. Batman, Superman, Spiderman…they're all ripped, and this representation has found its way into kids' dress-up costumes. While some parents have shunned the "traditional" pink princess outfits for their little girls, it doesn't seem to be an issue to dress little boys in costumes that are decked out with fake abs, biceps, and pecs! As I questioned in a 2013 *Parents Canada* article (Perks, 2013), most parents wouldn't find it appropriate to dress their daughters in costumes sporting fake boobs and bums, so why is it okay to dress little boys in the equivalent? What I can't understand is why our society thinks that bombarding young boys with images of unnaturally muscular or super-thin and waif-like males, won't have a similar impact as what woman have endured for generations?

## WHAT DOES THAT MEAN FOR MEN?

Stephen has suffered from body-image issues since he was a young child. Growing up in a household with three brothers, two older and one younger, Stephen always felt like an outsider. His construction of masculinity was conflicted from a young age. He was more comfortable in the quiet of the kitchen than the "stinky, sweary, loud, and angry" culture of the garage, where his brothers and father hung out. He was the smart one, the "beautiful" one, with long ringlets; he often had a to tell people he was a boy, not a girl.

Born with Gastroschisis, a birth defect where the baby is born with their intestines outside the body, Stephen had what he refers to as a permanent "fat roll" which, along with being shorter than the other boys, created a feeling of being "less-than" and "not as cool." His nickname growing up was "pudge."

Finding solace in food, he would eat until it hurt and continue. Food gave him comfort, though it was short lived, and he "would feel bad after," both physically and emotionally. Stephen struggled in silence. No one took him aside and suggested he diet. No one signed him up for the reigning exercise class of the time. No one stopped to see if he was okay. No one asked why he turned to food. Because boys don't have body-image disorders. But they do, and they struggle with it differently than girls do.

Zachary Ihli, a young man in his early twenties, suffered from anorexia. He dropped out of school, lost friends, gave up on his dreams. His life had crumbled before him. Finally, the time came when he realized he needed help. Zachary admits that, "The toughest step is admitting that you need help. Males, especially have trouble with this."

Like others who suffer from anorexia, food became an obsession. Zachary says, "My mind was constantly worrying about what I ate and what I was going to eat." In addition to eating disorders, men's body image disorders are often combined with body dysmorphic disorder, most commonly manifested in the form of "bigorexia." According to the American Addiction Centers, "These men are fully focused on how many muscles they have, and how many muscles they see on the bodies around them. They may think of themselves as tiny, weak, or puny, even when they are able to pick up hundreds of pounds of weight. To them, their bodies will always be just a little bit too small." While the physiological manifestation of these disorders may be similar between the sexes, the experiences are often different, and this is especially so when it comes to recovery.

Five years ago, when I wrote "Are superheroes and video games affecting boys' body image?" for *Parents Canada*, there were few treatment centres available for men and boys. While there are more options available today, men are still the minority of patients. As Zachary recounts, this isolation can make recovery more difficult: "I felt so alone being one of the only males in my treatment center. A lot of the other patients weren't able to understand where I was coming from. This made it difficult to open up during groups and therapy sessions."

## RECOVERY?

If happiness is a journey, not a destination, then I would say so is recovery. When we classify eating and body dysmorphic disorders as an addiction, the notion of recovery is complicated. The road to recovery is often hard to find, especially for men. Traditionally, men have not been taught to talk about their emotions and certainly to never show weakness. Tyson Busby (2015), an eating-disorder survivor, questions whether things would have been better "If I had been able to express my feelings or seek help without feeling like my peers were judging me for something that wasn't my fault, my eating disorder might not have developed. I got scared and held it in."

281

Eating and body dysmorphic disorders are clinical disorders as defined by the *Diagnostic and Statistical Manual of Mental Disorders* (DSM). There are some that also define these disorders as an addiction. And why not? They do have similarities: People suffering from body-image disorders may turn to food or lack thereof to make them feel better; they are unable to control the frequency of their food intake, purging, starvation, or physical activity; they have a compulsion to control their food intake, the shape of their bodies; and they continue the destructive behaviour, despite the consequences.

In this sense, the addictions model can be applied to body-image disorders, but less so when it comes to recovery. One of the primary recovery models for addictions is abstinence, and we can all agree that, when it comes to food, abstinence is certainly not an option. In addition, being pre-occupied with food intake or gym activity is not necessarily always a negative attribute. It only becomes an issue if it starts affecting your ability to be a productive member of society.

Survivors of body-image disorders have a healthy and balanced definition of recovery, with a focus on "Self-acceptance, living without a constant focus on food, and by their overall quality of life." When we look at the lives they live, this definition is a common theme. Like survivors of other addictions, there is a constant reminder of the addiction, or disorder, and each day they don't relapse is a check mark in the win column.

Stephen, although fit and athletic these days, still has "body issues." He still struggles with not wanting to gain weight and jokes about having recently gained a few pounds. It's not all encompassing, but it's still there. Rather than obsessing about what he was eating, Zachary is putting that energy towards rebuilding his life. His excitement is palpable: "Recovery is awesome. My passions and dreams now seem real to me. They are tangible goals I am working towards, instead of far-off fantasies when I was struggling with Anorexia." Recovery then, is perhaps better seen as a state of being or a mindset rather than a task to complete.

In the same way, I, too, have come to terms with my body-image issues. Sure, I still weigh myself daily and may occasionally still skip the odd meal if I feel like I've recently over-indulged. But I also don't fret about it. I run an average of three half-marathons a year and ran a full marathon in 2016. I am happy with my fit and healthy body and have (finally) come to terms with the fact that I will never be front-cover *Vogue* thin. And I'm fine with that.

## REFERENCES

American Addiction Centers. "Body Dysmorphia among Male Teenagers and Men: What to Know." Retrieved from: https://americanaddictioncenters.org/male-eating-disorders/body-dysmorphia/

Bordo, S. (2000). "Beauty (Re)Discovers The Male Body." In P. Z. Brand (Ed.). *Beauty Matters*. Bloomington: Indiana University Press.

Canadian Mental Health Association, British Columbia Division. "Eating Disorders." Accessed March 13, 2018. https://cmha.bc.ca/documents/eating-disorders-3/

"Finding New Ways to Define and Improve Recovery." *Eating Disorders Review.com*, 29(1). Retrieved from: http://eatingdisordersreview.com/finding-new-ways-define-improve-recovery/

Ihli, Zachary. "Recovery is Possible: A Male's Perspective." National Eating Disorders Association (NEDA). Retrieved from: https://www.nationaleatingdisorders.org/node/3037

Larbi, Miranda. "Shy Insurance Salesman is proof that beards can absolutely transform a man." *Metro*. February 15, 2018. http://metro.co.uk/2018/02/15/shy-insurance-salesman-proof

National Eating Disorder Association. "Statistics and Research on Eating Disorders." Retrieved from: https://www.nationaleatingdisorders.org/statistics-research-eating-disorders

Penny, Laurie. (2018, March 2). "A Generation of Shrinking Girls." *The New Statesman*. Retrieved from: https://www.newstatesman.com/politics/feminism/2018/03/generation-shrinking-girls

Perks, Naomi. (2013, June 17). "Are superheroes and video games affecting boys' body image?" *Parents Canada*. Retrieved from: http://www.parentscanada.com/family-life/are-superheroes-and-video-games-affecting-boys-body-image

Pope, H., Olivardia, R., Gruber, A., and Borowiecki, J. (1999, July). "Evolving Ideals of Male Body Image as Seen Through Action Toys." *International Journal of Eating Disorders*, 26(1), 65-72. Retrieved from: https://onlinelibrary.wiley.com/doi/pdf/10.1002/%28SICI%291098-108X%28199907%2926%3A1%3C65%3A%3AAID-EAT8%3E3.0.CO%3B2-D

Male Body Image as Seen Through Action Toys." *International Journal of Eating Disorders*, 26(1), 65-72. Retrieved from: https://onlinelibrary.wiley.com/doi/pdf/10.1002/%28SICI%291098-108X%28199907%2926%3A1%3C65%3A%3AAID-EAT8%3E3.0.CO%3B2-D

Busby, Tyson. (2015, Sept.11). "*A Man's Perspective*." The Looking Glass Foundation. Retrieved from: https://www.lookingglassbc.com/2015/09/a-mans-perspective

"The trajectory of my career
is one where I have had the significant honour
of working with both those with eating
disorders and those with addictions."

# ADDICTIVE THINKING AND THE EATING DISORDER MINDSET: SIMILARITIES AND DISCREPANCIES

8

Emily Orr

Substance use disorders (SUDs) and eating disorders (EDs) are two commonly occurring mental-health issues with chronic relapsing-remitting patterns. Although these conditions do occur in isolation, it is very common for them to be concurrent with other mental-health issues, and in fact, these disorders often occur in the presence of one another. Up to fifty percent of individuals with EDs will also meet diagnostic criteria for a SUD at some point in their disease trajectory. Similarly, up to a third of those with diagnosed SUDs also report clinically significant eating pathology (Brewerton and Dennis, 2014, ix). Despite the frequency of co-occurrence of these two disorders, clinicians who treat one are rarely cross-trained to treat the other. There is very little literature that addresses the treatment of both of these disorders when they occur concurrently (one ofthe few exceptions is a relatively new textbook by Brewerton and Dennis, 2014).

The trajectory of my career is one where I have had the significant honour of working with both those with eating disorders and those with addictions. The minor rotation of my clinical psychology residency involved working in an adolescent inpatient eating-disorder program. Subsequent to completing my residency, I was hired to be the clinical psychologist of an outpatient eating-disorder clinic in Sydney, Nova Scotia, working with people of all ages. In August 2016, I left Sydney and was hired by Calian Group Ltd., to work as a contract psychologist for Canadian Forces Base (CFB) Halifax. In this role, I work with the Addictions Prevention and Treatment (APT) team. This team provides services to Canadian Armed Forces (CAF) members with diagnosed substance use and addiction disorders. I offer this brief biography as it is against this background that I wish to discuss the similarities and differences in the cognitions associated with these disorders.

Distorted thinking in the domain of SUDs and addictions is often referred to as Addictive Thinking. The identification and modification of addictive thinking is often seen as a core element of treatment for SUDs, both in formalized treatment settings and in self-help organizations such as Alcoholics Anonymous (AA) (e.g., "stinking thinking"). Within the field of EDs, however, effective treatment remains far less developed (i.e., as compared to SUDs). What is considered the "gold standard" is Cognitive Behavioural Therapy that is Enhanced (CBT-E) for Eating Disorders. A core component of CBT-E is challenging what is known as the "Eating Disorder Mindset." In CBT-E, mindsets are considered, "a frame of mind that has multiple effects" (Fairburn, 2008, p.119).

Challenging the eating-disorder mindset is considered a fundamental feature of CBT-E.

In addition to behaviour change, the treatment targets for both SUDs and EDs are similar. As Brewerton (2014) identified, "Cognitive and affective distortions, which are often a target of treatment for both SUD and ED, impair perceptions and compromise the ability to deal with feelings, resulting in significant self-deception" (p. 274). However, little has been written about the similarities in overlapping cognitions (and discrepancies in cognitions) between these two disorders. The purpose of this essay is to start a dialogue about cognitions between these two fields that have, for too long, operated in independent silos. It is hoped that the emphasis on similarities between these disorders will help reduce fears that some clinicians might have about someone who presents with a disorder from the "unknown" field or, perhaps more likely, someone who is concurrently afflicted.

There are two categories of cognitions that this essay will address: the cognitions associated with active symptoms and the cognitions that maintain the disorders in between active symptomatic episodes. Many of the examples offered below are derived from my clinical experiences and the anecdotes relayed to me by clients. It is with great appreciation for these clients that I share these examples as an educational tool.

## SYMPTOMS AND ASSOCIATED COGNITIONS

During treatment, individuals with EDs and SUDs become increasingly aware of the thoughts that are operating during their active symptoms (i.e., of which they were previously unaware). These types of thoughts are in the service of justifying and/or continuing the symptoms. In other words, these thoughts rationalize maintaining the current (disordered) behaviours.

One category of cognitions that manifests in both those with EDs and with SUDs are those pertaining to lack of control around the preferred substance. A classic line from Alcoholics Anonymous states, "One is too many; 1000 never enough." This line is intended to convey the lack of control associated with alcohol consumption for those who identify as alcoholics. The same principle of lack of control is often seen in eating disorders, particularly with respect to binging. Many of my clients have reported that, with best intentions, they have attempted to consume a binge "trigger" food, only to have lost control. They initially tried to "test" themselves with a serving size of their trigger food, only to have the urge for more. This urge for more was not sated until they had eaten, uncontrollably, all that was available to them. Many clients have reported that, after tasting the initial bites, they thought, "Screw it all," and proceeded to binge. That is, they have tasted their substance of choice, labelled their consumption as a "failure," and decided to indulge. Often this is accompanied by distorted cognitions like justification thoughts (e.g., "I'll reset and try again tomorrow") or self-deprecating thoughts (e.g., "I'm a screw up, so I might as well enjoy this"). If this sounds similar to working with those with addictions, it should. This process (i.e., a lack of control over use) is often described by those with SUDs and has become part of the DSM-5 diagnostic profile for most addictive disorders (e.g., "unsuccessful efforts to cut down or control alcohol use.") (DSM-5; p. 490). As such, it should not be surprising that there is overlap in the content and quality of thoughts pertaining to the loss of control over one's addiction or eating disorder.

Both EDs and SUDs are disorders that can involve a protracted craving period leading up to use. Sometimes with and sometimes without an identifiable trigger, clients can experience the growth of an urge to use over several days. For those with addictions, the craving is often for the drug and/or its effects. For those with eating disorders, the craving is either for the taste of the "trigger" food, or for the physiological effects associated with eating (or purging if this is part of their disorder). The thoughts described by clients from each community in relation to this process are incredibly similar: "I just want [to do it]"; "The urge won't go away until I [engage in the symptom]"; or "I can't [outlast the urge]."

Another process often seen with both EDs and SUDS is using symptoms to distract from emotional pain. Whether through chemically induced changes to the brain (e.g., the release of "feel good" neurotransmitters) or through distraction (e.g., needing to remain focused on compensatory exercise), symptoms can often be relied upon to soothe emotional or cognitive distress. It should also be not-ed that severe nutritional restriction (such as that seen in anorexia nervosa) is often described by clients and the literature as having an affective numbing quality. Those with anorexia have described that in the height of their illness they did not "feel," and that this is one of the experiences they were seeking. In this way, the symptoms of both EDs and SUDs can be used to actively avoid potentially distressing thoughts or feelings. In fact, individuals can become reliant upon their ED or SUD to cope with distress.

SELF-DECEPTION

In addition to the cognitions and thought processes that are active during symptoms, there are often thoughts that help to maintain EDs and SUDs in between episodes. These are thoughts that are often used to convince the self (or others) that there is no problem, or less of a problem, than is actually the case.

Perhaps unsurprisingly, rationalization and minimization are the bedrock of maintaining cognitive distortions in both addictions and eating disorders. Rationalizations take on many forms, but can (in both fields) include statements such as: "My symptoms aren't as bad as they used to be," "I can stop any time that I want," and "At least it's not the worst it could be" (e.g., heroin use or binge/purge anorexia). Minimization (another form of rationalization) is a particularly powerful form of maintaining both EDs and SUDs. Specifically, self-comparisons to well-documented cases (e.g., Karen Carpenter, Amy Winehouse, Frank from the show *Shameless*), can be used by the afflicted individual to justify why their disorder "isn't so bad," doesn't need treatment, and can, therefore, continue.

While addictions counsellors are unlikely to be surprised when clients use blaming statements/thoughts in the service of rationalizing their behaviours (e.g., "She makes me drink" or "I drink because my boss is a jerk"), these types of thoughts are also common in those with eating disorders. These thoughts, however, may be somewhat obscured. For example, those with a propensity to binge may covertly blame someone else in the household for access to their trigger foods. This might sound like, "Well my husband has to have his chips, so I can't get rid of those from the cupboard," or "There is always cake in the workplace. I can't avoid it because we are always celebrating." Another form of blaming in eating disorders is when symptoms are triggered by the perception (or misperception) of others' intentions regarding the client's physical appearance. Those with eating disorders are well-versed in misperceiving others' statements, glances, or other behaviours as sinister commentary about their appearance. Often, the misperception is used to justify further eating disordered symptoms. Specific examples include, "No one asked me to the dance. This means I am hideous. If I restrict more and lose weight, then someone will ask me out," or "She told me I looked good. I must be gaining weight or she would have said I looked great. I need to work out."

Another cognition that helps to maintain both addiction and eating disorders is when these individuals convince themselves that

"No one knows." While those with SUDs often make such claims when they initially present for treatment, they often present for treatment because their problem has become evident to others (e.g., they have gotten into trouble with family, friends, or work because of their substance use). Once clients with addictions become engaged in the treatment process, they quickly uncover the lies and self-deceptions that they would tell themselves about being "too cunning" for other people to know that they were using. Outpatient eating-disorder clinics, however, are often quite different. Unless someone is acutely underweight, experiencing health consequences secondary to their eating-disorder symptoms, or there has been an environmental "tell" (e.g., the shower drains have become backed up with vomitus; there are remnants of a binge in the morning), eating-disorder patients are often right; "No one knows" unless they disclose. This process is clear when we look at media responses to celebrity disclosures of an (non-anorexia/restrictive) eating disorder. For example, media outlets expressed great interest (perhaps disbelief) at the disclosure of both singer Demi Lovato's and actor Bam Margera's (from *Jackass*) respective cases of bulimic symptoms. Unfortunately, because people often do not know that someone with an (non-restrictive) eating disorder is struggling; often, these issues go both undiagnosed and untreated. In EDs, the thought "no one knows," is often accurate, sometimes with deadly consequences.

SUMMARY

This essay has outlined anecdotal accounts of similarities and discrepancies between cognitions that occur in substance use disorders (SUDs) and eating disorders (EDs). By no means was this essay intended to be a comprehensive overview of the thoughts of those with SUDs and EDs. Rather, it was intended to be a starting point; a means of opening the lines of communication between these two fields in relation to thoughts processes. As the co-morbidity between these two fields becomes increasingly appreciated, researchers will need to pay greater empirical attention to the similarities and discrepancies between their symptomatic expression (both diagnostic and anecdotal). This research will be necessary in the pursuit of evidence-based concurrent treatments.

REFERENCES

American Psychiatric Association. (2013). *Diagnostic and Statistical Manual of Mental Disorders* (5th ed.). Arlington, VA: American Psychiatric Publishing.

Brewerton, T.D. (2014). "Are eating disorders addictions?" In T.D. Brewerton and A. Dennis (Eds.), *Eating Disorders, Addictions and Substance Use Disorders: Research, Clinical and Treatment Perspectives*, 267-299. Heidelberg, Germany: Springer.

Brewerton, T.D., and Dennis, A. (Eds.). (2014). *Eating Disorders, Addictions and Substance Use Disorders: Research, Clinical and Treatment Perspectives*. Heidelberg, Germany: Springer.

Fairburn, C. G. (2008). *Cognitive Behavior Therapy and Eating Disorders*. New York, NY: Guildford Press.

# CONTEMPORARY DISCUSSION OF ADDICTIONS IN CANADA: STEPS FORWARD

"Locking up the most vulnerable and traumatized men in our communities
(and they are part of our community)
without intervening in a compassion-focused and specialized-treatment
oriented way is adding to the damage
and harm that already exists."

## IMPRISONED BROKEN MINDS: UNSEEN, UNHEARD, AND FORGOTTEN MEN

Davis Laine Smith

It is vital that a therapeutic mental-health and addiction, evidence-based approach be utilized in the care and rehabilitation of offenders at Nova Scotian provincial correctional facilities in a responsible and comprehensive manner. The relationship between *care* and *control* needs to shift to make space for treatment of addiction and mental-health issues. It has only been five years since social workers have been hired as part of the team at Nova Scotia correctional facilities and use a case-management approach. The *care* aspect within corrections is in its infancy. I have worked within the field of addiction for over twenty years and have worked with persons who have been incarcerated while struggling with both addiction and mental-health concerns. These same clients, due to their actions when unwell, broke the law and became incarcerated. Sadly, none received addiction or mental-health treatment while they were housed at these correctional facilities.

I had the privilege of working at a correctional facility in Nova Scotia. I want to acknowledge the amazing work currently being done by the staff. This essay is not meant as a criticism of the work currently being done, as their jobs are very challenging, especially with the fiscal constraints and limited resources afforded. Nationally, combined childhood physical and/or sexual abuse is more common among males (thirty-two percent) than females (twenty-seven percent) (Statistics Canada, 2017). Canadian men also account for the most significant proportion of admissions to adult correctional services (eighty-four percent versus sixteen percent), with Indigenous males accounting for twenty-six percent of male admissions to provincial and territorial sentenced custody (Reitano, 2017); Black offenders are also disproportionately represented. Many of these men have been diagnosed with ADHD, and have other concurrent mental-health disorders and addictions. This article is meant as a call to action for the shift in the structure of the system by which it is governed. I believe there needs to be a shift in thinking to include the missing therapeutic component for both offenders and the staff who control them. In order for this to become tabled as a priority, there needs to either be community-driven political pressure for it to be seen, or at the very least, therapeutic voices at the helm of the decision-making hierarchy. The Department of Justice needs to hold hands with Healthcare at this table and develop a long-term provincial strategy, a strategy that measures existing mental illness and addiction, and provides appropriate treatment while incarcerated through education, counselling, and drug therapy by a collaborative team of qualified specialists in the area of addiction and mental health.

We know that a large majority of crime for which adult offenders are incarcerated in Nova Scotia is drug and alcohol related (Kitchin, 2006). We also know that these same offenders report a strong interest in taking substance-abuse programming (Kitchin, 2006). There are currently substance-abuse educational programs being provided in group settings. However, education is not a substitute for therapeutic intervention. This education is provided by correctional officers who do a fantastic job, but they are educators, not therapeutic staff. At the very least, there needs to be therapeutic staff trained in mental-health and addiction assessment and treatment. Therapeutic staff would include Masters level clinical social workers and psychiatric nurses, who have face-to-face access to psychiatry in the diagnosis and treatment of offenders, and who would work collaboratively as a team in the delivery of quality healthcare.

This is currently not happening, and I am not sure why. I realize that resources may be seen as a barrier, but such a view is very short sighted, so short sighted that data on inmates is not clearly known. Currently, we are not collecting healthcare data about mental illness and addiction. Ignorance is bliss if turning a blind eye equates to less resources needing to be allocated in the aspect of care. If we do not know the extent of the issue, then perhaps we cannot be held liable for not instituting the necessary resources. Presently, we have a handful of bachelor level social workers to work with all adult offenders in the entire province. They are not governed or guided by mental-health or addictions mandate. We do not have community-outreach staff to bridge the gap between incarceration and community. No staff at this facility were trained in mental-health and addiction treatment. These are significant and important healthcare issues. Why are offenders receiving substandard healthcare? Is healthcare a right or a privilege? And who gets to decide this? Who is advocating that we do better?

I have had the privilege of working with many people who struggle with addiction and mental health. Their stories are laden with trauma, pain, neglect, loss, and hopelessness. Incarceration does not improve this reality. Not only is it inhumane to allow people to suffer unnecessarily with addiction and mental illness and not provide treatment, but it actually makes people worse. Locking up the most vulnerable and traumatized men in our communities (and they are part of our community) without intervening in a compassion-focused and specialized-treatment oriented way is adding to the damage and harm that already exists. Spiritual guidance, bachelor level social work, and "contracted-in" nursing is not enough. Bringing in volunteer community groups such as Alcoholics Anonymous is not enough.

According to one study in Nova Scotia, close to seventy-seven percent of adult provincial inmates are challenged by substance abuse, and 85.5 percent of surveyed offenders revealed that substances were related to their crimes (Kitchin, 2005). It seems we have a lot of work to do in shifting our thinking to prioritize resources that include quality care of this vulnerable population. Providing methadone maintenance for opiate addiction does not alone warrant a treatment plan; it merely manages withdrawal symptoms. Reacting to mental-health concerns only in crisis situations (such as suicide attempts), due to lack of resources in psychiatry and therapeutic staff, forces a constant state of triage and does not constitute adequate healthcare for mental-health concerns. It also breeds an unnecessary and unhealthy work environment for correctional officers in the management of behaviours that occur due to mental-health decline.

We need to be progressive in looking "upstream." With predictable recidivism rates among the incarcerated, we know there are opportunities to effect meaningful change and provide therapeutic interventions. We also need to continue this support and navigation up to six months post-discharge with community-outreach workers. Currently, they do not receive therapy despite being a willing captive audience with lots of free time for self-reflection and growth, and despite most of them being victims of horrific violence and traumas. As humans, when we know better, we do better.

We need to begin with capturing data. Are correctional facilities asking the right questions in their data collection? Are assessment tools and screens for depression, anxiety, PTSD, Bi-Polar, Psychosis, substance use, etc. being administered by therapeutic staff in a comprehensive and equitable way? We need to provide a voice for inmates to share their concerns; we need to hear their stories and ask them for input in making changes. We also need a community action group whose mandate it is to advocate and ensure that offenders are getting adequate care. We need to bridge relationships between care and control so they are not competing for resources in the current state of fiscal constraints. We also need to be protecting correctional officers from PTSD and the trauma they experience as a result of their jobs and have timely supports and protocols in place for treatment when incidents occur.

Currently, social workers who are working in the provincial facilities are not considered to be part of the healthcare team, which complicates using a collaborate approach to treatment and information sharing. Also, in the facility in which I worked, inmates had to be sent out to another facility to receive psychiatric assessment because they could not recruit a psychiatrist, and this care was only achieved in reaction to dire circumstances.

Even if you do not believe the inmates are worthy of the money it would take to provide therapeutic services, and you operate from a punitive and gleeful point of view that these individuals are "getting what they deserve," can you consider the actual costs of not doing it? Consider the costs of continuing to pay for their incarceration when they re-offend, the costs of community services because they cannot get real jobs to support themselves, the ongoing healthcare, legal, and rippling social costs of maintaining their criminogenic lifestyles. Inmates are part of our community and will be returning to our communities.

I believe most of those who are incarcerated can be helped, and from my own experience, they are crying to get access to decent and humane healthcare. There are many evidence-based approaches that are available, and it seems ignorance is the only real barrier. These interventions would make such a profound difference in the lives of the offenders and, consequently, the correctional officers. We need to stop undervaluing addiction treatment and mental-health care. We are just as obligated to treat a broken mind as we are a broken bone. We need to come together and break down the barriers between care and control. We need a collaborative and comprehensive approach to healthcare in our correctional facilities from the top decision makers to those working on the ground floor. We have to stop operating from a "We don't know what we don't know" approach, and include specialized therapeutic insight steeped in trauma and addiction, at the decision-making table in an equitable way. It is negligible and short sighted to think otherwise. People can heal, and there is hope. This is a call to action to start a movement pushing for policy that is equitable, necessary, and humane for some of our most vulnerable, damaged, and forgotten members of our society.

REFERENCES

Kitchin, H. (2006). "Addictions programming: A perspective on corrections in Nova Scotia," Correctional Services Canada. http://www.csc-scc.gc.ca/research/forum/e181/e181c-eng.shtml

Kitchin, H. (2005). "FORUM on corrections research." http://www.csc-scc.gc.ca/research/forum/e181/e181c-eng.shtml

Reitano, J. (2017, March 1). "Adult correctional statistics in Canada, 2015/2016," *Juristat*, 85-002-X. Retrieved from https://www150.statcan.gc.ca/n1/pub/85-002-x/2017001/article/14700-eng.htm

Statistics Canada. (2017, February 16), "Family violence in Canada: A statistical profile," *Juristat*, 85-002-X. Retrieved from https://www150.statcan.gc.ca/n1/daily-quotidien/170216/dq170216b-eng.htm

"For many women who have come
in conflict with the law, their use of drugs or
alcohol is directly or indirectly related to
their crimes, e.g., selling drugs to address
poverty; stealing money to pay for
drugs/alcohol."

# SUBSTANCE USE AND ABUSE: THE ROLE THAT DRUGS AND ALCOHOL PLAY IN THE LIVES OF CRIMINALIZED WOMEN

Jane E. Barker AND D. Scharie Tavcer

It is fair to say that we all cope with the stresses in our lives in different ways. By definition, any behaviour a person uses to deal with a difficult situation, or a stressor, can be thought of as a coping strategy. These strategies are not always functional though, and many people adopt avoidant coping strategies in order to distance themselves from the problem without trying to deal with it (Skinner, Edge, Altman, and Sherwood, 2003). This in turn can lead to additional problems.

To decide whether someone's coping strategy is considered

functional or dysfunctional is a value judgment. A coping strategy used by an individual in one situation could be viewed as dysfunctional while that same strategy used by another person could be considered functional. However, for women in conflict with the law, there is an additional complication to navigate, that of systemic oversight, which convolutes their attempts to cope with the stressors they face. While in Canada the percentage of women living in low income is similar to the percentage of men, there are more women than men who are single-parenting children and living in low income. Reported sexual victimization as a child is three times higher among women than men. And if she is Indigenous, she is 2.7 times more likely to experience violent victimization than non-Indigenous women, and Indigenous women are over-represented within the prison system (Indigenous women represent approximately forty percent of the female prison population compared to five percent of the total female population in Canada) (Mahony, 2011).

The term *criminalization* refers to the process or processes by which individuals are transformed and labelled as criminals. Our society surveils, disciplines, manages, corrects, and punishes women, and many support strategies have been used to address the impact of imprisonment and the systemic abuses against poor and racialized women. Women in conflict with the law do so through multiple forces that come together and influence a woman's decision(s) to resist her experiences and violate the law. And in doing so, she is then labelled a "criminal" and further disciplined and punished, which in turn can result in continued coping with drugs and alcohol. A women's pathway into and out of crime cannot be understood without understanding the ways in which violence, race, class, and gender intersect to shape and guide that pathway.

For women who find themselves incarcerated for the first time, there is a lot to learn, a lot to get used to, and a lot to cope with all at once. While criminalized women may use a variety of coping strategies in their lives, for the purpose of this essay, we will limit our exploration to the area of substance abuse (alcohol and drugs). Using alcohol is socially acceptable (and using some drugs may be too) and may start out as functional (e.g., smoking, using prescription medication, having drinks after work, etc.). It can also be a way of responding to or resisting the victimization she experiences (marginalization, domestic abuse, poverty, etc.). All of this, then, can turn dysfunctional over time. For example, having a glass of wine or a beer as a means to relax after a difficult day may seem like a reasonable way to cope, but overtime, and without addressing the difficult or distressing experience, it can lead to excess use or abuse, or both. For many women who have come in conflict with the law, their use of drugs or alcohol is directly or indirectly related to their crimes, e.g., selling drugs to address poverty; stealing money to pay for drugs/alcohol. The fact that a large percentage of criminalized women have had problems associated with drugs or alcohol is well documented in the research literature. A recent study of incarcerated women serving federal sentences found that seventy-six percent met the criteria, using lifetime estimates, for an alcohol or substance use disorder (Derkzen, Barker, McMillan, and Stewart, 2017). Further, approximately forty to fifty percent of crimes committed by a Canadian sample of male and female offenders were attributed to drug and/or alcohol use or abuse (Pernanen, Cousineau, Brochu, and Sun, 2002).

Most police-reported drug crimes (two out of every three) are related to cannabis, with cannabis possession accounting for more than half (Cotter, Greenland, and Karam, 2015). As is the case with other crimes, more men are charged with drug-related crimes than are women. In 2013, only eighteen percent of those charged with drug-related offences were female, and in 2016, only fourteen percent were female (Mahony, 2011). A larger proportion of women (twenty-nine percent) were charged with the import or export of drugs in 2013 than were charged with possession (seventeen percent) (Cotter et al., 2015). For women who are involved in the drug trade, they are found in low ranking, high-risk positions that often involve smuggling or transporting illicit substances (Cotter et al., 2015), a role that is likely heavily influenced by poverty and/or coping with their traumatic experiences. Incarcerated women with substance-abuse problems appear to have more social and psychological needs than those who don't abuse substances. These women tend to hold more antisocial attitudes and associate with people who share similar attitudes. They also have more employment problems, marital/family problems in addition to the substance abuse (Dowden and Blanchette, 1999). Additionally, they may experience more mental-health issues, are separated from their children, and have self-esteem and self-concept problems. Because of the number of life areas where substance-abusing women appear to experience challenges, it is very possible that their substance use might have served as resistance to or a coping mechanism for these other areas of life. Alternatively, the relationship could be multi-directional: substance abuse may serve as a coping strategy *and* be a source of stress for these other life areas, *or* substance abuse serves as a resistance strategy to gain power and control over the abuse *and* becomes a source of stress for other life areas.

Most criminalized women have themselves made a link between their criminal behaviour and their use/abuse of alcohol or drugs. Victimization in childhood, e.g., sexual, physical and/or emotional abuse, or as an adult, e.g., intimate partner violence and/or sexual assault, have all been identified as factors relating to women's involvement in substance use and other illegal behaviours, including crime. In an attempt to dull the pain associated with prior victimization, women may choose to use substances as a way of self-medicating, or as a way of increasing their perception of power or control, i.e., resistance to the abuse. Criminalized women may be no different from many others in society who choose to self-medicate to deal with stress, a coping strategy that may be considered functional; however, when the consequences of a criminalized woman abusing drugs or alcohol are evaluated, their behaviour may be viewed as considerably more dysfunctional given their situation, experiences, and challenges.

The Correctional Service of Canada has recognized that a high level of substance abuse problems exists for women offenders who are incarcerated federally, and that many incarcerated women are survivors of past trauma (Furlong and Grant, 2006). In an evaluation of an intensive therapeutic substance-abuse treatment program, the researchers found that the majority of women who participated indicated they had used substances as a way to cope with their traumatic experiences. After program completion, the women showed significant improvements in their ability to cope. In this same evaluation, the majority (ninety-one percent) of the women reported they were under the influence of drugs or alcohol when they committed their offence(s). And of those who had used drugs, almost three-quarters of the women believed their crime was directly related to their involvement with drugs, and nearly half of those who had used alcohol came to a similar conclusion.

If a criminalized woman decides to use substances for coping with a stressor(s) in her life, then she may face some disastrous consequences. If she is caught using substance while incarcerated she will be disciplined, managed, corrected, and punished in some manner: she may receive institutional charges, her security classification may be reviewed and increased, and she may be transferred to a more secure living unit or even another correctional facility. Once released from prison, if the conditions of her parole state that she must not use drugs or alcohol and she is caught violating that condition (through a positive urinalysis test), she risks having her parole suspended or revoked, which results in her returning to prison. And if she has children, they may return as wards of the state and into foster care. These consequences are serious and have long-lasting effects for her and her children, all as a result of a behaviour that many others in society engage in daily.

Once cannabis use is legal in Canada, women on parole will likely be faced with the same inequitable predicament as they now face with respect to alcohol. Although possessing and consuming cannabis (less than thirty grams or four plants) will be legal, as is alcohol, if their parole condition stipulates abstinence but they test positive for it, they could be sent back into custody. Even though cannabis possession and consumption will no longer be considered illegal for Canadians (under specific conditions), the ramifications of using cannabis for those on parole may be more serious.

We all must cope with life's stressors, and women who are criminalized are no different from anyone else in this regard. Some turn to strategies that have worked for them in the past, but become ultimately problematic for both now and in the long-term. Drinking and drug use have been identified as common coping strategies be they positive or negative, functional or dysfunctional, good or bad. But whichever coping strategy a woman in conflict with the law chooses, the role of alcohol or substance use and abuse in their criminalization is complex.

Portions of this essay have been previously published in Barker, J., and Tavcer, D.S. (2018). *Women and the Criminal Justice System: A Canadian Perspective*. Toronto, Canada: Emond Montgomery Publishing Limited.

REFERENCES

Cotter, A., Greenland, J., and Karam, M. (2015), "Drug-related offences in Canada, 2013." *Juristat*, 35(1). Retrieved from www.statcan.gc.ca/pub/85-002-x/2015001/article/14201-eng.pdf

Derkzen, D., Barker, J., McMillan, K., and Stewart, L. (2017). *Rates of current mental disorders among women offenders in custody in CSC* (Emerging Results in Research ERR-16-23). Ottawa: Research Branch, Correctional Service Canada. Retrieved from http://www.csc-scc.gc.ca/005/008/092/err-16-23-eng.pdf

Dowden, C., and Blanchette, K. (2002). *An investigation into the characteristics of substance-abusing women offenders: Risk, need and post-release outcome* (Research Report R-81). Ottawa: Correctional Service of Canada.

Furlong, A., and Grant, B.A. (2006). "Women offender substance abuse programming: Interim results." *Forum on Corrections Research*, 18(1), 45-48.

Mahony, T. H. (2011). "Women and the Criminal Justice System. in Canada: A component of Statistics Canada Catalogue no. 89-503-X." *Women in Canada: A Gender-based Statistical Report*. Retrieved from https://www.statcan.gc.ca/pub/89-503-x/2010001/article/11416-eng.htm

Pernanen, K., Cousineau, M., Brochu, S., and Sun, F. (2002). *"Proportions of crimes associated with alcohol and other drugs in Canada."* Canadian Center on Substance Abuse. Retrieved from http://www.ccsa.ca/Resource%20Library/ccsa-009105-2002.pdf

Skinner, E.A., Edge, K., Altman, J., and Sherwood, H. (2003). "Searching for the structure of coping: A review and critique of category systems for classifying ways of coping." *Psychological Bulletin*, 129(2), Doi: 10.1037/033-2909.129.2.216

"He went from what he described as a high-dose opioid prescription, managed by a physician, to street drugs while, at the same time, public-health officials were scrambling to stem a growing epidemic of illicit opioid deaths."

# PRESCRIPTION LIMITS DRIVING SOME PATIENTS TO STREET DRUGS

Amanda Preffer

In thirty years on powerful pain medication for Crohn's disease and colitis, John never overdosed. Not once. That changed in the spring of 2017.

"I have overdosed twice since my pain medication has been discontinued by having to resort to street drugs," said John.

He went from what he described as a high-dose opioid prescription, managed by a physician, to street drugs while, at the same time, public health officials were scrambling to stem a growing epidemic of illicit opioid deaths. John is not his real name. CBC agreed to protect his identity because of the stigma connected to illegal drug use when we first published his story in the fall of 2017. The street drug he resorted to is heroin. At the time of our interview, he'd been using for six months. He had replaced a prescription mostly covered through the Ontario Disability Support Program with an $80 a day heroin habit. He lost his home when self-medicating took priority over the rent.

Two weeks prior to our interview in the fall of 2017, he survived his second overdose. In that incident, he landed in hospital after paramedics administered several doses of the antidote naloxone to revive him. His story illustrates for some clinicians and patient advocates how drug policy has conspired to make a bad situation much worse for former prescription patients now using deadly street drugs to treat chronic pain.

HIGH-DOSE OPIOID PRESCRIPTIONS

John has been on prescription drugs to treat his condition since the age of twelve, he said. By his late teens, doctors began prescribing opioids. Thirty years later, he was being prescribed doses of opioids the US Centers for Disease Control and Prevention decided should never be prescribed to future patients ever again. It introduced new guidelines, which helped inform the revision of the Canadian standard set out in a new *2017 Canadian Guideline for Opioids for Chronic Non-Cancer Pain* (Busse, J., 2017).

What to do with the thousands of patients who already exceeded the new guidelines has been the object of new policy, but with little monitoring of outcomes.

COLLEGE CRACKING DOWN

By November 2016, the College of Physicians and Surgeons of Ontario (CPSO) had updated its own prescribing policy to reflect the changes in the federal guidelines. It also began investigating the prescription practices of doctors flagged through the province's narcotics monitoring system (see Ontario Ministry of Health and Long-Term Care).

The doctors under investigation had several patients on "extremely high doses" of prescription opioids, according to a CPSO spokesperson. One of the eighty-four doctors named by the college matches the name identified by John as his own physician. The investigations would have been getting underway while the doctor-patient relationship between John and his physician was falling apart. John said his doctor told him his prescription had been identified by the college as a problem.

"He told me I was his worst patient," said John. But he said his life was turned upside down by the efforts to taper him from his medication. "It was too fast," he said. "Even my hair hurt. I got very sick."

The physician did not respond to our efforts to contact him for this story.

EXPERTS RAISE ALARM

Experts in the field of pain management have been raising the alarm about the lack of alternative therapy to help those patients as their doses are diminished.

"We're causing a lot of harm to people who actually had never gone to the street for an opioid," said Dr. Hance Clarke, whose specialized pain clinic at the Toronto General Hospital has a unique and formal strategy for weaning patients off high-dose medication.

"We know we need to educate our doctors, and that will come. But we have hundreds of thousands of individuals out there, just in Ontario alone…that we need to get safely from where they are (high dose opioids over 90mg of morphine equivalents) to where they need to be."

Our investigation found neither the CPSO nor the province is monitoring the long-term impact on patients affected by the new guidelines, including the patients of the eighty-four doctors involved in the CPSO review.

## SCALE OF PROBLEM UNKNOWN

"So there has been an impact, I understand that," said Peter MacDougall, director of pain management at the Ottawa Hospital. "We've seen individual cases, but haven't understood the scale."

Certainly the authors of the new Canadian guidelines are becoming aware of the risks for existing high-dose patients. The main editor of the guidelines, Dr. Jason Busse, wrote as early as December 2016 about the "limitations" of the original CDC guidelines, writing in the *Canadian Medical Association Journal* about British Columbia's attempt to adopt the guidelines but found "some patients have sought illicit opioids in the wake of reduced prescribing by physicians. With the profusion of counterfeit fentanyl in Western Canada, the consequences could be fatal" (Busse, Juurlink, and Guyatt, 2016).

## LACK OF TREATMENT OPTIONS

The Canadian guidelines state, "Some patients are likely to experience significant increase in pain or decrease in function...tapering may be paused and potentially abandoned in such patients" (p. 71).

MacDougall describes how these patients build their tolerance to eventually very high doses of opioids, "But they are not out of control in their use, they're using them as prescribed."

"Patients who have trouble adapting to lower doses should be referred to a specialized pain clinic," said MacDougall, conceding, however, there are long delays getting that referral: "Therein lies the rub, of course."

The wait for such treatment for non-cancer patients can be months. A call to MacDougall's Ottawa clinic in the fall of 2017 confirmed it would take six months to one year to get a consultation. Pain experts have been warning about the lack of alternative therapies for high-dose patients even as public policy was being introduced.

"It's well known we have an underfunded system," said Dave Walton, a pain researcher and professor with the School of Physiotherapy at Western University. "It means there's little access to see psychiatrists, psychologists, or get into a treatment centre," he said.

Walton was also concerned about a decision by the Ontario government to delist high-strength painkillers available to patients covered by the province's benefit program (see "Ontario to stop paying…"). Walton worried it too could wind up "trading one public health concern for another."

The province's drug program covers some prescription drugs for patients sixty-five and over, as well as for those receiving support though Ontario Works and the Ontario Disability Support Program. The change, billed in a 2016 news release as a strategy to deal with the "growing problem of opioid addiction in Ontario," went into effect in January 2017, affecting 9,127 patients, John included.

John said he's taking things one day at a time. He had in fact been referred to a pain clinic by his former physician a year before he stopped seeing him. In the fall of 2017, he was still waiting for that appointment.

He was left, in the meantime, finding relief the only place he can—on the streets.

REFERENCES

Busse, J. (Ed.) (2017). "The 2017 Canadian Guidelines for Chronic Non-Cancer Pain." McMaster University: Hamilton. Retrieved from http://nationalpaincentre. mcmaster.ca/documents/Opioid%20GL%20for%20CMAJ_01may2017.pdf

Busse, J., Juurlink, D., and Guyatt, G. (2016). "Addressing the limitations of the CDC guideline for prescribing opioids for chronic noncancer pain." *Canadian Medical Association Journal* (CMAJ), 188, 17-18.

CPSO News Release. Retrieved from: CPSO News Release: http://www.cpso.on.ca/Whatsnew/News-Releases/2017/CPSO-Releases-Interim-Opioid-Strategy-Progress-Upd

Dowell D, Haegerich TM, Chou R.(2016). "CDC Guideline for Prescribing Opioids for Chronic Pain – United States." MMWR Recomm Rep 2016:65 (No RR-1): 1—49. Retrieved from http://dx.doi.org/10.15585/mmwr.rr6501e1

Ontario Ministry of Health and Long-Term Care. *Narcotics Monitoring System.* Retrieved from http://www.health.gov. on.ca/en/pro/programs/drugs/ons/monitoring_system.aspx

"Ontario to stop paying for higher-strength opioid painkillers." (2016, July 25). CBC News. Retrieved from http://www.cbc.ca/news/health/opioids-ontaio-delisting-1.3693862

Portions of this essay have been previously published in Pfeffer, A. (2017, Oct. 20). "*Prescription limits driving some patients to street drugs.*" CBC News. Retrieved from http://www. cbc.ca/news/canada/ottawa/prescription-limits-driving-patients-street-drugs-1.4351816

"Finally, there is an ever-increasing awareness of the presence, importance, and complexity of physician addiction amongst the profession itself."

# PHYSICIAN ADDICTION IN CANADA: STAKEHOLDERS, SERVICES, AND DETERMINANTS

Derek Puddester

Physicians are vulnerable to substance-use disorders like any other Canadian; however, there are a few things that may increase their risk. First, some forms of substance use, i.e., binge drinking of alcohol or excessive use of caffeine, are still normalized in training and learning culture, although this seems to be shifting. Second, physicians have unique access to substances that can be abused, i.e., narcotics, stimulants, benzodiazepines, from product samples, pills returned by patients, leftover medication from procedures and interventions, or sourced from fraudulent prescriptions. Third, some physicians struggle with the trauma, stress, and pressure of medical training and practice and develop co-morbid mental-health problems like depression, post-traumatic stress disorder, or anxiety. The stigma related to help-seeking behaviours may lead some physicians to self-diagnose and treat, both of which may lead to substance-use disorders. Finally, physicians, like their patients, may carry genetic risk, have been exposed to early life experiences that increase risk, or develop maladaptive coping strategies in response to life's stresses and challenges.

Health promotion and disease-prevention initiatives are increasingly common. Many medical schools emphasize compassionate self-care, peer support, and wellness during their orientation experiences. Courageous practitioners, or more senior classmates, often share their stories of illness, impairment, and recovery, immediately clearing the stage of stigma and normalizing help-seeking behaviour. Providers of academic, physical health, mental health, and advocacy services are introduced, often in the context of adding rocket fuel to the learner's efforts at success. Finally, many programs emphasize the importance of fitness, nutrition, stress management, and mindfulness, all efforts that shape the physician's perspective on health and wellness.

Schools also have committed to educational standards in addiction medicine. Discussions about the role of the physician in the prevention, intervention, assessment, treatment, and monitoring of substance-use disorders begin early in training and are often complimented by input from those directly affected, such as people in recovery, or family members or friends. Family medicine, psychiatry, and internal medicine all have streams that lead to enhanced competence in addictions, and more learners are interested in serving this population than ever before.

Universities also have committed to training in physician health. As much of this work is dedicated to helping prevent or treat impaired physicians, particular attention is paid to substance-use disorders in this population. The Royal College of Physicians and Surgeons of Canada has anchored physician health in their professional role competency, ensuring that all physicians receive training and evaluation in self and peer care, including substance-use disorders.

Finally, there is an ever-increasing awareness of the presence, importance, and complexity of physician addiction within the profession itself. Most medical organizations in Canada, i.e., student and resident associations, provincial and national associations, specialty societies, and medical education organizations, actively discuss physician health at their conferences, publish research in their journals, develop policies and action papers, and are engaged in disease prevention and health-promotion strategies for their members.

Medical regulation is also an area in which Canada has much expertise. Simply put, every province has a college that ensures physicians have the proper credentials to be granted the privilege of a medical license to practice. Further, colleges have a role to play in reasonably ascertaining a physician's fitness to practice, investigating concerns about fitness, and supporting and monitoring a physician's recovery to ensure the public is appropriately protected from potential harm.

Physicians also have a risk-management partner, known as the Canadian Medical Protective Association. CMPA services help physicians seek advice from peers with expertise in health law and medical ethics, and also access legal services in the event of a complaint or lawsuit. CMPA vigorously supports the health and well-being of its members, perhaps with the knowledge that healthy physicians practice better medicine.

Canada also pioneered the development of physician health programs, often stand-alone clinical services, that provide support to ill or impaired physicians. These programs are often funded by physicians themselves and managed either outside of, or in collaboration with, the public health system. Physician health programs have been traditionally focused on substance-use disorders and are increasingly supporting physicians with mental-health disorders and behavioural problems, i.e., disruptive behaviour, gambling disorder. These programs have provided exemplary service, but are not yet subject to accreditation, regulatory oversight, or regular review or audit. This situation has led programs to be questioned by the public (e.g., do they help protect the public from ill or impaired physicians?) and members of the profession (e.g., are they an extension of the regulator?).

There are times when an ill or impaired physician is affected by all of these systems. A resident who has diverted narcotics from the emergency room may choose to reach out to their family physician for treatment advice, or perhaps their senior resident or supervising faculty will compassionately facilitate a referral for assessment, while also removing them from duty. The college may receive a complaint from a concerned patient, or other member of the public, and reach out to the resident to investigate the situation, often directing the resident towards treatment and recovery services along the way. Physician health programs may meet with them in their community, offering understanding, expertise, and compassion as they identify specific issues and opportunities for intervention. Specialized treatment services, often addiction treatment programs for physicians and other healthcare providers, may become involved and engage the learner in active treatment and recovery. CMPA may represent the resident should they need advocacy as they prepare to return to work, or if the situation has been entirely misunderstood. Finally, colleges and/or physician health programs may monitor the resident's recovery for a few years—random testing, reports from family and treatment providers, updates from the workplace—all to ensure a healthy and full recovery.

Physicians suffering from advanced burnout may be at a higher risk of depression and addiction (Trollope-Kumar, 2012). In Canada, an estimated thirty-seven percent of the physician population may be experiencing burnout characterized by a high level of emotional exhaustion and/or depersonalization (Canadian Medical Association, 2017), while overall burnout rates may well exceed half of all practicing physicians (Shanafelt, Dyrbye, and West, 2017), and even be as high as sixty to seventy-five percent, according to some studies (see Wallace and Ghali, 2009). Intimidation, harassment, and bullying within the medical workplace (Vogel, 2017), coupled with disturbing numbers of physicians confronting verbal abuse, threats with weapons, property damage, and even physical attacks at the hands of their patients and patients' relatives—some of which result in serious or fatal injury (Mittal and Garg, 2017)—all contribute to physician ill-health. Increasingly, governments are accused of treating physicians with disdain (e.g., Ontario has not had a contract with its physicians for many years), disrespecting a mutually established business model for practice, and unilaterally increasing taxes and cutting physician compensation. Considering taxes and business expenses, many physicians work for many months to pay overhead expenses, and many contribute over fifty percent of their remaining income in taxes at the federal and provincial level. Most physicians have no workplace benefits (e.g., retirement plan, paid leave, health insurance), and access to specialized addiction services for health professionals is challenging, expensive, and stigmatizing. These issues are tough to continuously ignore, and are determinants of physician health that ought to be addressed in a reasonable and thoughtful process.

Canadian physicians have many stakeholders dedicated to promoting their health and well-being. Most importantly, we are seeing the profession becoming more aware of the need for work/life integration and compassionate self-care. By promoting the health of all healthcare professionals, Canadians will benefit even more from its publically funded healthcare system.

REFERENCES

Canadian Medical Association (CMA). (2017, October). *"Background to CMA Policy: Physician Health."* Ottawa: CMA. Retrieved from http://policybase.cma.ca/ dbtw-wpd/policypdf/BACKGROUND%20TO%20CMA% 20POLICY%20ON%20Physician%20Health.pdf

Mittal S. and Garg, S. (2017). "Violence against doctors—an overview." *Journal of Evolutionary Medicine*, 6(33): 2748-2751, DOI: 10.14260/Jemds/2017/592. Retrieved from: https://jemds.com/data_pdf/Shilekh--.pdf

Shanafelt, T., Dyrbye, L., and West, C. (2017). "Addressing Physician Burnout: The Way Forward." *Journal of the American Medical Association (JAMA)*, 317(9), 901-902. doi:10.1001/jama.2017.0076. Retrieved from: https:// internalmedicinefaculty.wustl.edu/wp-content/up-loads/2017/04/2017-JAMA-Shanafelt-editorial-physician-burnout.pdf

Trollope-Kumar, K. (2012). "Do we overdramatize family physician burnout? No." *Canadian Family Physician* (CFP), 58(7), 731-733. Retrieved from: https://www.ncbi.nlm. nih.gov/pmc/articles/PMC3395503/

Vogel, L. (2017, Sept. 11). "Doctors dissect medicine's bullying problem." *Canadian Medical Association Journal (CMAJ)*, 189(36), E1161-E1162. doi: 10.1503/cmaj.1095484. Retrieved from: http://www.cmaj.ca/content/189/36/E1161

Wallace, J., Lemaire, J., and Ghali, W. (2009). "Physician Wellness: a missing quality indicator." *The Lancet*, 374(9702), 1714-1721. Retrieved from: https://soci.ucalgary.ca/fypp/sites/soci.ucalgary.ca/files/unitis/publications/233-32917/physician%2Bwellness%2Bmissing%2Bquality%2Bindicator.pdf

"Leaving my home, all my belongings,
my dear cat, my husband, all seemed so
   overwhelming as I stood in the women's
shelter trying to figure out a plan
   on how to get my children back."

# PARENTS WITH ADDICTIONS SHOULD NOT HAVE TO BATTLE CHILDREN'S SERVICES, TOO

Melanie Carefoot

The online Oxford Dictionary defines addiction as, "*the fact or condition of being addicted to a particular substance or activity.*" What does this mean in real terms for individuals who are caring for children? How much is too much, and when does this present a safety concern? Addictions can take many forms, including religion, work, keeping fit, but these are rarely seen as being negative. In fact, people are often praised for their dedication to such pursuits without consideration being given to any potential negative impact on parenting. A call to children's services alleging substance misuse will be treated very differently from a call with concerns about a parent being a workaholic. An intake that references alcohol or drug use will likely move to an assessment or investigation. A children's services title alone can cause anxiety and stress to clients, especially those who believe that their lifestyle may be viewed as socially unacceptable for parents.

The two words, investigator and assessor, are interchangeable in some jurisdictions, but the connotations can be viewed very differently, with clients feeling that an investigator is searching for information to prove a hypothesis while an assessor is looking at all the facts to make an informed decision. An investigator may also view himself or herself differently from an assessor; although both roles require an inquiring mind and a wish to get to know the client and their circumstances, and how any issues might affect their function as a parent. Dependent on how the children's services workers view themselves and their role, investigators begin by looking for evidence: Are there garbage bags around the property full of recyclables? Is there a smell of marijuana? Are there any discoloured spoons in the sink? Is the client unkempt or dishevelled? If any of these things are noted, it may lead a worker, who sees their job as validating the intrusiveness of children's services intervention, to confirm their original suspicions that the parent is using substances. Information may be taken at face value without positive inquiry and critical thinking. An individual who identifies positively with their role as an assessor will ask questions about the environmental factors that may be concerning, without having preconceived ideas of possible explanations. If clients believe the intention is to gather information that will be used against them, then the guarded, defensive responses will hinder a collaborative working relationship between client and children's services worker.

Recent social-work philosophies, such as Signs of Safety and Solution Focused practice, encourage children's services to work in a way that allows parents to be truthful without the fear of hopelessness or powerlessness. A child's safety is still the primary focus, with the objective being that the parents rely on informed natural supports for assistance. This approach requires children's services workers to build trust with clients, take a less punitive approach, and to explore levels of risk, all of which are more time consuming and require more skill. The client often has to make a shift from minimizing any concerning behaviours to being open and honest, in the belief that there is a commitment to work together for family preservation. The difficulties faced by large government agencies in the standardization of service delivery are overwhelming. In each large urban area throughout Canada, there are multiple offices delivering child protection services, all of which are required to work within the provincial legislation in conjunction with the province's policies and procedures.

Safety planning for children being raised by a parent who is an addict is imperative, but that does not mean the safety plan has to begin at the most intrusive and punitive point. It is important for clients of children's services to understand on what criteria they are being judged. Professional interpretation of these mandates varies widely and is the result of subjective factors and personal biases. If a parent is labelled as an addict, what standardized scale is being used to confirm this opinion? Individual workers have different tolerance levels, which are influenced by personal experiences, their own interactions with people who use drugs or alcohol, religious beliefs, education, training, personal philosophy on harm reduction or abstinence, and community standards. Factors such as these will influence case planning but are not known to the client. File determination, case planning, and agency response to families where addiction is an issue should not be inconsistent and variable, which is often the case.

Parents who have their children apprehended by child-protection agencies as a result of addiction report feeling hopeless, afraid, and alone. As a social worker assisting clients in their interactions with children's services, I have been fortunate to be able to remain connected with four families who had children apprehended during the past five years as a result of their addictions. Court applications for permanent guardianship orders were filed for all six children before the parents sought support and assistance. All the children remain in the care of their parents after being returned to parental care by the courts and currently range in age from four to eleven. The parents all report similar emotional responses at the time their children were in care, with two of them sharing a small part of their experiences.

Laura is a teacher who is now in her mid-thirties. She started using cocaine after her first baby was born, and he was apprehended at eighteen months, just before Laura gave birth to her daughter. Feeling overwhelmed and attempting to get sober was made that much more difficult when her newborn was apprehended from the hospital and demands were made of her to leave her home and husband. She had told the workers that there were no beds at the shelter for a woman who didn't have her children with her; she was not a priority, but was told to figure it out. After numerous attempts, Laura was able to secure a room at the local shelter and reflects, "Leaving my home, all my belongings, my dear cat, my husband, all seemed so overwhelming as I stood in the women's shelter trying to figure out a plan on how to get my children back." Laura remembers that the child-protection case worker changed three times. Each new worker came with a new set of expectations, viewpoint, and trajectory, for when she would be able to resume care of her children. As Laura was on maternity leave, her feelings of being alone and unsupported were magnified. In addition to these feelings were emotions of anger and frustration when she found out that a friend with identical issues, in another quadrant of the city, had been supported by children's services and allowed to keep her children. Laura asks, "How can one agency in the same city have such different outcomes?" Although children's services knew she had no other commitments and all of her days were available, they did not offer daily visits with her newborn baby and toddler son. Some of the most frustrating times for Laura were trying to convince the case worker that she was sober and feeling doubted no matter how much she did, being connected to paid in-home support services, and developing a close relationship with the worker that abruptly ended with no closure, and the lack of planning when children's services decided to return the children. Laura states, "If I hadn't been on maternity leave for a further six months, I have no idea how I would have reconnected to my children successfully, and once the file closed, no one at children's services cared." Laura took it upon herself to stay connected to the foster parents who had cared for her babies, which was never a suggestion made by the agency. Laura understands the need for child protection when addiction impacts children, but she still has many questions about the process and the government's commitment to meeting the needs of families.

Laura's story is heard repeatedly by people who have both lost guardianship of their children or who have been successful in their endeavours to have them returned. Fighting addiction for Steve, a father of two in his early thirties, was easy, he says, compared to fighting children's services in an attempt to have his children returned to his care. Having attended a rehabilitation program to deal with his drug and alcohol abuse, he found that the worker always doubted his sobriety, despite negative, random screenings. Steve says, "She didn't like me. She was rude and dismissive, and at times she swore at me. I was too frightened to stand up for myself and knew that she had the power to have my children adopted, as she often threatened." Steve felt powerless, and without any knowledge of the legislation or policies, he was not able to attend meetings informed, and never knew what to expect. Steve was determined to stay clean and prove to the worker that he could care for his children, but admitted that staying sober when under so much pressure was a tremendous task: "All my parenting time was supervised, and I was constantly under a microscope. I didn't know that I was allowed to ask for a review if I didn't agree with a decision made by the worker." Steve found connecting with an advocate who understood the child-protection system invaluable, and it gave him the support he needed to challenge the system in an appropriate manner. "When they agreed to change the case worker, I felt that I might finally get a chance to have my successes acknowledged." After being in care for almost three years, Steve's children were returned to his care; he is enjoying raising an eight and ten year old as a single parent.

Parents who have addiction issues regularly face other parenting challenges, including mental-health concerns, domestic violence, poverty, and inadequate housing. Trauma is often identified in the client's history, but this becomes lost in the children's services response, with the agency concentrating on the presenting problem without addressing the root cause. As the opioid crisis in Canada continues to escalate, children's services casework practice needs to be reevaluated in an attempt to address child-protection concerns while supporting families, and allowing relationships to be sustained wherever possible between children and their parents.

REFERENCES

"What is Signs of Safety" (2018). Resolutions Consultancy Pty Ltd.: https://www.signsofsafety.net/what-is-sofs/

"Addiction." (2018). In *English, Oxford Living Dictionaries*. Oxford University Press: https://en.oxforddictionaries.com/definition/addiction

"The courts will have sympathy for their struggles; however, the more important consideration will always be the best interests of the children and their right to a secure and stable home."

# OPIOID ADDICTION: PROACTIVELY ADDRESSING LEGAL CONCERNS WITH CHILD CUSTODY

6

Lisa Gelman AND David Frenkel

The opioid epidemic has infiltrated cities throughout Canada and the U.S. at an alarming rate, and the help for the individuals that need treatment is not reaching them quickly enough. For those parents with addiction issues that are caring for children, the repercussions may be even more severe and requires a proactive legal approach.

Recent family-law jurisprudence has indicated that drug use can create a "destructive and dysfunctional lifestyle, one which is marked by criminality, chaos and conflict." In order to support the lifestyle, the user "lies, steals and manipulates." Compounding the problem is that family members may exacerbate the situation by failing to recognize or report the concerns relating to the drug use. By failing to report the signs of the drug use, the family member would be placing the individual drug user's interests above the interests of the child and thus failing to adequately protect the child (*Nova Scotia (Community Services) v. CML*, 2017 NSSC 204).

Furthermore, the drug user often has other mental-health disorders which impair his or her ability to parent and increases the risks of harm for children in the drug user's care. For example, when the doses increase to the level of being high and chronic, the associated risks may include lower alertness for safety-related activities such as driving, unpredictable and potentially toxic interactions with other substances, increased pain sensitivity, impulsivity, erratic behaviour, and alterations in mood and personality (*British Columbia (Director of Child, Family and Community Service) v. K. (D.L.)*, 2016 BCPC 29).

For lawyers, it is important to proactively address the warning signs when advising clients with children and who may require opioids for a pain condition and that also may be at risk for addiction. One option to consider would be for the client to sign an "Opioid Treatment Agreement" in which the client acknowledges that he or she is receiving opioid medication but also agrees to follow certain conditions. The following is an example of such an agreement (J. (R.), Re, 2017 SKQB 126):

1.  I will not seek opioid medications from another physician. Only Dr. WR will prescribe opioids for me.

2.  I will not take opioid medications in larger amounts or more frequently than is prescribed by Dr. WR.

3.  I will not give or sell my medication to anyone else, including family members; nor will I accept any opioid medication from anyone else.

4. I will not use over-the-counter opioid medication such as 222s and Tylenol No. 1.

5. I understand that if my prescription runs out early for any reasons (for example, if I lose the medication or take more than prescribed) Dr. WR will not prescribe extra medications for me, I will have to wait until the next prescription is due.

6. I will fill my prescription at one pharmacy of my choice; pharmacy name: Rexall.

7. I will store my medication in a secured location.

Often times, courts will impose random drug tests to the individuals abusing drugs that are in a custody dispute. These tests can include monthly hair tests and weekly urine tests. However, how a court assesses the results of the tests may not be so predictable. For example, in S. *(C.M.L.) v. S. (F.C.M.)*, [2016 BCSC 1298], Verhoeven, J. noted that the mother's failed drug tests must be viewed in proper context as there were a large body of drug test results during a span of three years. Although the mother's credibility was in suspect and there were positive results for cocaine in year one, the results for opiates such as Percocet and OxyContin were not found more than two years prior to trial. The significance of the distinction was likely that the opiates were the subject of the mother's addiction and not the cocaine.

In addition to signing an Opioid Treatment Agreement, lawyers advising clients may also want to consider the following additional plans of action:

1. Having the client stop using the drugs in their entirety for a significant period of time.

2. Ensuring the children are not exposed to any violence in the home or the community.

3. Not using certain drugs in the presence of children.

4. Using all prescription drugs strictly in accordance with the prescribed dosage.

5. Cooperating with the Children's Aid Society.

6. Permitting social workers to interview the children in privacy at home and/or in the community.

7. Signing consent forms requested by the society such as release of medical information of the parent and/or child.

8. Attending random drug testing.

9. Attending a methadone program.

10. Attending Narcotic Anonymous meetings.

11. Seeing a regular counsellor specific to his or her recovery from drug addiction.

The above list is not exhaustive, but does address a number of ways lawyers can assist individuals caught in the middle of their battle in court and the battle with their addictions. Unfortunately, by the time parents find themselves in the lawyer's office, their dependency for drugs has often already consumed them. Consequently, the opioid crisis needs to be curtailed in a significant way before more and more parents add a custodial fight to their internal one with drugs. The courts will have sympathy for their struggles; however, the more important consideration will always be the best interests of the children and their right to a secure and stable home.

This article originally appeared on *The Lawyer's Daily* website published by LexisNexis Canada Inc.

"Young adults are an important population to target early, not only because most mental-health issues develop in young adulthood, but also because this population often slips through the gaps of health care."

# ONE SIZE DOESN'T FIT ALL FOR ADDICTION TREATMENT

Kathryn Dalton

The term "one size fits all" is commonly used in clothing stores, and we all know that is never the case. Why? Because everyone is unique. It is fairly easy for the general public to understand that something as simple as a T-shirt is not going to fit everyone the same way, and to disregard something when it reads, "One size fits all." If it is easy to understand that everyone is different in terms of the way clothes fit, then why is addiction medicine taking a universal approach to treatment for something as complex as an individual's mental health?

In Canada, the economic burden of mental health and addiction is estimated at $51 billion annually, including healthcare costs, lost productivity, and reductions in quality of life (CAMH Facts and Statistics). Approximately seventy percent of adult mental illness originates in childhood, adolescence, and young adult years; young people between the ages of fifteen to twenty-four are more likely to experience mental-health and substance-use disorders than any other age group. Young adults are often caught in the web of addiction and concurrent mental-health disorders, which further complicates treatment. These young adults often experience higher rates of unemployment, school drop-out, crime, recurring hospital visits, and suicide, incurring greater costs through the use of multiple health, justice, and social services. Young adults are an important population to target early, not only because most mental-health issues develop in young adulthood, but also because this population often slips through the gaps of health care. Increasingly, researchers are recognizing this, and urging providers to accommodate young adults as a unique treatment population.

The World Health Organization (WHO) defines adolescents as those people between ten and nineteen years of age, youth as fifteen to twenty-four, and young people as ten to twenty-four, a term used by WHO and others to combine adolescents and youth. However, pediatric care is under eighteen, and adult care is eighteen and above. The transition from pediatric care to adult care happens overnight, causing individuals between the ages of eighteen and twenty-five to fall through the gaps of health care. Recently, this population is beginning to be regarded as its own distinct developmental group. Jeffrey Jensen Arnett is a psychologist who has been researching the eighteen- to twenty-five-year-old population for decades. He discovered that this population shares a perception of feeling "in between." They feel distinct from the youth (under eighteen) population because they no longer have the stable and structured routine of an adolescent in grade school and living in the parental home. Due to their unprecedented degree of freedom and identity exploration, they also feel distinct from adults twenty-six and over. Therefore, Arnett (2000) proposes that the best term to encompass this age group is *emerging adults*. There are a few distinct features that separate them from their younger and older counterparts: emerging adults are in a stage of life where they are unsure what they want out of life, work, and worldwide views. Most emerging adults do not consider themselves adults yet. Therefore, they are at an age of being "in between." This is also an age of instability marked by not being financially stable yet, and frequent moves in and out of the parental home, differing roommates, and also differing countries. This is also an age of daunting possibilities: emerging adults have the opportunity to set the groundwork for their future or to go down a path of risky life decisions.

These emerging adult life characteristics can also be explained by their stage of brain development, which does not finish until the mid-twenties (around twenty-five). This developmental stage is marked by an imbalance in fully matured brain regions. The imbalance is between the prefrontal cortex developing later, and the striatal regions developing earlier. The prefrontal cortex is responsible for cognitive control, specifically self-regulatory capacities, such as controlling impulses and emotions. In an adult with a fully developed prefrontal cortex, the brain works to evaluate choices and make the right decisions. This brain region evaluates a situation and helps us answer the question of, "Is this a good or bad decision?" and ultimately helps us to act accordingly in each situation. In comparison to an emerging adult with a developing prefrontal cortex, the brain doesn't quite work like this yet. Individuals without a fully developed prefrontal cortex show signs of increased risk taking and need for social approval. In addition, the brain regions sensitive to novelty and reward-seeking behaviour develops earlier than the prefrontal cortex (Casey and Jones, 2010). The imbalance between brain regions may partially explain the higher prevalence of drug and alcohol use among this population. When an emerging adult is in a situation with alcohol and other drugs, their brains may not be helping them weigh the risks of engaging in this activity, due to the lack of a fully developed prefrontal cortex. Furthermore, the striatal regions early development makes alcohol, other drugs, and peer influence more appealing. Thus, the stages of brain development amongst emerging adults help explain the high prevalence of alcohol and other drug use in this population. In addition, some of the brain regions involved in addiction are among the last to develop, which can also explain the fact that most treatment programs are dominated by the eighteen- to twenty-five-year-old population: they are engaging in high alcohol and other drug use, and also their stage of brain development plays a role in increased risk for the development of long-term substance-use disorders.

The risky and impulsive behaviour of an emerging adult may also explain the problems associated with remaining in treatment programs. It has been well established in research that eighteen to twenty-five year olds drop out of substance-abuse treatment much sooner than adults twenty-six and older (Schuman-Olivier et al, 2014). Staying in treatment is important because it is positively correlated to a range of outcomes including reduced drug use, a higher social functioning, and a higher quality of life (Feelemyer, Des Jarlais, Arasteh, Abdul-Quader and Hagan, 2013). Unfortunately, emerging adults frequently fall victim to a "one size fits all" approach in addiction treatment. This approach ignores recent insights into the developmental and life differences of emerging adults in comparison to their older and younger counterparts. Standard in-patient treatment is typically a "cookie cutter" approach where each patient follows the exact same schedule of varying behavioural therapies and also pharmacotherapies, if needed. Patients' needs may not be individualized, and even worse, someone who is eighteen may be treated the same way as someone who is in his or her sixties. We all know this isn't how life works, regardless of a medical issue. People aged eighteen to twenty-five are going to be living a life quite different from those in their forties, fifties, sixties, etc.

Current research on emerging adults is limited with substance-abuse disorders (SUDs), with much of the research evaluating age differences in treatment retention; there is less research examining ways to improve treatment for this population. Indeed, the goal of increasing long-term sobriety should be two-fold: to gain a better understanding of which treatment interventions work best for this population and to better design the most effective treatment options with enhanced long-term outcomes, for this particularly vulnerable population.

REFERENCES

Arnett, J. J. (2000). "Emerging adulthood: A theory of development from the late teens through the twenties." *American Psychologist*, 55(5), 469-480. http://dx.doi.org/10.1037/0003-066X.55.5.469

"CAMH: Mental Illness and Addictions: Facts and Statistics." Camh.ca. 2017 from http://www.camh.ca/en/hospital/about_camh/newsroom/for_reporters/Pages/addictionmentalhealthstatistics.aspx

Casey, B., and Jones, R. (2010). "Neurobiology of the Adolescent Brain and Behavior." *Journal of The American Academy of Child and Adolescent Psychiatry*, 49(12), 1189-1201. http://dx.doi.org/10.1097/00004583-201012000-00005

Feelemyer, J., Jarlais, D. D., Arasteh, K., Abdul-Quader, A. S., and Hagan, H. (2014). "Retention of participants in medication-assisted programs in low- and middle-income countries: an international systematic review." *Addiction*, 109(1), 20–32. http://doi.org/10.1111/add.12303

Schuman-Olivier, Z., Weiss, R. D., Hoeppner, B. B., Borodovsky, J., and Albanese, M. J. (2014). "Emerging adult age status predicts poor buprenorphine treatment retention." *Journal of Substance Abuse Treatment*, 47(3), 202–212. http://doi.org/10.1016/j.jsat.2014.04.006

"We propose that evolutionary motives
may offer insight into people's modern
    social-media behaviour, including addiction
and overuse of social-media technology;
        this may help to better explain why some
individuals are compelled to engage
in acts like taking 200 selfies per day."

# AN EVOLUTIONARY
# PERSPECTIVE ON SOCIAL-
# MEDIA ADDICTION

Steven Arnocky, Shafik Sunderani AND
Darren W. Campbell

Human beings are an extraordinarily social species. The need to belong, or feel connected and accepted by others, is one of the fundamental motives underlying human behaviour (Baumeister and Leary, 1995). From an evolutionary perspective, this complex system of interconnectedness was necessary for maintaining social coalitions once crucial to basic survival. With the emergence and spread of online communication and social-media platforms available today, people are developing and monitoring social connections in a manner that is very different from our ancestral past. We propose that evolutionary motives may offer insight into people's modern social-media behaviour, including addiction and overuse of social-media technology; this may help to better explain why some individuals are compelled to engage in acts like taking 200 selfies per day:

> Danny Bowman, 19, spent ten hours a day taking up to 200 'selfies' of himself on his phone. "I was constantly in search of taking the perfect selfie and when I realized I couldn't I wanted to die, ... I lost my friends, my education, my health and almost my life... People don't realise when they post a picture of themselves on Facebook or Twitter it can so quickly spiral out of control. It becomes a mission to get approval and it can destroy anyone. It's a real problem like drugs, alcohol or gambling. I don't want anyone to go through what I've been through."
>
> – Danny Bowman (quoted in Aldridge and Hardin, 2014, the *Daily Mirror*)

Indeed, there are many immediate reasons why people use social media: a) generating social connections; b) managing one's online identity; c) forming new relationships (online dating); d) staying aware; e) remaining socially connected (i.e., fear of missing out); f) intellectual stimulation (e.g., discussion groups); g) simple pleasures (e.g., humour); h) erotic pleasures; i) video gaming; j) stalking; and k) online aggression (See Alt, 2015; Meshi, Tamir, and Heekeren, 2015).

Considering the multiple reasons why people utilize social media on a regular basis, it is not surprising that it can also lead to overuse and addiction. People who use social media excessively can display aspects of addiction such as "neglect of personal life, mental preoccupation, escapism, mood modifying experiences, and concealing the addictive behaviour" (Kuss and Griffiths, 2011,

p. 3529). Social-media addiction is proposed to develop when people rely on social networking to relieve stress, loneliness, or depression (Xu and Tan, 2012). Social networking accounts for twenty-eight percent of all media time spent online. Users now spend over thirty percent of their online time (roughly two hours daily) using social-media platforms such as Facebook, Twitter, and Instagram (Global Web Index, 2017). Some researchers estimate that nearly ten percent of young adults engage in disordered online social networking (Hormes, Kearns, and Timko, 2014). Other researchers propose new addiction disorders, such as "smartphone addiction" and "internet addiction" based on clear functional impairments associated with their misuse (e.g., Lin et al., 2016; Pies, 2009).

Current knowledge about the causes of social-media use or addiction is very limited. Below we offer a sampling of evolutionary explanations for social-media use. Specifically, we propose that the appeal of social media, including its addictive properties, is at least partially rooted in the adaptive value of social connectedness and reward-based neurophysiological responses associated with social connectedness within our species.

THE EVOLUTION OF THE SOCIAL BRAIN

Evolutionary processes have favoured human social relations, including socially monogamous mating, bi-parental care of offspring, and alliances with extended family and non-kin community members. These interpersonal relations require sophisticated and dynamic social thinking, planning, and interaction. Neuroimaging research has identified several brain systems that play a central role in these interpersonal processes. Below we discuss these brain systems, point out their relevance to evolutionarily motivated social behaviours, and propose how these systems support the development of addictive versions of these social behaviours in person and online.

Three brain systems are central to social thinking, planning, and interacting. The mentalizing network is crucial for understanding the goals and intentions of others (Molenberghs, Johnson, Henry, and Mattingley, 2016). The limbic brain network is central to emotional responses associated with social encounters (Bressler, and Menon, 2010). A third, somewhat overlapping neural network is the brain's reward circuit, which is more directly linked to the experience of pleasure. Each of these brain systems likely underlies the social and emotional responses necessary to the pursuit of mating opportunities, competing for resources, or forming alliances.

With the current focus on social-media addiction, we will focus our discussion primarily on the brain's reward circuit. Mammals have evolved reward circuitry fundamentally tied to social interaction. This neural circuitry typically fires in response to events that provide external rewards, enhance survival, or support reproduction, such as increased social status, access to nutritious foods, and opportunities for sex. This pleasure response in the brain encourages people to engage in those actions which promoted such events again in the future.

However, this reward circuitry is also susceptible to addictive processes. Addiction is a condition that results when a person ingests a substance (e.g., drugs) or engages in an activity (e.g., gambling) which initially is pleasurable, but then becomes compulsive and interferes with ordinary aspects of life. Specific addictions also undermine people's enjoyment of naturally pleasurable events which emerged through natural and sexual selection. This undermining process is referred to as the "high-jacking of the reward circuit" because natural pleasures no longer activate people's reward circuit sufficiently.

People can become addicted to socially focused activities as well as consumption-related activities. During the addiction process, however, people will begin to engage in extreme levels or versions of the social activities to generate stronger feelings of reward and greater responses in their reward circuit. The link between social interactions and the reward is evident in both animal and human studies. Mice, genetically engineered to produce more dopamine in the reward circuit, show a marked increase in social interaction, whereas mice with a decrease in dopamine production in this area show decreased social interactions (Gunaydin et al., 2014). In humans, a similar increase in reward-circuitry activity is associated with increases in social reputation perceptions (receiving positive social feedback) (Meshi, Morawetz, and Heekeren, 2013).

Today, people can monitor and maintain their social reputations through social-media outlets such as Facebook, Instagram, and Twitter. These sites allow one to cultivate a particular social image, and to compare themselves to others. Evidence shows that reward circuitry (in this case, the left nucleus accumbens) becomes activated when people's social reputation increases, but they show no such activation when they see other people's social reputation rise (Meshi et al., 2013). Furthermore, this neural activity predicts people's Facebook use (Meshi et al., 2013).

The reward system also is associated with social-media addiction. Turel and colleagues (2014) had participants complete a Facebook addiction questionnaire, consisting of behaviours surrounding withdrawal, salience, relapse, loss of control, and conflict. People who scored higher on Facebook addiction tendencies showed more activation in the amygdala-striatal region when exposed to Facebook images. Together, these early findings suggest that social-media use activates the brain's reward system. A reward system that evolved ancestrally to promote activities that increased survival and reproductive fitness (i.e., the likelihood of passing one's genes on to the next generation). This begs the question: What evolutionarily adaptive goals might contemporary social-media use satisfy?

ADAPTIVE FACTORS POTENTIALLY UNDERLYING SOCIAL MEDIA USE

Below we highlight an initial list of adaptive challenges which may be relevant to contemporary social-media use. This list is not meant to be exhaustive or invariable, but rather to act as a starting point for further discussion on the potential evolutionary factors underlying the manner in which we use social media.

## 1. Signalling

*Altruism*. Altruism is any act that benefits another person at a cost to the altruist. Within some hunter-gatherer societies, successful hunters who altruistically share meat with others receive greater reproductive access to females. In contemporary Western society, individuals who engage in altruistic acts toward unrelated others report more mating success (see Arnocky et al., 2017 for review). Some researchers have suggested that altruism directed toward unrelated others functions as a signal of personal qualities that are otherwise difficult to observe, but that are desirable in an ally or mate. For example, donating money to a charity can signal to others that one is kind, cares for others, and has enough resources that they can afford to give some away without any expectation of reciprocity. To the extent that modern social-media altruism is widely observable to the other members of one's social network, engaging in online acts of kindness may bolster one's value as a friend or mate. Many social-media charitable campaigns have been highly successful. For example, the Facebook organ-donor initiative allows users to officially register as an organ donor as part of their online profile. This viral initiative resulted in nearly 40,000 new registrations over a two-week period. Charity campaigns such as the ice-bucket challenge, whereby participants dump a bucket of ice water over their heads in support of Amyotrophic Lateral Sclerosis (i.e., Lou Gehrig's disease), was once widely popular, garnering over twenty-eight million participant videos that were viewed over ten billion times. Such acts performed over social media allow users to signal their altruistic proclivity. However, social media has simultaneously enabled individuals to feign altruism without actually donating time, effort, or resources, and yet still receive altruism-related social-status benefits. The ice-bucket challenge is an example of feigned altruism. According to some reports, the majority of the participants (nine out of ten) did not actually donate any money to the charitable cause of ALS (Maguire, 2014). This hyper-proliferation of "non-costly signals" (i.e., a low effort; high reward ratio) is much easier since the advent of social media in which a person can benefit from appearing altruistic even with minimal investment of their time, effort, and money.

*Sex differences in self-presentation.* Women and men also differ in their social-media self-presentation tendencies in ways that conform to evolved sex difference in fitness-promoting characteristics. For instance, Buss (1989) found that in each of thirty-seven cultures studied, men more than women desired partners who were youthful and physically attractive (i.e., women's mate-value relies more upon their physical attractiveness relative to men). This may explain why teenage girls are more likely than boys to post overtly seductive photos of themselves (Sorokowski et al., 2016). Buss (1989) also reported that characteristics considered "attractive" are remarkably consistent across cultures, ostensibly because these features signal underlying genetic quality, overt health, or fertility. Some researchers suggest that such very conventional beauty standards and aesthetics draw women to sites like Instagram (see Seligson, 2016). Given the technological advancements in personal photography, image manipulation is much easier today. From an evolutionary perspective, we predict that women are more likely to manipulate their personal images to conform more closely to conventional beauty standards than men. However, future research is needed to test this hypothesis. Buss (1989) also reported that men's mate-value, in contrast to women's, relies more upon resources and status. Consistent with this finding, men were more likely than women to have posted a photo which implied that they were staying, eating, or visiting somewhere more expensive than their reality (as reported in Renzulli, 2017). In summary, these sex differences in online behaviour are consistent with efforts at demonstrating mate-value within the context of intersexual selection (dating and mating competition).

## 2. Monitoring of Intrasexual Rivals

*Social comparison.* Social-media use extends beyond intersexual selection behaviours. People are able to cultivate particular social images. They can highlight select social group memberships and showcase certain personal interests, values, or traits. However, people often evaluate themselves and their self-worth in how they compare to others. Social-media sites support these social comparisons. Research has demonstrated that when women evaluate images of other women on Facebook and Instagram as more physically attractive than themselves (i.e., an upward social comparison), they are more likely to report a negative mood and engage in dieting and exercise in an attempt to personally match these physical ideals (Fardouly, Pinkus, and Vartanian, 2017). Social comparison has been proposed by some evolutionary psychologists as a cognitive mechanism that evolved to allow for individuals to gain important information about where they stand on important mate-value characteristics (Arnocky et al., 2012). Frequent social comparisons can motivate specific goals and behaviours aimed at competing or "keeping up" with others. This perpetual process of self-refinement approximates some of the addiction tendencies described earlier.

### 3. Relational Maintenance

*Mating relationships.* Social media not only allows people to monitor and manipulate their own social persona, it also supports the monitoring of other people's social persona and affiliations. From a mating perspective, regular surveillance of a partner's online behaviours may serve to circumvent partner infidelity or a same-sex rival's attempts at poaching (i.e., stealing) one's partner. Ancestrally, losing a reproductive mate is very costly resulting in lost reproductive and survival related resources. Similarly, partner infidelity may result in cuckoldry and relationship termination. Thus, from a mating perspective, frequent monitoring of a partner's online actions (i.e., recent updates; newly added friends) may not simply reflect "pathological," "abnormal," and/or "dysfunctional" online behaviours. Instead, this online vigilance represents a tactic for ensuring and preserving the self from emotional harm and loss of reproductive resources.

Excessive online social-media vigilance may lead to psychological problems and relationship problems. Muise et al. (2009) surveyed undergraduate students asking them questions such as "How likely are you to become jealous after your partner has added an unknown member of the opposite sex?" and "How likely are you to monitor your partner's activities on Facebook?" Results indicated that social media may trigger "potentially jealousy-provoking information" (p. 443). A recent review reported that, in about thirty percent of marriages, one partner secretly read the e-mails or text messages of their partner (Utz and Beukeboom, 2011). Social signals, including social-media postings, are often ambiguous (e.g., friendly or flirty) in their meaning. In an attempt to determine whether their lover's online interpersonal communications with others are benign or threatening, the weary and distrusting partner within the romantic dyad may ramp up surveillance of their lover's social-media connections and communications (Muise et al., 2009)—often for good reason. This oversensitivity to a romantic partner's social-media behaviour as potentially threatening simulates the mental preoccupation and compulsive behaviours found in addiction.

*Non-mating alliances.* Use of social-networking sites can strengthen relationships with friends and acquaintances. For instance, previous research (as reviewed in Utz and Beukeboom, 2011) found that SNS are useful for generating *bridging capital* (i.e., maintaining weaker ties with acquaintances) and *bonding capital* (i.e., maintaining strong ties with close friends). In primates, including macaques, chimpanzees, and human hunter-gatherers, evidence suggests that social ties, including those of an indirect nature, can predict reproductive success (e.g., Page et al., 2017).

## 4. Intrasexual Competition

Interpersonal aggression, as one form of intrasexual (i.e., same-sex) competition, may have evolved to help our ancestors solve problems related to status generation, resource access, and mate acquisition (e.g., Arnocky and Vaillancourt, 2017). Beyond the prototypical examples of overt aggression, such as a physical fight between two men, indirect (i.e., surreptitious) forms of aggression, such as gossip, rumor spreading, and social exclusion, are more common and can be effective at inflicting harm to one's competitors while improving one's own access to mates (Arnocky and Vaillancourt, 2012).

Aggression is commonplace on social-media sites. Today, seventeen percent of Canadians between the ages of fifteen to twenty-nine report having been victims of online aggression such as cyberstalking or cyberbullying (Hango, December 2016). In one survey of teens, more than half reported witnessing cyberbullying on social media; twenty-five percent of teens reported a later face-to-face confrontation with their cyberbully (Cox, 2014).

Cyber-aggression seems to conform to established sex differences in aggression. Females have evolved to employ less physically risky aggression tactics, in part, to remain alive for offspring survival (see Arnocky and Vaillancourt, 2017 for review). For example, females are more likely than males to post gossip on the Internet to hurt other people they might know. In contrast, males are more likely to attack others directly with violent threats and homophobic insults (Marcum et al., 2012).

Given that human reproduction does not provide males with paternity certainty, males have evolved to prefer mates who are sexually faithful. Women who are sexually unfaithful and/ or promiscuous are susceptible to increased criticism and derision (see Buss and Dedden, 1990). Perhaps, unsurprisingly in the context of the cyber-world, woman more than men report online aggression which is largely focused on their sexual activities too. Marcum et al., (2012) provided a relevant example: "A few guys posted a naked picture of a girl I know on Facebook for everybody to see and called her a slut." Conversely, males are more likely to be victimized via attacks of their skills and talents.

Interestingly, social-media use alongside romantic motivations and social comparisons (described earlier) have been identified as important predictors of online aggression (Young, Len-Ross, and Young, 2017). Moreover, recent research has linked Internet addiction to a greater propensity for aggression (Ko et al., 2009). Future studies will be needed to determine whether Internet addiction has any causal influence upon either online or offline aggression.

## Conclusion

Researchers have proposed that various online activities, including but not limited to social-media use, can be pathological. Yet little research has examined the underlying etiology of this proposed clinical disorder. Among the limited research available, the focus has been on proximate social-cognitive and reward-based mechanisms rather than evolutionarily based mechanisms. Neurophysiology is implicated insofar as production of pleasure-related neurotransmitters (e.g., dopamine) coincides with resolving socially and sexually relevant adaptive challenges. However, an understanding of social-media addiction is incomplete without considering the evolutionary mechanisms underpinning our need for social affiliation rooted in our ancestry. By taking into account evolutionary processes, both researchers and clinicians alike could be better equipped to assess, diagnose, and provide treatment for people afflicted with social-media addiction.

## REFERENCES

Aldridge, G., and Hardin, K. (2014). "Selfie addict took two hundred a day—and tried to kill himself when he couldn't take perfect photo." *Daily Mirror*. Retrieved from: https://www.mirror.co.uk/news/real-life-stories/selfie-addict-took-two-hundred-3273819

Alt, D. (2015). "College students' academic motivation, media engagement and fear of missing out." *Computers in Human Behavior*, 49, 111-119. doi:10.1016/j.chb.2015.02.057

Arnocky, S., Piché, T., Albert, G., Ouellette, D., and Barclay, P. (2017). "Altruism predicts mating success in humans." *British Journal of Psychology*, 108(2), 416–435. doi: 10.1111/bjop.12208

Arnocky, S., Sunderani, S., Miller, J., and Vaillancourt, T. (2012). "Jealousy mediates the relationship between attractiveness comparison and females' indirect aggression." *Personal Relationships*, 19 (2), 290–303. doi:10.1111/j.1475-6811.2011.01362.x

Arnocky, S., and Vaillancourt, T. (2017). "Sexual competition among women: A review of the theory and supporting evidence." In: M.L. Fisher (Ed.), *The Oxford Handbook of Women and Competition* (pp. 25–39). New York: Oxford University Press. ISBN:978-1-63463-131-0. doi: 10.1093/oxfordhb/9780199376377.013.3

Arnocky, S., and Vaillancourt, T. (2012). "A multi-informant longitudinal study on the relationship between aggression, peer victimization, and adolescent dating status." *Evolutionary Psychology*, 10(2), 253–270.

Baumeister, R. F., and Leary, M. R. (1995). "The need to belong: Desire for interpersonal attachments as a fundamental human motivation." *Psychological Bulletin*, 117(3), 497-529. doi:10.1037/0033-2909.117.3.497

Bressler, S. L., and Menon, V. (2010). "Large-scale brain networks in cognition: emerging methods and principles." *Trends in cognitive sciences*, 14(6), 277-290.

Buss, D. M. (1989). "Sex differences in human mate preferences: evolutionary hypotheses tested in 37 cultures." *Behavioral and Brain Sciences*, 12(1), 1–49. doi:10.1017/S0140525X00023992.

Buss, D.M. and Dedden, L.A. (1990). "Derogation of competitors." *Journal of Social and Personal Relationships*. 7(3), 395-422. doi: 10.1177/0265407590073006

Cox. (2014) "Cox 2014 Internet Safety Survey." The Futures
Company. Retrieved from: https://www.cox.com/content/
dam/cox/aboutus/documents/tween-internet-safety-
survey.pdf

Global Web Index (2017). "Digital vs. Traditional Media
Consumption." Retrieved from: https://www.global
webindex.com/reports/traditional-vs-digital-media-
consumption

Gunaydin, L. A., Grosenick, L., Finkelstein, J. C., Kauvar, I. V.,
Fenno, L. E., Adhikari, A., Lammel, S,... and Deisseroth, K.
(2014). "Natural Neural Projection Dynamics Underlying
Social Behavior." *Cell*, 157(7), 1535–1551. doi:
10.1016/j.cell.2014.05.017

Hormes, J. M., Kearns, B., and Timko, C. A. (2014). "Craving
Facebook? Behavioral addiction to online social networking
and its association with emotion regulation deficits."
*Addiction*, 109(12), 2079–2088. doi: 10.1111/add.12713

Ko, C. H., Yen, J. Y., Liu, S. C., Huang, C. F., and Yen, C. F.
(2009). "The associations between aggressive behaviors and
Internet addiction and online activities in adolescents."
*Journal of Adolescent Health*, 44(6), 598–605.
doi:10.1016/j.jadohealth.2008.11.011

Kuss, D. J., and Griffiths, M. D. (2011). "Online social networking
and addiction—A review of the psychological literature."
*International Journal of Environmental Research and Public
Health*, 8(9), 3528–3552. doi:10.3390/ijerph8093528

Lin, Yu-Hsuan, Chiang, Chih-lin, Lin, PoHsien, Chang, Li-Ren,
Ko, Chih-Hung, Lee, Yang-Han, and Lin, Sheng-Hsuan.
(2016). "Proposed diagnostic criteria for smartphone
addiction." *PLoS ONE*, 11(11), e0163010. Retrieved from
https://doi.org/10.1371/journal.pone.0163010

Maguire, J. (2014, Sept. 14). "How many people donate after ice bucket challenge?" *BBC*. Retrieved from: http://www.bbc.com/news/av/uk-29170642/how-many-people-donate-after-ice-bucket-challenge

Marcum, C. D., Higgins, G. E., Freiburger, T. L., and Ricketts, M. L. (2012). "Battle of the sexes: An examination of male and female cyber bullying." *International Journal of Cyber Criminology*, 6(1), 904–911.

Meshi, D., Morawetz, C., and Heekeren, H. R. (2013). "Nucleus accumbens response to gains in reputation for the self-relative to gains for others predicts social media use." *Frontiers in Human Neuroscience*, 7, 439. doi: 10.3389/fnhum.2013.00439

Meshi, D., Tamir, D. I., and Heekeren, H. R., (2015). "The Emerging Neuroscience of Social Media." *Trends in Cognitive Sciences*, 19(12), 771–782.

Molenberghs, P., Johnson, H., Henry, J. D., and Mattingley, J. B. (2016). "Understanding the minds of others: A neuroimaging meta-analysis." *Neuroscience and Biobehavioral Reviews*, 65, 276-291.

Page, A. E., Chaudhary, N., Viguier, S., Dyble, M., Thompson, J., Smith, D., Deniz Salali, Mace, R., G., and Migliano, A. B. (2017). "Hunter-Gatherer social networks and reproductive success." *Scientific Reports*, 7, 1153. doi:10.1038/s41598-017-01310-5

Pies, R. (2009). "Should DSM-V Designate 'Internet Addiction' a Mental Disorder?" *Psychiatry*, 6(2), 31–37.

Renzulli, K. A. (2017). "More Than 33% of Men Say They've Faked a Vacation Photo." *Time Magazine*. Retrieved from: http://time.com/money/4823463/men-women-vacation-spending-social-media/

Sorokowski, P., Sorokowska, A., Frackowiak, T., and
    Oleszkiewicz, A. (2016). "Sex differences in online selfie
    posting behaviors predict histrionic personality scores
    among men but not women." *Computers in Human
    Behavior*, 59, 368–373. doi: 10.1016/j.chb.2016.02.033

Hango, D. (2014, December 19). "Insights on Canadian Society:
    Cyberbullying and cyberstalking among Internet users aged
    15 to 29 in Canada." *Statistics Canada*. Retrieved from:
    https://www.statcan.gc.ca/pub/75-006-x/2016001/article/
    14693-eng.htm

Turel, O., He, Q., Xue, G., Xiao, L. and Bechara, A. (2014)
    "Examination of neural systems sub serving substance and
    gambling addictions and Facebook 'addiction'." *Psychologi-
    cal Reports*, 115(3), 1–21. doi: 10.2466/18.PR0.115c31z8

Utz, S., and Beukeboom, C. J. (2011). "The role of social network
    sites in romantic relationships: effects on jealousy and
    relationship happiness." *Journal of Computer Mediated
    Communication*, 16(4), 511–527. doi: 10.1111/j.1083-6101.
    2011.01552.x

Xu, H., and Tan, B. C. Y. (2012). "Why do I keep checking
    Facebook: Effects of message characteristics on the
    formation of Social Network Services addiction."
    International Conference on Information Systems, ICIS, 1,
    812-823. ScholarBank@NUS Repository. Retrieved from:
    http://scholarbank.nus.edu.sg/handle/10635/78432

Young, R., Len-Ross, M., and Young, H. (2017). "Romantic
    motivations for social media use, social comparison,
    and online aggression among adolescents." *Computers in
    Human Behavior*, 75, 385–395. doi:10.1016/j.chb.2017.
    04.021

"Each of us likely meets the criteria for
an addiction via our pet habits, our manias and
passions, as well as our phobias and hates.
Our addictions—be they to coffee, tea, ice
cream, peanut butter, crosswords, nicotine,
alcohol, sex, drugs, gambling, speeding, or
cleaning, all reveal our biases."

## THE INTEGRITY MODEL: *TO BE* OR *NOT TO BE* AS A FUNCTION OF OUR VALUES

9

Nedra R. Lander AND Danielle Nahon

Our encounters with individuals who are grappling with addictions began in the late 1960s, when I (Nedra) began working with my mentors, the respected psychologists Dr. O. Hobart Mowrer and his wife Dr. Molly Mowrer at the University of Illinois. It was a rich and unique journey in large Integrity (Therapy) groups that were the precursors of much of the current work in recovery from addictions. In these Integrity groups, the role of leader was rotated amongst the group members, and the therapists did as much personal work in the group as the other participants. For me, this was a challenging and remarkable opportunity for personal growth and self-work that has left a defining mark on my life ever since. As we note in our book on The Integrity Model (TIM) (Lander and Nahon, 2005), I feel that the Mowrers left a lifeprint on my mind, heart, and soul.

Many of the individuals in these Integrity groups were physicians grappling with addiction issues. At the time, this was not a well-known area in psychotherapy, and thus I had an opportunity to work with them and to discover that the Integrity (Therapy) group approach was very meaningful for them, as it had been for me. A few years later, while working in a hospital setting in Ottawa, I again found myself working with a growing number of individuals who were trying to understand and find a resolution to their addictions and carve out a more meaningful existence. The referring psychiatrists were startled to learn that I did not view these issues as comprising a psychiatric illness of any sort, and that I felt these individuals would find their way through this challenging journey as would any other person seeking to redefine who they were within their unique life spaces. I was seeing real people with dilemmas in living; I did not deny the unique situational or historical issues that could impinge on them and on their lives. While I understood that part of their dilemmas around their addictions may have been specific to them, their overall quest to rediscover the self and to like what they saw was clearly part of a universal journey.

I (Danielle) began to work with individuals grappling with addictions issues in my community psychological practice over two decades ago. I found that these individuals were deeply responsive to TIM, a holistic approach to doing life well and with a sense of meaning. Furthermore, I discovered that as individuals grew through their Integrity work, they reached a point in their personal journeys whereby their addictions no longer had Integrity for them; in many cases, they took a brief hiatus from therapy, enrolled in a recovery program, and having reached abstinence/sobriety, promptly returned to therapy where they continued to work on sustaining their recovery.

TIM was evolved by Dr. Nedra Lander, in later collaboration with Dr. Danielle Nahon, from the work of O.H. Mowrer and his Integrity (Therapy) groups, which he devised and implemented from the mid-1940s to the mid-1980s. TIM is the very first wellness- and values-based model of psychotherapy. It is based on Mowrer's view of the human being as a valuing animal. As we have discussed in our writings (e.g. Lander and Nahon, 2010; Nahon and Lander, 2014), the basic underlying principle of TIM is that the degree of distress or angst in one's life reflects the degree of personal violation of one's personal value system. We and Mowrer define Integrity as comprising a three-legged stool of honesty, responsibility, and emotional closure/community as follows: (a) Honesty means being open and truthful about one's feelings, and acknowledging past or present wrongdoings; (b) responsibility means taking 100 percent ownership of one's fifty percent in conflict situations; and (c) what Mowrer referred to as community, which we later evolved to emotional closure—referring to the intent of any actions as "closing the psychological space" or increasing one's sense of community with self and others. Integrity requires all three components to be present in order for Integrity to exist at a given time in a given context. Consequently, any interaction (verbal or behavioural), any decision by a person, institution, or government, any product or service can be analysed as to its level of Integrity by the presence or absence of the three components.

We understand stress and distress as reflecting a clash of values, and an Integrity crisis as occurring when any one of the three components of Integrity—honesty, responsibility, and emotional closure/community—are absent. Guilt comprises an important aspect of TIM. We understand it as reflecting the violation of one's values and their discrepancies with one's actual deeds done rather than feared (Lander and Nahon, 2017; Nahon and Lander, 2016).

THE INTEGRITY MODEL AND WORKING WITH ADDICTIONS

Dr. Mowrer was a pioneer in introducing many key concepts in psychotherapy, including the importance of morality, mindfulness, spirituality, and the self-help group—his work paralleling that of Bill and Dr. Bob in the foundation of the twelve-step program of Alcoholics Anonymous (AA). Beginning with Mowrer's early work, TIM assists individuals in addressing issues of addictions with a profound complementarity to the twelve-step programs. Mowrer played a key role in designing and implementing several twelve-step recovery programs, such as *Daytop Village* and *Synanon*. As we note in Lander and Nahon (2005), Mowrer's paradigm of Integrity, operationalized as a three-legged stool of honesty, responsibility, and increased emotional closure, is reflected in the twelve steps of AA (Alcoholics Anonymous World Services, Inc., 1952) as follows:

> Honesty is reflected in step one ("We admitted we were powerless over alcohol—that our lives had become unmanageable" (p. 5)); step four ("Made a searching and fearless moral inventory of ourselves" (p. 5)); step five ("Admitted to God, to ourselves, and to another human being the exact nature of our wrongs" (p. 6)); and step ten ("Continued to take personal inventory, and when we were wrong, promptly admitted it" (p. 7)).

> Responsibility is reflected in step eight ("Made a list of all persons we had harmed, and became willing to make amends to them all" (p. 7)); and step nine ("Made direct amends to such people wherever possible, except when to do so would injure them or others" (p. 7)).

> Increased emotional closure is reflected in steps eight and nine, as well as step twelve ("Having had a spiritual awakening as a result of these steps, we tried to carry this

message to alcoholics, and to practice these principles in all our affairs" (p. 8)) (Lander and Nahon, 2005).

## TIM AND MOTIVATIONAL INTERVIEWING

Through an introduction by a colleague who saw striking similarities between TIM and Motivational Interviewing (MI), we had the opportunity to meet Dr. William R. Miller, founder of the MI approach towards the process of change in acknowledging and addressing addictions. In a lengthy review of Lander and Nahon (2005), Miller opined that not only was he working on a parallel path, but that TIM was helpful to him in understanding his own journey and that of others. In 2012, Miller and Rollnick pointed to the complementarities between TIM and MI, and the role of TIM in providing a helpful framework in assisting individuals to become aware of their values and to behave in accordance with these.

## TIM AND VALUE CLARIFICATION

TIM is an existential model that focuses on the individual, on one's value system, and on the prices that one is willing to pay for these values. In this model, there is no psychiatric labelling or psychological/psychiatric jargon. TIM views the individual as reflecting a value system which forges an identity of self revealed in one's behaviours. It asks each one of us to rank our values, including how we rank those whom we perceive as different from ourselves. Individuals who are grappling with addictions across the spectrum— including drugs, alcohol, gambling, sexual addiction, etc.—are invited to examine (a) the values that they currently hold; and (b) the values of the person they would like to be, as well as the specific behaviours that are the reflection of those values. We then invite individuals to examine the price tags that they pay for these respective values.

This becomes a key step in the therapeutic process of Integrity-based recovery, as individuals begin to examine the value clashes that they have, both within themselves as well as with the important others in their lives as a consequence of their addictions. They begin to reflect on the price tags that they would have to pay if they were to change these values. They also reflect on whether there may be alternative values of the self that might place a higher valuing on abstinence and/or sobriety and that would be unique to them and their own selves, rather than to any other individuals or groups.

Values are gained from family, religion, society, peers, media, and ultimately as a result of our personal choices. TIM asks each of us to consider whether the values that govern our lives are our own or someone else's (e.g. Nahon and Lander, 2016). In either case, one must choose whether or not to keep these values, and if kept, how one will rank them. It is important that no value is ranked too rigidly, as life requires the valuing of flexibility to meet contextual demands. Sometimes one is more easily able to identify a value when it emerges behaviourally; the choice then becomes whether to continue to value it, to make it a project to work on, or perhaps to discard it.

## FINDING CREATIVE WAYS TO DEAL WITH RAGE

One example of the behavioural expression of a value is that of rage. Rage is one of our favourite emotions, as it provides us with useful feedback regarding the presence of an Integrity issue or value clash that needs to be dealt with (Nahon and Lander, 2016). It is not a pleasant emotion to feel; however, the Integrity challenge is to find ways of being furious in ways that allow one to like the self. This often means that the person receiving the anger is neither hurt nor humiliated by it, but rather feels drawn closer because of the manner in which the anger is expressed.

For individuals grappling with addictions, discovering one's individual thumbprint in being able to do this is another key step in the journey of repair and healing. TIM suggests that in any relationship, one can only take one of three stances: to move towards, away from, or against another (Nahon and Lander, 2016). Especially when we are angry, this is a very important existential choice that we must make. Integrity is about daring to resolve value clashes with others in a manner that allows us to move towards rather than away from or against the other–especially when we are angry. Most individuals find that this work becomes a quintessential component of their recovery journeys in comprising a profound vehicle for the repair and healing of their relationships with both self and others.

DISCUSSION

Each of us likely meets the criteria for an addiction via our pet habits, our manias and passions, as well as our phobias and hates. Our addictions—be they to coffee, tea, ice cream, peanut butter, cross-words, nicotine, alcohol, sex, drugs, gambling, speeding, or cleaning, all reveal our biases. Our perceptions of others reveal these biases; consequently, to paraphrase Jean-Paul Sartre, "In order to know myself I must first know another." Mowrer would often remind us of the old saying that "If you point the finger at someone else, there are three fingers pointing back at you" (Lander and Nahon, 2005). This saying challenges us to look at and to own our own levels of humanity, compassion, and generosity versus those of another.

Mowrer reminded us that we are all somewhere on the road to recovery, which allows us to choose whether or not to increase our identification and validation of those travelling just steps behind us, and our capacity to care for them. To do otherwise would be to risk self-deception and to see those as somehow less than or beneath us, which is not honest, not responsible, and certainly does not close the psychological space with others travelling on their own path of recovery.

Existence is personal and unique to each individual, and thus an individual grappling with addictions is both unique and may also share many similarities with one another and with humanity as a whole. Suffering is a fact of life, and one can only choose whether to suffer meaningfully or meaninglessly. Giving up an addiction requires courage and grit—and, as someone we once worked with pointed out, grit is the "root word" of Integrity (Lander and Nahon, 2005). The journey of recovery requires grit from each of us if it is to be lived meaningfully and with a sense of fidelity to our values. Simply put, it is about Hamlet's dilemma of whether *to be* or *not to be*. Only we can decide on this, as well as on the prices that we are willing to pay in order to be. Living with Integrity also means resisting labelling and therefore resisting the devaluing of others that inevitably leads to values justifying behaviours of marginalization, rejection, and aggression. The individuals we work with have the same hopes, dreams, and fears as others, with the added focus on the roles of their addictions in their lives. This focus in itself does not really separate them from their humanity and the multi-faceted nature of their identities as unique individuals.

As we have recently written (Lander and Nahon, 2017), a profound metaphor for the journeys that we see individuals go through as part of their Integrity-based recovery work is that of the hermit crab who, as a species, is unable to generate a new shell. As it outgrows its shell, the crab must go out to hunt for a new one. When it moves from one shell to another, there is a brief moment when it becomes completely vulnerable to predators and to the tide. However, it is driven to grow and thus undertakes this challenging journey. In going through the seeming Scylla and Charybdis of this voyage of transformation, it is through the Integrity to one's values that one is able to find safe passage.

REFERENCES

Lander, N. R., and Nahon, D. (2005). *The Integrity Model of Existential Psychotherapy in Working with the 'Difficult Patient'*. London, UK: Routledge.

Lander, N. R., and Nahon, D. (2010). "A meaningful death as a function of a meaningful life: An Integrity Model perspective." *International Journal of Existential Psychology and Psychotherapy*, 3(2), 34-61.

Lander, N. R., and Nahon, D. (2017). "An Integrity Model, existential perspective in clinical work with men from a gender and health perspective." In M. P. Sánchez-López and R. M. Limiñana-Gras (Eds.), *The Psychology of Gender and Health, 1st Edition: Conceptual and Applied Global Concerns* (pp. 251-273). Amsterdam, NL: Elsevier.

Nahon, D., and Lander, N. R. (2014). "Working with men in individual psychotherapy from an Integrity Model perspective: The unsung heroes." *The Journal of Men's Studies*, 22(3), 194-206.

Nahon, D., and Lander, N. R. (2016). "The Integrity Model: Working with men, their intimacy issues and their search for community." *The Journal of Men's Studies*, 24(1), 89-116.

"Getting past an addiction isn't about quitting the drug or reducing harm. It's about getting a life. For someone actively pursuing a meaningful life, addiction serves no purpose. That's why even those burdened with ongoing medical, financial, and family hardships as a result of drug use can flourish in recovery."

## TREATING ADDICTION AS A PROBLEM OF MEANING

10

Geoff Thompson

This thing we call *addiction* is complicated. We've been studying it for decades, and regardless of what we examine—effects of drugs on the physical brain, on thinking or emotions, on family or society—we've found that addiction stamps itself into every aspect of the drug user's life. We've treated it as a brain disorder, behavioural conditioning, self-medication for an underlying issue, faulty thinking, a response to an unbalanced family system, and a counterfeit search for spirituality. But none of these efforts has led to any inspired success. Most of us who work in the field identify with psychologist Warren Bickel and psychiatrist Marc Potenza (2006) when they lamented, "Why is addiction so difficult to treat?" (p. 8).

Attempting to answer this question, a small but growing number of experts propose that addiction is a problem of meaning. The great Viennese psychiatrist, Viktor Frankl (1984), stated this formally in his book, *Man's Search for Meaning*, when he declared, "Alcoholism ... [is] not understandable unless we recognize the existential vacuum underlying [it]" (p. 129). According to Frankl, this vacuum arose in those who were persistently frustrated in their attempts to live a personally meaningful life. The vacuum was particularly devastating, said Frankl, because the search for meaning was the single, most powerful human motivation. Alcoholic drinking was one way to fill the void, even if it was ephemeral and doomed.

Lots of psychologists disagree that meaning is *the* motivation in human beings, but they all agree that we are meaning-seeking and meaning-making creatures. Without meaning, life is dull and empty, a tedious and dreary existence. Addiction, thus, serves a purpose. It helps a person live more comfortably in a life that is hollow at the core. Research has moved well beyond Frankl's original work, but it has affirmed his idea that those who experience life as meaningless, monotonous, and boring are vulnerable to chronic drug use.

It's important to appreciate that interpreting addiction through the lens of meaning does not deny that it has a physical substrate in the brain. It does not deny that addiction can be a habit or a way to escape painful feelings, that muddled thinking plays a role, that troubled families influence it, or that the social stigma promotes it. What it does argue, however, is that if we want to make sense of addiction as it really is, then we need to recognize that it operates at the level of an innate and primary motivation to pursue a meaningful life.

The solution is obvious. Those suffering from addiction have to figure out how to live in such a way that they feel significant and fulfilled. Getting past an addiction isn't about quitting the drug or reducing harm. It's about getting a life. For someone actively pursuing a meaningful life, addiction serves no purpose. That's why even those burdened with ongoing medical, financial, and family hardships as a result of drug use can flourish in recovery.

Where I work, a residential facility for men suffering from addictions and other disorders, we use Meaning-Centred Therapy (MCT), based on the work of psychologist Paul T. P. Wong (2012). MCT (and meaning) is all about sense-making. How does this client make sense of himself, his world, and how he fits in that world? How does he make sense of his drug use? MCT does not treat an *addict* or an *addiction*. It treats a whole, complicated human being whose way of making sense of things has led to problems. This isn't a new idea, by the way. Two thousand years ago, the ancient Greek philosopher, Epictetus, said that we don't react to anything as it really is; we react to the *meaning* that we give to it, often a warped or mistaken meaning, as Epictetus liked to point out.

A key principle of MCT is that each client is the author of his life. It is the client's responsibility to make decisions that will determine how well he lives. Therapists don't tell clients what to think, feel, do, or say; that's the client's job. The goal of MCT is, of course, to help them pursue a personally meaningful life. Any intervention that helps achieve this goal is useful. A client suffering from post-traumatic stress disorder (PTSD), for example, may believe that PTSD is so overwhelming that it controls him, and he's relied on alcohol for relief. Medications, grounding exercises, and hypnotherapy can help the client manage nightmares, anxiety, and other trauma symptoms. But easing symptoms never led anyone to the good life. People are not built to live by reducing or avoiding what they don't want; they are built to pursue what they do want.

Interventions that ease suffering don't work very well to help the client figure out who he is and what he wants out of life. We use narrative and existential therapies to help the client know himself and to gain awareness that he is the author of his life and is capable of going after the life he chooses, in spite of trauma. (In fact, research has shown that engaging in meaningful activity, by itself, reduces PTSD symptoms.) In MCT, each intervention, from psychotropic medications to existential therapy, works in harmony with the others, all directed toward helping the client get a life.

Living a personally meaningful life has to do with self-awareness, relationships, and motivations. Contented people, those who feel their lives are significant, are not attracted to chronic intoxication. They have a good understanding of who they are and why they get out of bed each morning. They can tell you what is truly important to them, their strengths and limitations, their wants and desires. They have genuine connections with others, able to care even for the stranger. Based on their internal anchor of self-awareness, they reach out into the world, making choices that affirm and nurture who they are and what they want from life. Contented people live purposeful lives.

But this is not the how the clients I work with function. When we deconstruct their lives in therapy, the first phase of MCT, we discover that they rely on the external world to tell them who they are and what they should do. The obvious example of this external orientation is, of course, that they depend on a chemical substance, not themselves, to feel a certain way. But reliance on the outside world is far more than reaching for a drug. Asked to describe himself, one client said, "My friend thinks I'm a pretty good guy." Another client entered treatment a month after he tried to commit suicide. Asked to describe what was going on for him at that time, he could say only, "The police officer on the scene said it didn't look like I had much to live for."

In large part, they lack self-awareness because they don't think about themselves very much. Charles, a successful fifty-seven-year-old investment banker, told his life story in group therapy. Group members pointed out that his story was simply a series of incidents in chronological order. Charles never said how an incident affected him or what it meant to him. Each time when asked, he replied, "I don't know." A client who was a theatre director told me he loved reading plays because he learned from the various characters how other people experienced life. When I asked him if he had learned anything about himself from these characters, he was silent. The idea had never occurred to him. Of course, some clients tell me, at least in the beginning of therapy, they know themselves pretty well. Patrick made sense of himself as an Irish drinking man: "If you don't drink in Ireland, people don't trust you. In Ireland, you don't see people walking down the street with a coffee. They have a pint." Yet, as open as he was about his Irish drinking identity, he was silent on specifics of his life, such as his loveless marriage, problems at work, and legal hassles. He disagreed when our psychiatrist diagnosed him with severe Alcohol Use Disorder.

Relationships for clients are weak and superficial. When their addictions became public, for example, all relationships became warped. The mother of a client I worked with told me that she gave her son a cellphone, telling him that she appreciated he was broke, and wanted to help him out. In reality, she wanted to investigate whom he was calling, which she could do by tracking the calls on the bill. More than one partner has greeted her lover with a kiss, close enough to smell alcohol or cannabis. Those with addictions are exquisitely attuned to society's shaming finger. Lies and manipulation are barriers to real relationships, but they are necessary tactics to keep doing something that society stigmatizes.

With only a weak sense of who they are, they rely on the external world for direction. Carson told me he "hated every day" of his four years studying engineering in university. Asked why he put himself through this hell, he explained, "My father thought it was a good idea." A common complaint is "Sundays are boring." When most people are happy with a free day to pursue personal interests, those who don't know themselves rely on the world to keep them entertained. What goals they admit to are usually superficial and depend on others to pat them on the back, such as "making lots of money" or "being a successful musician." "I just want my old life back" is a common goal, without considering that whatever that life was, it had led to addiction. "I just want a normal life" is also common, without realizing that what they really want is to feel energized and fulfilled, regardless of what *normal* is.

Drug use is their response to feeling that the external world is in control. It's an act of agency, the time when they pay attention to themselves. One client described how he spent his workdays doing what his boss told him to do. After work, he was taxi driver for his kids' soccer practices and music lessons. On the weekends, he fixed leaky faucets and weeded the garden. But at night, after all this was over, when he no longer felt controlled by the boss, kids, or chore lists, he used heroin. "It's my reward," he said, "It's my time."

Why drugs? If their sober experience of life is meaningless, monotonous, and boring, their intoxicated life sparkles. It's curious that most clients have never really thought about intoxication beyond a method to "numb myself" or "help me sleep" or "to keep from getting dope sick." Processing the experience of intoxication in therapy, they begin to appreciate that it's more than an escape hatch. Under the influence, boredom melts away. Music is richer and jokes are funnier. Intoxication makes a meaningless job more interesting. Even vacuuming or mowing the lawn can be entertaining. Creativity comes easier when making music or finding solutions to a problem at work. There is an emotional intensity to an intoxicated life, which sobriety denies. But little else. Nothing is accomplished under the influence. There is no progress, no thought of how to make things better. Intoxication serves mainly to keep itself going. Still, if one feels life is impotent and boring, then intoxication is a way to feel vital and alive, if only temporarily. Those who suffer from addictions live with a drug-fuelled intensity as a substitute for living meaningfully.

After deconstructing how clients make sense of themselves, relationships, and motivations, MCT helps reconstruct their lives, but this time in a way that reflects what is genuinely important to them and an acceptance of their situation. The first step is, of course, self-awareness. Getting to know themselves is a process, slow and strewn with obstacles. Jason declared, "I'm totally lost, out of control." I pointed out to him that he'd dressed himself, combed his hair, put his watch on, and showed up to our session on time. Martin stated with conviction, "I don't like to be around other people. That's just who I am." After processing this in therapy, he realized that he had mistaken a coping skill to protect himself for a personality trait. MCT helps clients connect with their physical bodies, emotions, thoughts, values, assumptions, and coping skills, which provide answers to *Who am I?*

Developing authentic connections with other clients and staff seems to have the most powerful therapeutic influence on those who have relied on drugs to feel more comfortable in the world. Research indicates that we are hard-wired for relationships, and they are essential for self-awareness and motivations. Clients learn about themselves from feedback and noticing how they are different from others. Relating with others is also necessary to set goals. Meaning-centred theorists and therapists are convinced that attaching life to something greater than the self is the way to flourish.

It is far more powerful to pursue goals that match personal values, than those that come from others. But clients don't get very far shifting from their reliance on the external world to looking within for direction. This makes sense, of course, because they don't really know themselves after only a month or two of therapy. What they do have is, as one client put it, "a roadmap." They recognize that allowing the outside world to direct their lives has led only to misery. Authorship, being true to themselves, is the path to the good life.

By the end of treatment, clients typically say they're optimistic about the future. It's an odd thing. They haven't figured it all out yet. They're returning to wary families, drained bank accounts, angry bosses, and few friends, hardly the ingredients for optimism. But their optimism is not about looking forward to a pleasurable life, free from suffering. It's what Viktor Frankl called a "tragic optimism":

> … an optimism in the face of tragedy and in view of the human potential which at its best always allows for: (1) turning suffering into a human achievement and accomplishment; (2) deriving from guilt the opportunity to change oneself for the better; and (3) deriving from life's transitoriness an incentive to take responsible action. (p. 162)

This optimism is about digging deep within and finding courage and perseverance to take responsibility for their lives, to become their own author, regardless of personal limitations and environmental pressures.

Some experts believe that those in recovery require such a radical change in thinking and behaviour that they become, essentially, different people. A meaning approach disagrees. Recovery demands the authentic person emerge and make choices that reflect personal values. The good news is that, at some level of awareness, clients already know who they are and what they want from life. MCT provides space for them to discover it.

REFERENCES

Bickel, W. K., and Potenza, M. N. (2006). "The forest and the trees: Addiction as a complex self-organizing system." In W. R. Miller and K. M. Carroll (Eds.), *Rethinking Substance Abuse: What the Science Shows and What We Should Do about It*, 8–24. New York: Guilford.

Frankl, V. E. (1984). *Man's Search for Meaning*. New York: Vintage.

Wong, P. T. P. (2012). "From logotherapy to meaning-centered counseling and therapy." In P. T. P. Wong (Ed.), *The Human Quest for Meaning: Theories, Research, and Applications* (2nd ed.), 619–647. New York: Routledge.

# SERVICE PROVIDERS

"Our support meetings are facilitated by peers *for* peers; addiction and mental-health providers who are in recovery themselves and receive ongoing professional development training in the field of concurrent disorders."

## PROGRESS PLACE AND THE DOUBLE ROOM RECOVERY PROGRAM

Kathryn Eve

Progress Place, a recovery centre for people living with mental illness, hosts a comprehensive network of services that include employment, education, recreation, and housing. Our innovative approach to psychosocial rehabilitation is progressive and world-renowned. Mental illness need not be an obstacle to fulfilling one's dreams. We are committed to helping people stay out of hospitals, achieve their personal goals, and contribute to the community in which they live.

Housed within Progress Place, Double Recovery is a medication-friendly, twelve-step support program for people who are diagnosed with a substance dependency and a psychiatric disability. Double

Recovery differs from conventional twelve-step programs in that we offer a safe, non-stigmatizing environment to comfortably discuss our substance abuse and other mental-health issues. Our confidential support meetings are facilitated by peers *for* peers. By sharing our experience, offering positive strategies for healthy sobriety and mental wellness, as well as practical solutions to help us better cope with life's daily challenges, we discover new insights for living.

Dual recovery ultimately empowers us to be the best that we can be!

PROGRESS PLACE

Progress Place is a community-based mental-health recovery centre. Our vision is that all people living with mental illness have the opportunity for full recovery. Our mission is dedicated to improving the lives of those living with mental illness. We offer programs and services, which provide meaningful opportunities for recovery through social connections that lead to friendships, employment, education, housing, and recreation in a welcoming, accessible environment of support, respect, and dignity.

Progress Place was founded by Brenda Singer, who introduced a new way of working in mental health, and a new philosophy of treating people with mental illness as equal partners. This was ground-breaking territory in the 1970s and 1980s as she developed programs which offered hope, respect, and opportunities for personal development for those previously marginalized by the community. This was the beginning of a succession of achievements in breaking down barriers for people living with mental illness.

Brenda believed what people living with mental illness lacked were opportunities to have meaningful day activities, a range of employment positions, social activities on the weekend and in the evening, supportive housing, and education. Too often, people were told by well-intentioned professionals, families, and friends, that they were unemployable. Consequently, many developed low self-esteem. They were faced with few options and little hope. Fortunately, Brenda knew different.

As far back as 1981, she had the foresight to envision more options for people than wiling away their days doing arts and crafts or other recreational activities. While working at a social recreation centre, she made it her goal to develop a psychosocial rehabilitation centre for people living with mental-health issues. One day Brenda told the recreation program participants about Fountain House in New York City. They decided to watch a film about this clubhouse and how it functioned. Participants were called "members." They could choose their activities and fully partake in operating the clubhouse together with a handful of staff. Thus began Progress Place's journey, which is modelled after Fountain House. This was in sharp contrast to people living with mental illness in other parts of America and Canada who were discharged from psychiatric hospitals and spent their days in donut shops or hospital day programs.

For over thirty years, Progress Place has been a recognized leader in psychosocial rehabilitation throughout Canada, the international clubhouse community, and mental-health recovery movement. It has become Canada's first program using the clubhouse approach of psychosocial rehabilitation for people living with severe and persistent mental illness. The clubhouse model focuses on people's strengths and recognizes that mental illness need not be an obstacle to fulfilling one's dreams. The clubhouse model believes that people need to be recognized for their full potential to lead satisfying and productive lives, which is why everyone is truly needed and wanted in the program. Everyone can contribute. At Progress Place, we believe that recovery from mental illness is possible when it involves the individual in a community—one that offers hope, respect, and opportunities for personal development.

DOUBLE RECOVERY

Double Recovery is a medication-friendly twelve-step self-help program for people between the ages of sixteen and sixty-five years old, who are diagnosed with both a substance abuse/dependency and a psychiatric disability. Double Recovery differs from conventional twelve-step groups in that we offer people a safe, non-stigmatizing environment to comfortably discuss their substance abuse, psychiatric disabilities, and medication. We are an innovative community-based program, designed to holistically address the needs of people in dual recovery.

Double Recovery started as a grassroots initiative in 1989 under the original title Double Trouble in Recovery (DTR) in New York State by Howie V. based on his own experiences of dual recovery. As a long-time member of AA, he found the traditional twelve-step groups inadequate for those with added psychiatric issues. Hence, the genesis of a tailored self-help program to meet the special needs of those who are dually diagnosed. Regular DTR meetings are now nation-wide in the US. Progress Place agency has adopted the DTR model in Toronto, Canada, under the revised name Double Recovery.

Our program reaches over 5,000 group participants per year through our sixteen weekly recovery meetings in Toronto, including a wellness yoga class, which focuses on the relationship between mood management and the mind-body connection. It is a combination of breathing, gentle movement, postures, mindfulness, and music. The sessions are designed for all levels, offering options for beginners and regular practitioners as part of a regular treatment plan for anyone dealing with various conditions including stress, anxiety, depression, and addiction.

Our support meetings are facilitated by peers *for* peers: addiction and mental-health providers who are in recovery themselves and receive ongoing professional-development training in the field of concurrent disorders. This mobile team meets at a variety of easily accessible sites in conjunction with our clinical and community partners. To service people where they are at, we offer groups in psychiatric wards, detox centres, addiction hospital units, community drop-ins and hostels.

Together we share our experience, offer positive strategies for a healthy sobriety, and practical solutions to cope with mental-health challenges. Double Recovery offers a safe, confidential space where we can surround ourselves with others who understand our journey and remind us that we are not alone. By building a network of support and encouragement, we discover new insights for living and inspire each other to achieve a better quality of life, ultimately empowering ourselves.

Our program motto is simple: We all deserve a good life in recovery!

Double Recovery Program at Progress Place: www.progressplace.org

"Recognizing that addiction negatively impacts aspects of an individual's life,

CCFA provides a client-centered approach, where together with the client, our

clinical team of addiction counsellors and therapists work to create a recovery

program that best suits the individual's unique needs."

## CANADIAN CENTER FOR ADDICTIONS (CCFA)

Seth Fletcher

The Canadian Center for Addictions (CCFA) is a fully accredited residential treatment facility located in Port Hope, Ontario, one hour west of Toronto. CCFA specializes in helping people who are addicted to alcohol and other drugs learn the skills required to successfully live an alcohol and drug free lifestyle. Recognizing that addiction negatively impacts aspects of an individual's life, CCFA provides a client-centered approach, where together with the client, our clinical team of addiction counsellors and therapists work to create a recovery program that best suits the individual's unique needs.

CCFA provides addiction and detox services in a luxury retreat atmosphere in a 17,000 square foot heritage Victorian home overlooking Lake Ontario. Luxury amenities and services help provide a level of comfort that enables our clients to focus solely on their recovery program.

## OUR VISIONS AND VALUES

CCFA is committed to helping individuals and families heal from addiction and discover the freedom of being well. We provide a safe and private environment where our tremendous team of professionals uphold CCFA's vision and values by providing all services with compassion, care, dignity, and respect to all clients.

## MISSION

To help individuals and families heal from addiction and discover the freedom of being well.

## WHAT MAKES CCFA DIFFERENT?

The Canadian Centre For Addiction recognizes that addiction is the symptom! Authentic recovery lies in the identification of core and underlying issues that led to the addictive behaviour in the first place. Once this has been identified, our therapeutic staff can connect clients to the appropriate modalities of therapy, resources, and coping mechanisms to more effectively manage the underlying issues, emotions, and feelings. The following will highlight the experiences that are most common during an inpatient treatment program at CCFA as well as bring attention to the spectrum of professional addiction services that CCFA provides. The treatment experience has been organized into five distinct phases:

1.  Pre-Admission Assessment

2. Intake and Admission
3. Withdrawal Management / Detox / Medical Support
4. Program and Therapies
5. After-Care and On-going Case Management

## 1. Intrasexual Competition

Upon establishing a desire to enter CCFA for substance-abuse rehabilitation services, admissions staff gather preliminary information concerning a client's specific situation (mental health, substance of choice, medical concerns, medications). If CCFA's program is deemed to potentially be a good fit by admissions staff, the potential client is then assessed further by CCFA medical staff by way of telephone interview or consultation. The purpose of this protocol is to gather all necessary information to ensure that the withdrawal management protocols required, as well as the treatment and therapeutic environments, are within CCFA's services scope and are consistent with the potential client's immediate needs. CCFA physicians are consulted in this process for pre-admission approval if required.

## 2. Intake and admission

Clients arrive at the Canadian Centre For Addiction (CCFA) most often with family/loved ones, or with CCFA staff. The first objective is to put the client and their families at ease by answering any of their questions and further communicating the scope in which treatment will occur. Our priority is to make our clients feel that they are in a safe place and to build good rapport from the onset. CCFA takes great pride in providing a safe, secure, and controlled environment for clients to achieve their recovery goals. To help achieve this result, client belongings are searched to ensure that no illicit drugs and/or contraband items are being brought into our facility. CCFA takes the safety of all our clients and staff very seriously, and these search protocols help achieve that endeavor. At this time, CCFA intake staff will gather important information and perform industry-approved screening tools to assess the individual's addiction and specific needs. This information is extremely important so that CCFA can begin to tailor the recovery program to the client's individual needs.

### 3. Withdrawal management / detox / medical support

All clients are medically monitored 24/7 throughout the entire duration of their treatment program. Based on the information acquired during the pre-assessment and intake procedures, an appointment will be scheduled with a CCFA physician to medically assess the client to ensure that all medical and withdrawal management needs for the client are completely supported. Urine analysis and a physical exam (including vitals) will be conducted. Blood work may be required as part of the medical intake. Medical staff work diligently and collaboratively with the intent of keeping all clients as comfortable as possible through the mitigation of their withdrawal symptoms. This individualized care is provided immediately.

As part of the screening process, all clients are administered a urine test to ascertain which substances are in their system and to help the CCFA physician put an effective medically supervised detox plan in place. This entails the client's medical history and background, and promotes individualized client-centered care. It is mandatory that each client complete industry-approved screening tools with a certified clinician. These screening tools are evaluated, and the client is assigned a primary counsellor immediately. Clients undergoing detoxification frequently present with medical and psychological conditions that can greatly affect their overall well-being. These may simply be pre-existing medical conditions not related to substance use or the direct outcome of the substance abuse. CCFA provides both medical and psychological support for these symptoms.

### 4. Program and therapies

When a client is physically able, they will be encouraged to participate in the program portion of their treatment. The client will have already been assigned a room and given all program supplies that he/she will require. The client is given a program schedule. To address the biopsychosocial implications that led to addiction, all clients receive one-on-one sessions with their assigned primary counsellor. All other counselling staff are available seven days a week to provide peer support for all recovery initiatives. Industry-approved screening and assessment tools are administered. For those clients that have been assessed to require further psychological support, their treatment program will be augmented with the necessary one-on-one sessions with a psychotherapist. Other professional care is available through CCFA's network of clinicians and will be provided based on the individual needs of each client. Group therapy is intertwined with individual counselling as program components include classes that explore a variety of treatment methods and modalities.

Yoga and personal training are often included in a client's recovery plan. Our program caters to all active learning styles and focuses on abstinent-based empowerment and trans-theoretical clinical models. CCFA also utilizes solution focused brief therapy, cognitive behaviour therapy, and twelve-step modalities of programming. A client-centred approach is the hallmark of CCFA's treatment philosophy. Nutrition, mindfulness, and physical activity are important components of the treatment program as well. Red-Seal chef prepared menus, clinical workshops, mindfulness, meditation, and yoga are provided to all clients. Certified personal training is available to advocate for the importance of physical activity in a healthy recovery plan. Program support is provided to families as well through CCFA's family services coordinator, who is available daily and to facilitate weekly family workshops at Port Hope's facility.

### 5. Aftercare and ongoing case management

As part of each client's relapse prevention plan, all clients who graduate from any length program at CCFA will receive a comprehensive, personalized exit plan that will connect clients with resources and services that are local to their communities. The Canadian Centre For Addiction's network of professional services is Canada wide and includes psychiatrists, psychologists, psychotherapists, and certified addiction counsellors. These resources are researched and set-up in a collaborative treatment effort between the client and their primary counsellor and reviewed by the clinical director. This exit plan provides the continued support to manage the client's individual triggers and to continue to address the underlying issues that the client has presented with.

CCFA continues to provide support to clients even after their inpatient treatment is complete. A lifetime enrollment is included with every treatment program. Aftercare meetings are run every Wednesday in our Toronto outpatient office. These interactive sessions are also available online, allowing clients from all over North America to remain in touch and to participate in these insightful and important support meetings. Included in CCFA's aftercare package is the lifetime membership in our alumni support system, which includes a half-day program, meetings, guest speakers, and meals at our Port Hope location. The alumni support program runs every weekend.

For those clients who complete a forty-five-day recovery program or longer, they are eligible for CCFA's guarantee. The guarantee provides a fourteen-day relapse prevention program free of charge for those clients who need to revisit some of their recovery goals, objectives, or strategies.

OTHER SERVICES PROVIDED INCLUDE

*Intervention services*: For those individuals who may still be in a pre-contemplative or contemplative stage of the trans-theoretical model (TTM). CCFA can provide intervention services for families who are looking to help expedite their loved one's acceptance for positive behaviour change. Interventions are conducted from a position of compassion and support with emphasis on healthy boundaries and a balanced family dynamic. CCFA interventions result in an eighty-five percent success rate of admission into a CCFA's substance abuse program.

*Out-patient addiction counselling*: Out-patient addiction counselling is provided by certified addiction counsellors at CCFA's Toronto office and via on-line.

*Keynote speaking on issues of addiction*: Keynote speaking, webinars, media appearances, and educational interviews regarding issues of addiction are services that CCFA offers.

"JACS' clinical approach and physical environment feel safe and almost informal, as if you have entered a trusted friend's living room. This welcoming model has allowed many people intimidated by clinical uniforms, long waiting lists, paperwork, and stark environments to turn to and find recovery at JACS."

# JEWISH ADDICTION COMMUNITY SERVICES (JACS)

David Kaufman

Founded in 2000 by concerned community members, the not-for-profit Jewish Addiction Community Services (JACS) has been on the front line of addiction treatment, outreach, and education. JACS assists individuals, families, and the larger community to effectively treat the problem of addiction where it exists and helps prevent it from spreading. JACS helps people without question of their religion or ethnicity. As JACS' executive director, Ori Goldstein, proudly says, "Addiction does not discriminate, so neither do we."

JACS' clinical approach and physical environment feel safe

and almost informal, as if you have entered a trusted friend's living room. This welcoming model has allowed many people intimidated by clinical uniforms, long waiting lists, paperwork, and stark environments to turn to and find recovery at JACS. Zalman Goldman, current chairman of the board of directors, and JACS' managing director, from 2000-2018, stated, "If you create enough welcoming, non-judgmental doors to walk through, those struggling with addiction will come seeking a solution."

Each year, JACS' clinical staff together hold over 1000 individual counselling sessions for those struggling with addiction, and their families. Our clinical/counselling team work together and meet weekly for peer supervision to ensure that each client is receiving the best therapeutic support and services available.

Our outreach to adolescents, young adults, and parents, finds us in schools, places of worship, and community centres, throughout the greater GTA. This year alone, our education programs will reach over 6000 people through interactive workshops, lectures, and Q and A sessions, offering help to youth, parents, educators, therapists, and clergy. Our successful educational and treatment programs are substantiated by evidence-based research and studies.

JACS' philosophy uses these evidence-based best practices, whether it's counselling, running support groups for addicts, parents, spouses, or siblings, or in schools, running educational programs. Following our motto of meeting the client where they're at, JACS' addiction treatment model moves clients, at any stage in their relationship to their addiction, closer to healthy life choices, from people in the pre-contemplative stage, who still doubt they have a problem, to those in longstanding recovery, who may continue to struggle even years after becoming sober.

JACS' use of support groups helps newcomers feel more emotionally stable after what, for many, has been years of denial, moving from one crisis to another:

When you first walk into to the meeting, you may feel uncomfortable admitting out loud to yourself and others about your situation, as we did. However, our experience has been that in exchange for those few minutes of feeling unsettled, you will gain a lifetime of knowledge, empowerment, and support. You can come just to listen or share. There is no pressure. All things discussed in our meetings and contact with JACS are 100% confidential.

*–Mothers Support Group Brochure, JACS*

JACS provides education, guidance, support, and hope to those struggling with, or affected by, addictive behaviours. JACS places a special emphasis on helping family members deal with the collateral damage that living with someone struggling with an addiction often brings to the lives of others. Parents, siblings, and the extended family and community are in need of help, too. A top priority at JACS is helping family members take responsibility for their own well-being, regardless of their loved one's success in dealing with their addiction. A heavy emphasis is placed on teaching people how to care for themselves, and creating healthy boundaries:

A lack of clear boundaries, and knowledge of how you want to treat yourself and be treated by others, invites chaos and lack of respect. People struggling with addiction are unable to maintain healthy boundaries. Their addiction makes them relentless in their desire to get what they want, often with little regard for who gets hurt along the way. When you find yourself (as someone who is interacting with an active addict) falling apart, feeling burnt out, manipulated, exhausted, resentful, and angry, ask yourself if you have set or kept healthy boundaries, and looked after your needs? The answer more often than not will be, "No." – *Creating Healthy Boundaries*, JACS

With an eighteen-year record of success, JACS' infrastructure includes a quick response intake program, counselling, and continuing group support, for individuals and family members, all free of charge, aside from counselling which is offered on a sliding scale. In the last five years, JACS has opened satellites in Vancouver and Winnipeg, and regularly fields questions about addiction issues from all over North America. Over 700 people walk through the doors of JACS every week seeking education, guidance, and hope for themselves or those they love. JACS daily programs include:

- Individual counselling to those who struggle with addiction of all types
- Family counselling
- Nine unique weekly support groups for addicts, parents, and family members
- JACS acts as a host to many "twelve-step" fellowship/support groups, such as Alcoholics Anonymous and Narcotics Anonymous
- Outreach educational programs and events to schools, youth groups, camps, PTA groups, adult groups, houses of worship, clergy, professional counselling associations, and medical professionals
- A speaker's bureau, sharing personal accounts
- 'Lunch and Learn' at professional corporations

For more information about how JACS can help you and those you love, or to help JACS carry out its life-saving mission by making a donation, please call 416-638-0350.

www.jacstoronto.org

"Smudging is a sacred act that is
recognized by many Indigenous peoples as
respecting the Great Spirit and the
ancestors. Sacred medicines such as sweetgrass,
sage, cedar, and tobacco are used
during each sharing circle. Drumming is used in
the circles to represent the heartbeat of the
Nation and the pulse of the universe.
Some songs are honour songs and were
sung to honour the Creator, the ancestors,
and particular individuals."

# IMPLEMENTATION OF A TWO-EYED SEEING TREATMENT MODEL IN AN INDIGENOUS RESIDENTIAL TREATMENT PROGRAM: BENBOWOPKA

Teresa Naseba Marsh AND Carol Eshkakogan

Indigenous peoples in Canada have experienced generations of traumatic events as a result of colonialism and the associated consequences, which include structural racism, residential school systems, oppression, and misguided policies (Kirmayer, Tait, and Simpson,Waldram, 2006). Two major consequences of these substantial challenges are intergenerational trauma (IGT) and substance-use disorders (SUD). Unfortunately, there is no currently available, culturally appropriate, evidence-based, integrative treatment for both conditions (Kirmayer, et al., 2009; Stewart, 2007).

Indigenous communities in Canada also experience mental-health problems, depression, anxiety, substance-use disorders (SUDs), and their consequences—such as violence, anger, and suicide—at significantly higher rates than the general population. Within this population, youth are the most dramatically affected. The disproportionately high prevalence of mental-health problems and SUD in Indigenous communities can be linked in part to a history of cultural disruption, oppression, marginalization, and the impact of ongoing colonization (Waldram, 2006). These factors have strongly contributed to the multigenerational grief and loss associated with intergenerational trauma (IGT) (Brant Castellano, 2004; Smith, 1999). Western treatments and conventional psychology have failed to understand holistic Indigenous wellness, spirituality, and traditional healing methods (Cote and Schissel, 2008; Evans-Campbell, 2008). It is therefore necessary to investigate treatments that are more relevant and incorporate Indigenous ways of knowing and approaches to healing.

ABOUT BENBOWOPKA TREATMENT CENTRE

Benbowopka Treatment Centre started in 1991 as a twelve-step Alcoholics Anonymous model of intervention to address alcohol addiction that was prominent in many First Nation communities during that time. However, the onset of prescription drug abuse on First Nation communities has shifted the need for addictions treatment towards harm-reduction models of service. This has

prompted Benbowopka Treatment Centre to go through a significant transformation over the last twenty-four months with regard
to ensuring its services are better able to address the SUD needs on
First Nations communities.

The abstinence model of service that was being delivered at
Benbowopka Treatment Centre was excluding many individuals
who were seeking residential addictions treatment for prescription
drug abuse. Individuals who were on prescribed medication, by
their physician, to address SUD or mental-health challenges, were
not eligible for admission to Benbowopka Treatment Centre because
of its abstinence-based model of services.

In 2014, Mamaweswen North Shore Tribal Council directed
Benbowopka Treatment Centre to move forward with a plan for the
realignment of its services to a harm-reduction model of service that
would follow the best practice strategies recommended for addressing
addictions treatment.

ABOUT THE INDIGENOUS HEALING SEEKING SAFETY
TREATMENT MODEL

Dr. Lisa Najavits developed the Seeking Safety treatment model
in 1992. The perspective of Seeking Safety is convergent with
Indigenous traditional methods. Because of the content and
delivery method of Seeking Safety, the program complements
traditional teachings such as holism, relational connection, spirituality,
cultural presence, honesty, and respect (Lavallée, 2009). Specifically, this model was chosen because it offered an individually
empowering approach to the treatment of trauma and substance-
use disorders (SUD) (Najavits, 2002).

The Indigenous Healing combined with Seeking Safety (IHSS)
stemmed from the research and work of Dr. Teresa Naseba Marsh.
The results from this new treatment model demonstrated that the

IHSS model was more than acceptable to many of the Indigenous participants struggling with intergenerational trauma and SUD, who reported that the blended approach was appealing, empowering, and healing. The IHSS program consists of up to twenty-five treatment topics that aim to teach participants a variety of skills. The majority of topics address the cognitive, behavioural, interpersonal, and case-management needs of persons with SUD and PTSD. To adhere to Two-Eyed Seeing and cultural sensitivity, the material is conveyed verbally. The facilitators encourage language that respects the participants' cultural values and beliefs. For example, the session on boundaries is explained through the role of the Seven Grandfather Teachings (Benton-Banai, 1988).

In the IHSS program, a holistic and philosophical quotation is used to start each session. Each sharing circle is opened with smudging, drumming, and singing. Smudging is a sacred act that is recognized by many Indigenous peoples as respecting the Great Spirit and the ancestors. Sacred medicines such as sweetgrass, sage, cedar, and tobacco are used during each sharing circle. Drumming is used in the circles to represent the heartbeat of the Nation and the pulse of the universe. Some songs are honour songs and were sung to honour the Creator, the ancestors, and particular individuals. These songs can have a profound healing effect on participants (Menzies, et al., 2010).

Sweat lodge ceremonies are available to the participants. Sweat lodge ceremonies provided a powerful way to bring forth a Two-Eyed Seeing as an Indigenous decolonizing methodology. The sweat ceremonies help repair the damage done to the spirits, minds, and bodies of the participants. During the sweat ceremonies, the Elder gives teachings about Indigenous traditional healing and its restorative power. Participants are also invited to share their stories and experiences.

The IHSS program ends each session with a checkout activity

where clients can give feedback about their experiences, report on what they liked or disliked, identify community resources that they may use, and discuss how they will continue their healing. In addition to this, each session closes with a Grandfather Teaching, Indigenous insight, prayer, or smudge. These techniques help traumatized individuals connect to the present, calm the nervous system, and help with difficult memories. In the sharing circles, grounding and centering is an important part of the healing process. During the ceremonies, the Elders and facilitators encourage participants to connect with Mother Earth and her elements. They teach participants to be aware of their feet connected to the Mother Earth, to feel Mother Earth's support, and to honour this feeling of connection. Moreover, during the grounding, participants are encouraged to drum, sing a sacred song, or burn a sacred medicine (see Marsh, Coholic, Cote-Meek, and Najavits, 2015).

Historically, the treatment program at Benbowopka merged IH with an abstinence-based residential treatment model. In 2016, Benbowopka modified their program to fully integrate Seeking Safety into a novel IHSS treatment intervention; this community led initiative—with a novel clinical treatment framework—presents a unique opportunity to study innovative approaches for Indigenous wellness.

THE IMPACT OF THE IMPLEMENTATION OF IHSS

The IHSS implementation project was originally designed to explore whether a blended approach could help Indigenous men and women with intergenerational trauma and SUD. The implementation of this model at Benbowopka profoundly affected the symptoms and behaviours related to intergenerational trauma and SUD in the participants, particularly over that past six months. From the Indigenous wisdom, the key healing following the experience of residential school abuse and its intergenerational effects lies in the area of reclaiming identity (Smith, 1999). Also, from the qualitative data and voiced experiences of participants who completed the twenty-eight day cycles, came testimonies that this blended implementation model enhanced their wellbeing and healing. Other changes included the request by many communities across Northern Ontario for the treatment of community members. The traditional healing practices, the land-based activities, the support from Elders and staff, and the knowledge and wisdom of the IHSS model, brought healing, connection, and hope to so many participants. As they move along the road to recovery, these participants will learn how to maintain balance and harmony in their mental, physical, emotional, and spiritual health via participation in individual counselling, group educational sessions, and talking circles; they will also learn relaxation techniques through yoga and drumming. Other areas include the importance of addressing their physical health through proper nutrition and exercise, and how to address their spiritual health through cultural activities and teachings.

REFERENCES

Benton-Benai, E. (1988). "The Seven Grandfathers and the Little Boy." *The Mishomis Book - Voice of The Ojibway*, 60-66. Hayward, WI: Indian Country Communications Inc.

Brant Castellano, M. (2004). "Ethics of Research." *Journal of Aboriginal Health*, 1, 98-114. Available: www.naho.ca/english/pdf/journal_p98-114.pdf (accessed 2011 Aug 14).

Cote, H., and Schissel, W. (2008). "Damaged children and broken spirits: A residential school survivor story." In Brooks, C. and Schissel, B. (Eds.), *Marginality and Condemnation: An Introduction to Critical Criminology* (2nd edition), 220-237. Black Point, NS: Fernwood Publishing.

Evans-Campbell, T. (2008). "Historical trauma in American Indian/Native Alaskan communities: A multilevel framework for exploring impacts on individuals, families, and communities." *Journal of Interpersonal Violence*, 23(3), 316-338.

Kirmayer, L. J., Tait, C. L., and Simpson, C. (2009). « The mental health of Aboriginal peoples in Canada: Transformations of identity and community." In L. J. Kirmayer and G. G. Valaskakis (Eds.), *Healing Traditions: The Mental Health of Aboriginal Peoples in Canada*, 3–35. Vancouver, Canada: University of British Columbia.

Lavallée, L. (2009). "Balancing the Medicine Wheel through physical activity." *Journal of Aboriginal Health*, 4(1), 64–71.

Marsh, T.N., Coholic, D., Cote-Meek, S., and Najavits, L.M., (2015a). "Blending Aboriginal and Western healing methods to treat intergenerational trauma with substance use disorder in Aboriginal peoples who live in northeastern Ontario Canada." *Harm Reduction Journal*, 12(1), 1-12.

Menzies, P., Bodnar, A., and Harper, V. (2010). "The role of the Elder within a mainstream addiction and mental health hospital: Developing an integrated." *Native Social Work Journal*, 7, 87-107.

Najavits, L. M. (2002a). *Seeking Safety: A Treatment Manual for PTSD and Substance Abuse*. New York, NY: Guilford.

Smith, L. T. (1999). *Decolonizing Methodologies: Research and Indigenous Peoples*. London, England: Zed Books.

Stewart, S. L. (2008). "Promoting Indigenous mental health: Cultural perspectives on healing from Native counsellors in Canada." *International Journal of Health Promotion and Education*, 46(2), 12-19.

Waldram, J. B., Herring, D. A., and Young, T. K. (2006). *Aboriginal Health in Canada: Historical, Cultural, and Epidemiological Perspectives* (2nd ed.). Toronto: University of Toronto Press.

"At SCHC, we work from the heart and recognize that all clients are unique.

We encourage honest self-reflection in a supportive atmosphere that helps foster real change and the pursuit of meaning and purpose. Science and research guide our program, and we are motivated by compassion and humanity."

# SUNSHINE COAST HEALTH CENTRE

Geoff Thompson

Sunshine Coast Health Centre (SCHC) is a forty-bed, private, residential facility for men suffering from addictions. Located in Powell River on BC's Sunshine Coast, SCHC is licensed by the Vancouver Coastal Health Authority and accredited by Accreditation Canada

The centre offers medical detoxification, mental-health and addictions treatment, and aftercare support. Professional staff includes physician, psychiatrist, nurses, registered massage therapist, exercise kinesiologist, psychotherapists, and therapists who specialize in family and trauma therapies.

HISTORY

The history of SCHC is the history of its evolving scientific, ethical, and humane treatment. When it opened in 2005, SCHC delivered a "twelve-step based" program, a model that had its origins in the 1950s and was used in more than eighty-five percent of residential programs. But research was indicating that therapy rooted in science and focused on the individual client's needs was more beneficial. SCHC soon shifted to a research-based model that put the whole, complex human being at centre stage, rather than treat an *addict* or an *addiction*.

This shift was reflected in its new mission statement: "At SCHC, we work from the heart and recognize that all clients are unique. We encourage honest self-reflection in a supportive atmosphere that helps foster real change and the pursuit of meaning and purpose. Science and research guide our program, and we are motivated by compassion and humanity."

Recognizing that addiction treatment has been impeded by a social stigma and by a struggle to translate research into practice, SCHC developed a new vision statement: "We strive to change the way society sees addiction and set a new standard for treatment."

TREATMENT APPROACH: MEANING-CENTRED THERAPY

SCHC's scientific model is Meaning-Centred Therapy (MCT), a name that confuses almost everyone who comes across it for the first time. MCT is based on the fact that human beings have a built-in need to make sense of their experiences. What meaning does this man give to having had a heart attack last year? If he thinks he's less of a man because he can't even shovel the driveway without risking a second heart attack, then he won't be comfortable with himself. What meaning does this woman give to her neighbour's rude behaviour this morning? If she thinks the guy's just being a jerk, then her relationship with him will suffer. But if she simply assumes that her neighbour is having a rough day, then she won't take it personally. The meanings that people give to their experiences determine the quality of their lives. Those with a positive attitude, who know their strengths and imperfections, who pursue goals based on what is important to them, who accept the world as it is, make sense of their experiences in a way that helps them flourish. But those who have only a weak understanding of who they are and what's important to them, who see the world as they wish it to be and not as it is, make sense of their experiences in a way that constricts their lives. They often believe they are defective human beings, feel victimized or confused by others and circumstance, and pursue goals that aren't fulfilling. The result is that they feel little meaning in their lives.

According to research, chronic intoxication is one response to a life that lacks personal meaning. Psychologist Jefferson Singer (1997) concluded that those suffering from "chronic addiction either had never found sufficient meaning in a sober life or through years of addiction had squandered any meaning they had once possessed" (p. 17). They score low on psychological tests of meaning and purpose-in-life and high on measures of boredom, the most common symptom of a lack of meaning. Other researchers tell us that those vulnerable to chronic drug use believe they are different from others, struggle to express what is genuinely important to them, and rarely examine their lives to determine if they need tinkering or an overhaul.

Addiction psychologists describe this life as "empty," "a void," or a "vacuum." One SCHC client put it this way: "I've always had this feeling that something isn't right. It's like when you leave the house in the morning, but you have this feeling that you've forgotten something. You don't know what it is, but something is missing. That's how I've felt my entire life." This condition is so uncomfortable that they are willing to endure the inevitable suffering that addiction brings just to find a brief respite.

Therapy explores with a client why he feels his life is empty or missing something. Perhaps he's bored at work because he finds no meaning in it other than a paycheque. Perhaps he experiences his intimate relationship as dull and monotonous. Perhaps he doesn't pursue outside interests that would bring new energy into his boring routine. Therapy typically discovers that the meanings a client attaches to experiences are warped or inaccurate. Why does this sixty-year-old client glorify the past and complain about smart phones and the rudeness of young people? He says it's because the world is deteriorating. But it's really about his feeling that he no longer belongs in the complicated and confusing modern world.

Guided by research on what makes life meaningful, therapists help clients find answers to: *Who am I? How can I feel comfortable with others? What do I want to accomplish?* One implication of a meaning approach is that addiction and recovery are inside jobs. If addiction is a response to a life that lacks *personal* meaning, then addiction must be in the person, not in the drug. There is something about the way this person or that person makes sense of their experiences that leaves them vulnerable to chronic drug use. Recovery, too, must be in the person. No one can tell another person how to live a personally meaningful life. That's something that the individual must minister to himself. This is a key principle of MCT: each client is the author of his life.

PROGRAMS: PRIMARY, FAMILY, TRAUMA

### 1. Primary Program

SCHC's primary program helps clients overcome addiction. Although the medical professions tend to see the problem in terms of specific drugs—such as addiction to alcohol or addiction to cocaine—

MCT works with any addiction. From the perspective of meaning, even those with non-drug addictions, such as gambling or gaming, also use these behaviours to ease a dull and impotent life. It's no accident, for example, that people with non-drug addictions are prone to boredom. Within a meaning framework, it doesn't make sense to offer different programs based on different addictions. It's always about how the individual person makes sense of things.

Psychologist Louis Hoffman (2009) helps us recognize that a meaningful life comes from different experiences. "The instillation of meaning is a primary component of ... psychotherapy. The deepest forms of meaning can be experienced on the various realms of biological, behavioural, cognitive, emotional, and interpersonal; in other words, it is holistic meaning" (p. 45). Therapy isn't about sitting around contemplating the answer to: *What is the meaning of life? What can I do to change the world?* Those answers are too high up and too far away. Therapy is more down to earth. You have to get your hands dirty digging through daily life. This *holistic meaning* is why MCT integrates medicine, exercise, nutrition, art, recreation, yoga, mindfulness, massage, career exploration, and family relationships with psychotherapy and psychiatry.

## 2. Family Program

Although the family program provides scientific information on the nature of addiction, its focus is on MCT's principle of *authorship*. Families typically struggle because their main coping skill is to manage their addicted loved one. "Yes, yes, I know he's thirty-four, but he acts like a twelve year old." Brandishing ultimatums, tearing up credit cards, hiding car keys, presenting them with bank receipts to confront lying, and keeping silent for fear of triggering an outburst are desperate attempts at control.

The family program helps the family come to terms with the

obvious: None of their efforts has stopped him from using drugs. But there is a more insidious problem at work. It's common for a family member to admit, "I've spent so much time focused on him that I've lost myself." It's as if the family's meaning and purpose in life has been to control the addicted family member. Therapy invites the family to recognize that each adult is the author of his or her life. The best support family members can give is to encourage their loved one to take responsibility for his life, to become his own author. This new way of thinking, of course, makes demands on families. It demands recognizing that their loved one is an adult and not a twelve year old. It demands accepting that his recovery belongs to him, not them. It demands confronting their fears of what will happen if they don't bail him out. And it demands that families become the authors of their lives.

### 3. Trauma Program

SCHC's adjunct trauma program is also meaning-centred. Research tells us that only a small proportion of people who experience a traumatic event go on to develop Post-traumatic Stress Disorder (PTSD). Why is this? The main reason is that PTSD arises when a person is confronted with an extreme real-life situation that severely conflicts with how he or she makes sense of self and the world. The consequence of PTSD even affects someone at the level of personal identity, giving rise to a sense they are no longer who they once were.

Imagine, for example, a young man with little going on in his life joins the military. He absorbs the military's values and ways of thinking. When he is ordered overseas on combat, he truly believes that he's one of the good guys sent to beat up the bad guys who are hurting the local population. He soon finds himself in a firefight. In the wreckage near the enemy a little girl jumps out. Out of reflex he shoots. At that moment, the way he makes sense of things is shattered. He is confronted with the fact that he shot an innocent local girl, an affront to his belief that he was there to save her. He works desperately to avoid thinking about it, but memories start intruding in his waking life and in his dreams. He feels helpless in the face of anxiety, nightmares, intrusive thoughts, and shame. He discovers that drinking a bottle of vodka eases stress and allows sleep. Although he doesn't understand what's happening to him, his psychological problem is that he cannot integrate the memory of this painful experience into his sure belief that he's one of the good guys saving innocent civilians.

Using medications and coping skills, therapy helps the client reduce trauma symptoms. But it also helps him make sense of things in a new way. MCT invites the client to examine whether his beliefs are accurate or helpful. Perhaps he sees himself as a defective soldier, rather than as an imperfect human being. Perhaps he interprets his actions as criminally negligent, rather than as a simple reflex honed by months of training. Perhaps he believes that combat is an orderly sequence of events with each soldier doing precisely as ordered, rather than the fog of war. Perhaps he believes he's doomed by PTSD, rather than recognizing that he is capable of pursuing meaningful goals in spite of trauma symptoms. A more sophisticated and accurate understanding of himself and the world allows him to make sense of his traumatic experience.

## A MEANING-CENTRED ENVIRONMENT AND WORKPLACE

Apart from its therapy, two features make SCHC unique. First, all staff members, from cook to counsellor, practice empathy, unconditional positive regard, and genuineness. Research has shown that a caring, non-judgmental, and transparent environment is necessary for clients to feel free to be themselves, a prerequisite for therapeutic success. At SCHC, a housekeeper is hired not merely to vacuum or clean the door handles, but also to interact with clients in a way that supports their progress. Therapy would be less effective if a client feels safe with his therapist but then runs into a cook who dismisses him, a maintenance worker who judges him, or an administrator who thinks he's a defective human being.

Secondly, SCHC is a meaning-centred workplace. If meaning is personal to the individual, then this must be true not only for clients but also for each cook, driver, support worker, administrator, nurse, doctor, and therapist. SCHC supports each staff member to pursue a personally meaningful working life. A job at the centre isn't simply a list of rules to follow and tasks to complete. It's tailored to the individual, because each staff member has his or her own aspirations and practical realities.

Research has shown that that a meaning-centred workplace benefits both employees and employer. At SCHC, it also has a positive influence supporting the therapeutic program. A staff member understands clients better because he or she is, in a very real sense, on the same journey.

ADDICTION AS A HUMAN PHENOMENON

Psychologist Stanton Peele (1998) tells us, "Human experience and its interpretation are central to the incidence, course, treatment, and remission of addiction" (p. ix). Addiction is not bizarre or alien behaviour. It's a very human response to a lonely, boring, and unfulfilled life.

One of those human things about addiction is suffering. To be bearable, suffering must have meaning. The Olympic athlete willingly endures extreme pain to win a medal. A mother rushes into traffic to save her child. Soldiers put themselves in harm's way for a cause. But those addicted to drugs have no goal or purpose or cause. A study of SCHC clients concluded that, before therapy, they could find no meaning in their suffering (Thompson, 2016).

MCT's greatest power may be to help clients make sense of suffering in a way that they can grow from it. Adversity is, after all, how we grow as human beings—but only if we listen to what it can teach us. Those who have pulled themselves out of the abyss of chronic intoxication describe a newfound confidence that they can endure any hardship, accept life as it is, live comfortably in the grey areas of life, recognize that to be human is to be imperfect, pursue what is truly meaningful to them, and feel an urge to get on with the business of living. SCHC suggests that this personal growth is what recovery from addiction is ultimately about.

REFERENCES

Hoffman, L. (2009). "Introduction to existential psychology in a cross-cultural context: An East-West dialogue." In L. Hoffman, M. Yang, F. J. Kaklauskas, and A. Chan (Eds.), *Existential psychology East-West*, 1–67. Colorado Springs, CO: University of the Rockies Press.

Peele, S. (1998). *The Meaning of Addiction: An Unconventional View*. San Francisco, CA: Jossey-Bass.

Singer, J. A. (1997). *Message in a Bottle: Stories of Men and Addiction*. Toronto, ON: The Free Press.

Thompson, G. R. (2016). "Meaning therapy for addictions: A case study." *Journal of Humanistic Psychology*, 56(5), 457–482.

**DOUGLAS GOSSE,**
PH.D., is the author of
*Jackytar* and a professor of
social justice and cultural
studies at Nipissing
University. He is a frequent
speaker and writer on human
rights, particularly for
marginalized men and boys,
and the LGBTTIQQ2SA
community.

Photo: Georgette Harris

## CONTRIBUTORS

**DR. STEVEN ARNOCKY** is an associate professor and founding director of the Human Evolution Laboratory at Nipissing University, Canada. His research is funded by the Canadian Foundation for Innovation (CFI), the Social Sciences and Humanities Research Council of Canada (SSHRC), and the Natural Sciences and Engineering Research Council of Canada (NSERC). His work broadly examines the evolutionary underpinnings of human mating. For more information, please visit: http://evolutionlab. nipissingu.ca.

**AISHA ASHRAF** is a full-time mum, freelance copyeditor, and writer of memoir and creative non-fiction. A member of the Writers Community of Durham Region and recipient of the Ann Weisgarber Scholarship for 2017, she splits her time between creative non-fiction, poetry, and proof-reading. She currently lives in Ontario, Canada, with her husband and three children. You can find her writing portfolio at aishaashraf.contently.com.

**JANE BARKER** is Chair and Associate Professor of the School of Criminology and Criminal Justice at Nipissing University. She is co-editor, with D. Scharie Tavcer, on the second edition of *Women and the Criminal Justice System: A Canadian Perspective* published in 2018 by Emond Montgomery Publications Ltd. Her research interests focus on issues related to women in conflict with the law, including mental health and addictions.

DR. JENNIFER BARNETT is a tenured associate professor at Nipissing University in North Bay, Ontario. She holds degrees in Sociology, Education, and Law. Her research focuses on how different segments of society seek to control and educate individuals and groups through cultural and legal politicking.

DR. DARREN W. CAMPBELL is an associate professor in the Department of Psychology at Nipissing University. His NICE lab focuses on social emotional evaluations, online communication, and chronic cannabis use effects assessed through behavioural and functional MRI assessments. For more information, please visit: https://faculty.nipissingu.ca/darrenc/.

MELANIE CAREFOOT is a registered social worker in Alberta. She worked for children's services from 2000 until the beginning of 2012 and since then has been in private practice at Positive Choices Counselling. Melanie and her colleagues specialize in assisting clients who have become involved with children's services, offering advocacy, support, and information on agency policies and procedures. They also provide a range of other therapeutic services, including divorce coaching, parenting coordination, and mediation. Before immigrating to Canada from England, she worked with diverse groups of clients including traveller, fairground and circus families, students at risk of being excluded from school, and marginalized youth. Melanie enjoys living in the foothills of Alberta where the view of the Rocky Mountains and the company of her family and dogs make the long commute from the office well worth the time.

ANDREW CARTER is a thirty-two-year-old recovering addict from St. John's, Newfoundland. He suffered for years with addiction and mental-health issues, and turned to crime to support his habits. After serving a five-year, federal sentence for armed robbery, Andrew changed his lifestyle and is now living a clean and sober life. Andrew is working as a skilled carpenter, and he is a devoted father and partner to his long-time girlfriend. Andrew owes his success to his girlfriend, family, parole officer, and close supports.

JIM CONLEY is a civil contracting estimator and writer. He holds degrees in English Literature and Construction Management and has published multiple magazine articles. The dialog above is one of nearly a hundred compiled in the collection *There Will Be Time* which remains in search of a publisher. He lives with his teenage son in Western Canada.

MELISSA COOK is an intergenerational residential and missionary school survivor, who testified as a living witness and survivor at the National Inquiry Into Missing and Murdered Indigenous Girls in October of 2017 at ground zero: Winnipeg, Manitoba. She has been published by *Residential School Magazine*, *The Mighty*, *Native Reflections*, and Red River College (curriculum). She is a mother of two, and now works facilitating workshops about crystal meth/addiction awareness, colonization and intergenerational effects awareness, lateral violence/bullying awareness, family tree and self-awareness, and much more. She shares her story of survival to reach out to others who are still struggling. Her message: "Never give up, and just keep going."

CASEY DALTON is a twenty-six-year-old, single mother of two children and lives in St. John's, Newfoundland and Labrador. She is currently studying Paralegal Studies at Academy Canada. She is passionate about helping people who have gone through similar struggles, and would like to set up a program to assist people who are in the process of coming off the methadone program.

KATHRYN DALTON is a Master of Science in Pharmacy student at Memorial University of Newfoundland (MUN). Kathryn completed a Bachelor of Science (Honours) in Neuroscience and Mental Health at Carleton University in Ottawa, Ontario. Kathryn's research interests are addictions and the brain, with a specific focus on the emerging adult (18-25) population, and the role of the developing brain in addiction and addiction treatment. Kathryn plans to pursue a PhD in a field involving addiction treatment, and hopes to ultimately work in research/academia or a clinical setting.

REBECCA DAWE is nineteen years old and lives in Conception Bay South, Newfoundland. She is a recent graduate from the Canadian Training Institute, as a heavy equipment operator. Rebecca loves sports, the outdoors, dogs, and of course, her family and amazing boyfriend.

ANDREW DRECHSLER was born in Charlottetown, Prince Edward Island. After attending Dalhousie University and living in Halifax for many years, he recently moved to London, Ontario, where he works as an insurance claims adjuster. Andrew enjoys painting and the company of his treasured schnauzers, Eddie and Patsy.

ANN DWYER GALWAY was a teacher in Newfoundland for twenty-nine years. Since retiring in 2003, she and her husband have been teaching in the Northwest Territories of Canada. They now live in Inuvik. Ann enjoys reading, writing, and travelling.

KIRSTEN EMMOTT is a family doctor in Comox, British Columbia. She is a former member of Vancouver Industrial Writers' Union. Her poetry collection, *How Do You Feel*, was published by Sono Nis Press. Her poetry has been included in numerous anthologies.

CAROL ESHKAKOGAN is an Anishinabe Kwe from Sagamok Anishinabek First Nation. Carol graduated from Cambrian College in 1989 with a diploma in Native Community Care: Counselling and Development and went on to receive an undergraduate degree in Public Administration and Governance with Ryerson University in 2004. Carol remains a candidate for the Juris Doctorate graduate degree at the University of Ottawa Law School. Carol's work experience spans over thirty-two years serving First Nations people at a community level and Tribal Council level from individual counselling to management and coordination of programs and services in the field of health and social services. Currently, Carol is the executive director of Benbowopka Treatment Centre and continues to develop the capacity of the area First Nations in addressing mental health and addictions, particularly opioid addiction.

KATHRYN EVE is an addiction and mental-health specialist living in Toronto, Canada, with her wife, Shana, and son, Noah. She is also a published writer and founder of MakePeace International. Kathryn graduated from the University of Toronto with a Bachelor of Arts degree in Psychology and English and a Master of Arts degree in International Relations from Deakin University in Australia. She recently completed certification in a two-year Spiritual Direction Training Program from Regis College in Toronto and the Urban Spirituality Centre in Portland, Oregon. Kathryn is a member of Spiritual Directors International.

SETH FLETCHER is a certified addictions counsellor and interventionist who brings many years of professional experience working the front lines of addiction in both the government and privatized sectors. In treatment centres, the classroom, or the executive boardroom, Seth has worked alongside and in conjunction with the Canadian Addiction Counsellors

Certification Federation (CACCF), INSITE Vancouver, the Canadian Centre on Substance Abuse (CCSA), the RCMP, Health Canada, Justice Canada, The Saskatoon Health Region, and the Addictions Foundation Manitoba (AFM) towards helping those suffering from substance abuse.

DAVID FRENKEL is an associate lawyer at Gelman and Associates. He has exclusively been practising family law for the past ten years.

LISA GELMANis the founder of Gelman and Associates in Toronto and has been in private practice for the last twenty years in the area of family law.

JENINE GLYNN lives in St. John's, Newfoundland, where she enjoys spending time with her husband, two children, and two dogs. Her love of lifting weights continues to grow, and she will compete in her first power-lifting competition later this year. Jenine contributes her success with staying clean to the love and support of her family and friends.

DR. BLAINE E. HATT is a professor of Education in the Schulich School of Education at Nipissing University. He completed his undergraduate and early graduate work at the university of New Brunswick and earned his doctorate at the University of Alberta. His research and writing interests include heart in teaching, imagination, and creativity in education (ICE), attending the empathic, transactional curriculum, and pre-service teacher education.

ERIKA HUNZINGER is a registered occupational therapist and mental-health specialist with additional training in medicine and spiritual care. She finds strength and renewal in her faith, practicing yoga, cat-cuddling, nature, and travel. Her passion is bringing hope, compassion, and inspiration to every encounter with individuals who struggle with mental-health concerns or addictions.

DAVID KAUFMAN is a warm and outgoing narrative and solution focused brief therapist and Canadian certified addictions counsellor, who provides education and guidance to those who struggle with, or are affected by, addictions. He is the director of outreach and education at the Jewish Addictions Community Services (JACS) in Toronto. He facilitates three weekly support groups, lectures about addiction wherever the opportunity arises within schools, houses of worship, and professional forums.

SHERI KILMURY-GINTHER is forty-five year old alcoholic/drug addict, living a life free of any substances, one day at a time. She currently resides in Winnipeg, Manitoba. Sheri has a great career today, working with women starting their own sober journey—her true passion in life.

DR. NEDRA R. LANDER is associate professor of Psychiatry, Faculty of Medicine, University of Ottawa, and has worked for thirty-five years as a clinical and health psychologist at The Ottawa Hospital. Dr. Lander is passionately committed to her collaborative work with Dr. Danielle Nahon in developing The Integrity Model (TIM)–the first values-focused and wellness-based therapeutic approach, providing a philosophical perspective for a mindful and meaningful understanding of self, life, and daily living. TIM has been implemented through an integrity- and values-based model of workplace stress and physician wellness across the healthcare spectrum, and has been presented in numerous national and international forums. Nedra and Danielle have disseminated their work through several hundred presentations at local, national, and international scientific meetings, and through thirty peer-reviewed journal publications and book chapters. Their collaborative book on The Integrity Model of Existential Psychotherapy was published by Routledge (London and New York).

MORGAN LONGJOHN is a Plains Cree First Nation woman from Sturgeon Lake First Nation. She was born and raised in Prince Albert, Saskatchewan. She has been clean and sober since May 20, 2017. She returned to live on reserve and is pursuing her goals and dreams after addiction. Today, she lives her life as a bible-believing Baptist Christian because her faith is what saved her from the living hell of addiction.

TERESA NASEBA MARSH, PhD, is an assistant professor of Clinical Sciences at Laurentian and Lakehead Universities. Teresa immigrated to Canada from South Africa in 1992 and continued to contribute to healing approaches to overcome suffering, trauma, addiction, historical trauma, and the aftermath of oppression. In her current book, *Enlightenment is Letting Go! Healing from Trauma, Addiction and Multiple Loss,* Teresa continues her dedication to this field by teaching people how to heal through participatory action, ancient spiritual methods, poetry, and the telling of stories. Indigenous Healing combined with the Seeking Safety (IHSS) model stems from Teresa's research work. The results from this new treatment model demonstrate that the IHSS can help clients cope with symptoms of addiction, post-traumatic stress disorder (PTSD), and intergenerational trauma, including terror, fear, intrusive thoughts, destructive behaviours toward self and others, loss of meaning of life, hopelessness, confusion, shame, guilt, isolation, and self-blame. Many clients who attend this program report that the blended approach is appealing, empowering, and healing.

RACHEL MARZETTI is thirty-nine years old. She is formally educated in both Gerontology and Nursing, though not currently employed in either specialty. She has a variety of interests and hobbies, which include art (sketching, drawing, painting) and reading. She has a love of music and is often described as having a very eclectic taste for it. She considers herself to be an introvert, though she does enjoy the company of her small group of friends and family.

KAILA MCANULTY is certified clinical counsellor and relationship and sex therapist in Prince George, British Columbia. She currently has her own practice as a sex therapist and also works in both the youth and adult correctional system. Kaila has been counselling for over twelve years and has eight years of education in psychology, counselling, and sex therapy. She also has expertise in Cognitive Behavioural Therapy (CBT) when working with patients with depression, anxiety, Obsessive Compulsive Disorder (OCD), phobias, etc. She has a unique ability to connect with her clients and provides a genuine, supportive, and non-judgmental approach.

STEPHEN MILLER was born in raised in Marystown, Newfoundland. He currently resides in St. John's with his girlfriend and their cat, Bella, both of whom are lovely. He is a journalist in training, an avid reader and writer, and a proud big brother of two amazing sisters. He is presently trying to be the best version of himself...It's a work in progress.

HAZEL MILLS is a middle-aged woman on a mission—to live life to the greatest extent possible. She grew up in a small rural town with a big family around her. Now living in a bigger town, she enjoys crafting, cooking for friends and family, and writing. Her favourite motto is, "You can catch more flies with honey than with vinegar."

GARETH MITTON is a professional writer living in St. John's, NL, with his wife, Jessica. He develops ad campaigns and is also a keen fiction writer, currently in talks to publish his first novel. A proponent of natural techniques for healthy living, Gareth pens a blog, *My Creative Life*, which can be viewed at garethmitton.com along with more information about his life and work.

RICHARD MORIN est né à Hauterive en décembre 1964. Joueur occasionnel dès l'âge de douze ans, joueur compulsif à l'âge de vingt ans, passionné du poker, des paris sportifs et des courses de chevaux jusqu'à l'âge de sa retraite du monde du jeu à trente-cinq ans. Il a fait des études en sciences humaines au Cégep de Hauterive de 1982 à 1984. Richard a complété un certificat en toxicomanie à l'Université de Sherbrooke en 2016. Actuellement, il étudie à l'université de Montréal en santé mentale. Sa plus grande réalisation à ce jour est d'être abstinent du jeu depuis le 6 mai 2000. «Actions speak louder than words» est sa devise préférée. Email : somwon4@gmail.com

AMANDA MURPHY is a twenty-nine-year-old recovering addict from Job's Cove, NL. She has a Bachelor of Nursing and hopes to resume working as a registered nurse in the near future. She enjoys going to the gym, spending time with family, defying stereotypes, and challenging closed minds.

DR. DANIELLE NAHON was a clinical psychologist with a community psychological practice, and associate professor of Psychiatry at the Faculty of Medicine of the University of Ottawa. She was co-chair of the Women Faculty Mentoring Program, Faculty of Medicine, University of Ottawa, and helped offer a series of Continuing Medical Education programs and mentoring evenings for women physicians/faculty. Based on her long-standing work in the arena of men's issues and the importance of men's health, and her experience in cofounding the first men's clinic in a tertiary care setting in North America, she co-hosted, along with Dr. Nedra Lander, the first Continuing Medical Education men's health conference in Canada, as well as the First International Multi-Disciplinary Congress on Men. Danielle received the Award for Advancement of Equity, Diversity and Gender Issues from the Faculty of Medicine of the University of Ottawa. Dr. Nahon passed away April 13, 2018.

EMILY ORR is a doctoral-level clinical psychologist. She has worked with individuals with substance-use disorders and/or eating disorders since 2009. She presently lives in Halifax and provides psychological services to members of the Canadian Armed Forces. Her essay in this anthology is dedicated to those clients with whom she has worked, both past and present.

MICHAEL PARSONS is a retired software engineer, amateur writer, poet, photographer, and fisherman living on what soon may be a resettled island (Little Bay Islands, pop. 42) in the North Atlantic.

NAOMI PERKS lived with her husband and two children in the suburbs of Vancouver. An unlikely marathon runner, she found her happy place running the streets of Vancouver and hiking the surrounding mountains. After spending six years researching about the crisis of masculinity, she is thrilled that others have begun taking it more seriously. She only wishes it were no longer necessary.

AMANDA PREFFER is a journalist with CBC based in Ottawa. Amanda has worked for the CBC across the country, before Ottawa, including Montreal, Vancouver, Fredericton, and Quebec City.

LISA PONT, MSW, RSW, joined the Problem Gambling Service at CAMH as a therapist in 2007. Lisa's experience in counselling, outreach, community work, and training, led her to her dual role as an educator and therapist at the Problem Gambling Institute of Ontario at CAMH in 2009. Currently, she is involved in responsible gambling industry training and specializes in the area of problem gaming, gambling, and Internet use. Lisa continues to provide group and individual counselling, and develops and delivers customized training programs. Lisa teaches both in professional development and continuing education programs at two Ontario universities and presents at domestic and international conferences. Her expertise has been sought out for print, radio, and, television. She has a Bachelor of Social Work from Ryerson University and a Master of Social Work from York University.

DEREK PUDDESTER, M.D., M.Ed., FRCPC, PCC, is an associate professor in the Faculty of Medicine at the University of Ottawa. A global expert, consultant, and educator in physician health and wellness, he has served as director of the Faculty Wellness Program at University of Ottawa, director of physician health at the Canadian Medical Association, and associate medical director of the Ontario Medical Association.

CHIARA (pronounced with a flourish as Key-ar-a!) STAGLIANO is a thirty-something recovering addict who emerged from very dark times and is now loving life and spreading sunshine to all those she meets. Her naturally loud voice will draw you to her, but you will stay for her generous heart and fun-loving nature. She loves the beach, books, chicken wings, and sparkly manicures. She always smell fantastic. She recently overcame her fear of large dogs and assembled a bed frame. These are two accomplishments that are a close second and third to kicking addiction's ass. She is now unstoppable!

ANGELA RINALDIS is a litigation lawyer in Vancouver, BC, practicing at her law firm Angela Rinaldis Law Corporation. Angela and her supportive husband, Clinton Bauman, share an adorable daughter, Sydney who was born December 30, 2016. Angela is also the president and founder of Project True, a not-for-profit organization supporting those who cannot afford their eating disorder treatment and working on breaking the silence around eating disorders. Angela suffered from anorexia and over exercise addiction for much of her teenage and early adult life. Recovery is a road Angela travels on a daily basis, and part of that recovery is sharing her story.

MARGARET SCOTT has been a teacher for thirty years. She has taught grades kindergarten to grade ten in three provinces. She enjoys time with her family, especially in the outdoors. Her pastimes include reading and listening to music. She has completed a number of special qualifications in education, including a Master of Education degree.

DAVIS LAINE SMITH is a therapist who specializes in addiction treatment in the Atlantic provinces. She is a community activist for social justice and is a passionate change maker. She lives by the belief that the essence of being human is to be loved, to heal, be kind, forgive, and belong.

WILLIAM STROMICH was born on Vancouver Island, and earned a Bachelor of Music. He lives in Vancouver with his husband. He enjoys hiking in the mountains and playing the piano.

DR. SHAFIK SUNDERANI is a practicing psychotherapist in the greater Toronto area. He provides psychological treatment for patients with a wide-range of clinical presentations, including but not limited to depression, anxiety, trauma, relationship concerns, and addictions. He has an educational background in both personality theory and evolutionary psychology.

MARK TANNOUS is an entrepreneur living in downtown Toronto, Ontario. In his spare time, he works out, eats healthily, and is surrounded by a broad circle of friends. He frequently attends events in and around Toronto, from plays to concerts and festivals. His outgoing nature, optimistic attitude, and drive define him.

D. SCHARIE TAVCER is an associate professor of Criminal Justice in the Department of Economics, Justice, and Policy Studies at Mount Royal University. She is co-editor, with Jane Barker, on the second edition of *Women and the Criminal Justice System: A Canadian Perspective* published in 2018 by Emond Montgomery Publications Ltd. Her research interests focus on violence against women, mental health, and occupational stress injuries, prostitution and sex trafficking, and the law, sentencing, and corrections.

GEOFF THOMPSON is program director at the Sunshine Coast Health Centre. He earned his M.A. in counselling psychology and Ph.D. in psychology. He has published journal articles and books on addiction, including co-editing *The Positive Psychology of Meaning and Addiction Recovery*.

KELLY S. THOMPSON is a writer and retired military officer with a Master's degree in Creative Writing from the University of British Columbia. Kelly won the House of Anansi Press Golden Anniversary Award, the 2014 and 2017 Barbara Novak Award for Personal Essay, and was shortlisted for *Room* magazine's 2013 and 2014 Creative Nonfiction awards. Her essays have appeared in several anthologies. Her military memoir will be released by McClelland and Stewart in Spring 2019.

RICARDO VILLELA was born in Sao Paulo, Brazil. He moved to Toronto to learn English at the age of nineteen, working in tourism and the financial industry. He is planning to return to Toronto in the near future.

DR. GRACE VITALE is a registered psychologist and obtained her PhD in 1999 from York University. She has been working as a school psychologist at the York Catholic DSB for the past twenty years, where she is now one of the supervising psychologists. She has also worked in various hospitals and treatment facilities and has taught undergraduate courses in Psychology at York University. In addition, she runs a private practice focusing on the assessment and treatment of children, adolescents, and families. She has also written children's picture books addressing topics such as depression and resiliency in children.

DR. JOHN VITALE holds a doctoral degree in Curriculum Studies from the University of Toronto (2002). He is currently a professor at the Schulich School of Education, Nipissing University, where he teaches a number of different courses at both the undergraduate and graduate levels. In addition to his ten years of service at Nipissing University, John also has fourteen years of experience as a teacher in the Ontario school system. John has numerous professional interests, including music education, arts education, technology education, and mental-health education. John has presented his research at dozens of national and international conferences, and is widely published in a number of books and peer-reviewed journals.

CHRISTOPHER K. WALLACE, advisor to men at ckwallace.com, author of *Drinker's Riddle* (2015), has a college background in the behavioural sciences and the street. At age fifteen, his father tossed him from a family of eleven, saying there was room for just one rooster there. Angry and aimless, a decade later he developed a hard drug habit. After an epiphany, he turned his life around. He works to help men use their power in service of themselves and their community. He believes this gives a man's life meaning and represents the keys to his freedom. The rooster is now his totem.

DAMASYA WING has been employed in both the physical-health and mental-health fields for over twenty years. She has a Master of Social Work, and currently works for a specialized mental-health program in Winnipeg. Her partner's recovery inspires her work daily.

BENJAMIN SHING PAN WONG, MA, RCC, is a clinical counsellor in British Columbia who treats behavioral addictions through www.Mindful Digitality.com. He is currently collaborating with the BC Responsible and Problem Gambling Program in their pilot of support and clinical initiatives to reduce the harm of gaming disorder in Metro Vancouver. Benjamin is an outspoken advocate for parental involvement from early infancy in children's development, and the responsible use of digital technologies to enhance learning, social skills, resilience, and mental-health fitness.

IAN YOUNG is a recovered addict from video games. Ian is twenty-eight years old, and works both full-time and contractually on side-projects. He seeks to not only end the stigma of video-game addiction, but also to quell the irresponsible and incredibly harmful understandings and assumptions regarding addiction in both our society and in our personal lives.